About the Author

Elaheh Rostami-Povey is a writer and researcher. She is a research associate at the Centre for Media and Film Studies and is affiliated to the London Middle East Institute, Centre for Iranian Studies and Centre for Gender Studies at the School of Oriental and African Studies, University of London. Her research focuses on Iran, Afghanistan and the Middle East, in particular on gender issues in Iran and Afghanistan. She is the author of *Afghan Women: Identity and Invasion* (2007) and *Women, Work and Islamism: Ideology and Resistance in Iran* (1999) under her pen name, Maryam Poya. Both books have been translated widely.

Iran's Influence

A Religious–Political State and Society in Its Region

ELAHEH ROSTAMI-POVEY

Zed Books

LONDON & NEW YORK

Iran's Influence: A Religious–Political State and Society in Its Region
was first published in 2010 by
Zed Books Ltd, 7 Cynthia Street, London N1 9JF, UK
and Room 400, 175 Fifth Avenue, New York, NY 10010, USA

www.zedbooks.co.uk

Designed and typeset in Monotye Joanna
by illuminati, Grosmont
Index by John Barker
Cover designed by Safehouse Creative
Printed and bound in Great Britain by
CPI Antony Rowe, Chippenham and Eastbourne

Distributed in the USA exclusively by Palgrave Macmillan, a division of
St Martin's Press, LLC, 175 Fifth Avenue, New York, NY 10010, USA

A catalogue record for this book is available from the British Library
Library of Congress Cataloging in Publication Data available

ISBN 978 1 84813 219 1 Hb
ISBN 978 1 84813 220 7 Pb
ISBN 978 1 84813 221 4 Eb

Contents

Preface and acknowledgements

This book is based on the testimonies of Iranians, Iraqis, Lebanese, Palestinians and Egyptians – activists, journalists, refugees, exiles and academics – with diverse political views ranging from Islamist modernists, the secular left, nationalists and feminists, whom I interviewed throughout 2007–09 in Iran, Lebanon, Syria, Palestine, Egypt and the UK. The level of violence in Iraq did not allow me to travel there; instead, I interviewed Iraqis in Syria, Iran and the UK. Many were curious about me: I looked like them, but was not speaking Arabic or wearing the Islamic hijab. 'Where do you come from?' they would ask curiously. When I replied 'I am Iranian', the immediate reaction was 'Welcome, *Ahlan wa Sahlan*, Iran good'. In one visit to Cairo, a middle-aged shoe keeper in a mosque in Islamic Cairo said 'Iran good, Bomb *Inshaallah*', indicating that he wished Iran to obtain the bomb. Every time I visited these regions, similar sentiments were repeated on a daily basis by taxi drivers and shopkeepers, and in restaurants. Their identification with my Iranian-ness was striking – not that I, a woman without a hijab from that part of the world, was Muslim, Shi'a, non-Muslim or secular, but that my being Iranian was good enough for them to express their support for Iran. Observing these sentiments triggered my interest in researching and writing about how Iran is perceived in these societies, as a country which is going through changes both internally and in terms of its role in the region and within global politics.

Thus my field research, in particular the interviews, constitute an important part of my analysis. I am grateful to many friends and colleagues, without whom I could not have written this book. My daughter Tara Povey and my partner John Rose have read the entire manuscript and have made detailed and insightful suggestions; I am indebted to both of them for their love and for their critical care, which has enriched my thinking. Laleh Khalili, Anne Alexander and Nur Masalha have read the chapters on Lebanon, Iraq, Palestine and Egypt; their incisive critiques have been crucial in making this book better. I am indebted to Sadaf Rostami and Behnam Tonekaboni for assisting me in my research. Sadaf worked hard to provide me with valuable statistics and Behnam researched the relevant books in Farsi and recommended which to read. Nariman Massoumi provided me with important articles and directed me to websites. Tamsine O'Riordan, my editor at Zed Books, was a tremendous intellectual support.

I am profoundly indebted to all those women and men whose interviews are presented in this book. In Iran my gratitude is extended to Elaheh Kollaee, Jamileh Kadivar, Eisa Saharkhiz, Mashallah Shamsolvaezin, Ataollah Mohajerani, Susan Shariati, Mohsen Kadivar, Fakhrolsadat Mohtashamipour, Minoo Mortazi, Habibollah Payman, Maliheh Aryan, Mohammad Adeli, Hassan Eshkevari and Ali Rahnema. My field research in Beirut and Syria would not have been possible without Laleh Khalili introducing me to amazing scholars and activists. I am most grateful to Sari Hanafi, Mona Harb, Mahmoud Zeidan, Saleh Agha, Fatemeh Mirzadeh, Ali Hamdan, Jean Said Makdisi, Jim Quilty, Amal Saad Ghorayeb, Reinoud Leenders, Roschanack Shaery-Eisenlohr, Manal Kortam, Ola Hanafi, Mohammed Hourani, Judith Palmer Harik, Ibrahim Mousavi and Haj Hassan Houssein. I am grateful to my friend Hossein Shahidi, who gave me shelter in Beirut and shared with me his years of experience in Lebanon. In Syria, I am also indebted to Mehri Honarbin-Holliday, Safa Kassab Hassan, Hala Sarraf, James Pope, Mazen Rabie, Cyrus Shayegh and

Shokri Rayan, who shared with me their valuable experiences. My gratitude goes to Rima Tarbadar and her family, who opened their home to me in Damascus; their hospitality and intellectual support were immeasurable. In Palestine, without Islah Jad, Fadwa Al-Labadi and Lisa Taraki I would not have been able to witness the suffering of Palestinians on a daily basis. I am also grateful to Ommar Barghoti, Eileen Kuttab, Simine Alam and Ammar Zorba. It was a memorable experience for me to meet Sameh, who was under house arrest in Um el Fahim. His family have lost their homes and lands to the Zionists and have been resisting the Israelis for generations. In Jaffa, Yousef's and Ruba's hospitality and generosity are unforgettable. They showed me their parents' and grandparents' family homes, which over the course of painful years were stolen by the Zionists. I am most grateful to Mohammed, who showed me most parts of Ramallah, where I witnessed the uprooting of the Palestinians by the Zionists. In Silwan men and women campaigners shared with me the ways they are resisting the Zionist destruction of their community. In London, my heartfelt thanks are also due to Sami Ramadani, Haifa Zangana, Maysoon Pachachi, Nadje Al-Ali, Hana Ibrahim, Tahrir Numan and Khaled Ziyada, from whom I learned a great deal about the reality of life in Iraq and Palestine. In Cairo, without Rabab Al-Mahdi I would not have been able to meet so many fine academics and activists. She also gave me shelter and intellectual support during my fieldwork. I am also indebted to Hossam el-Hamalawy, Omaima Abou-Bakr, Omayma Abdel-Latif, Ibrahim al-Hudaiby, Wafaa Al-Masri, Mohammed Sami, Gamal Nassar, Heba Raouf, Dina Samak, Ibrahim al-Sahary, Zeinab Afifi, Sameh Naguib, Mostafa Radwan, Hala Shukrallah, Mohamed Morsy El-aiat and Farida Makar, who kindly assisted me and translated the interviews from Arabic into English.

My heartfelt thanks go to my family, Lily, Farhad, Tara, John, Behrang, Behnam, Amy, Lara, Daryoush, Roya, Nahid, Ahmad, Jason, Jane, Siamak, Sanam, Sadaf, Maryam and Niloofar, for their love and support, which kept me going.

Glossary

In this book the transliteration of Farsi and Arabic words do not use diacritical marks. These words are translated in the text when they appear for the first time; thereafter the reader may need to consult the glossary. There are discrepancies in translation, partly because I have tried to follow what has become customary in the literature and partly because I have attempted to preserve the Farsi pronunciation of Farsi words and Arabic pronunciation of Arabic words in relation to each other. This has resulted in differences in spelling: I have given both Farsi and Arabic spellings.

Advare Tahkime Vahdat   Alumni organisation
Arbaeen   The 40th day of Muharram
Ashoura   The 10th day of Muharram
Aql   Reason
Bazaar   Traditional marketplace
Dieh   Blood money
Edalat   Justice
Fatwa   Religious ruling
Fiqh   Islamic jurisprudence
Fiqh Poya   Dynamic Islamic jurisprudence
Ghadir Khum   According to Shi'as, Prophet Muhammad declared Ali
   his successor in Ghadir Khum

Hadith   Tradition

Hijab   Islamic cover

Hokomate Ali   Imam Ali's governance in early Islam

Hokomate mardomi   People's governance

Hudna   Truth

Ijtihad   Application of human reason and rationality

Imam   Leader

Imamate   Leadership

Infitah   Opening

Intifada   Uprising against Israel's occupation of Palestine

Jihad   Striving against evil

Khaneghah   Sufi place of worship in Iran

Khoms   Religious taxes paid annually by Shi'as, one-fifth of the value
of their wealth

Mahr   Bride price

Majlis   Parliament

Majlis Khebregan   Assembly of Experts

Majma'e Tashkhis Maslehat   Assembly to Discern the Interests of the
System, also known as the Expediency Council

Mardom   People

Marja' al-Taqlid   The source of imitation

Marja'   Religious leader

Marja'iat   Religious leadership

Mote'ahed   Committed

Motehajer   Backward

Motekhases   Specialist

Muharram   The first month of the Islamic lunar calendar

Mujtahid   Learned religious scholar

Nabovat   The Prophet Muhammad's mission

Roshanfekrane dini   Religious new thinkers

Shahid   Martyr

Sharia   Islamic law

Shora   Council

Shoraye Negahban   Council of Guardians

Sighe   Temporary marriage

Sofra   Dinner table

Sunna   Traditional portion of Muhammadan law, based on Prophet
   Muhammad's words or acts but not written by him; accepted as
   authoritative by most Sunnis but not by most Shi'as
Tahkime Vahdat   To foster unity
Ulema   Religious authorities
Umma   Islamic community
Velayat-e faqih   Guardianship of the jurist
Waqf   Religious endowment
Zakat   Religious taxes donated by Muslims, intended to assist the
   poor
Zanan   Women

This book is dedicated to Lilys, Behrangs, Samehs, Mays, Rimas, Omimas, Omars and all those who have made sacrifices to end repressive local and global dominations

Introduction

My task in this book is twofold. First, I will discuss the internal political dynamics of Iran since 1979. Over the past three decades, Iran has emerged as a religio-political state – a state that is both religious and emphasises nationalist and anti-imperialist ideologies. My analysis of Iran since the 1979 revolution will demonstrate that the contradictions inherent in the Islamic state are shifting the boundaries of conservative Islam, leading to the emergence of an important democracy movement.

Second, I discuss the global and regional perception of Iran's foreign policy since the 1979 revolution, which has been popular with the majority of the people in the Middle East region. I will argue that Iran's influence reflects how various communities in different countries perceive Iran's foreign policy in contrast to US foreign policy. Despite diverse religious and nationalist identities, in the face of the 'war on terror', neoliberalism, neoconservatism and Zionism, a majority in the Middle East identify with Iran's stance against the USA and Israel.

This book contextualises the internal political dynamics of Iran and the influence of Iran in Lebanon, Iraq, Palestine and Egypt, within the wider historical context of colonialism, imperialism and Zionism. Subsequently, it discusses the impact of socio-economic development, nationalisms, Islamisms and the political trajectory of these experiences, which have produced distinct changes in each of these societies. In this context, I discuss the fall of the secular left and the secular nationalists, and chart the rise of Islamism as an alternative force; this involves consideration of the contradictions, limitations and the dynamic nature of political Islam, as these multiple factors have impacted profoundly upon the internal dynamics of Iran and the country's influence across the Middle East.

The internal dynamics of Iran

Most analysts in the West portray Iran simply as a religiously conservative 'fundamentalist' phenomenon, ignoring the very real socio-economic achievements brought about by the 1979 revolution. To ignore this side of Iran's development is a mistake, since it is the socio-economic transformation that has brought about the powerful democracy movement in the country, including women's-rights, student and trade-union activism.

Throughout the late twentieth century, and to date, there have been contradictory shifts and changes in both the economy and the society of Iran. Following the 1979 revolution, the Islamic state distributed wealth and provided social welfare to the majority of the population. This was in contrast to the secular pro-West state of the Shah in the 1960s and 1970s, which served only to enrich a small elite and did little to develop the rest of the country. The economy of Iran depends on its oil revenues – 80 per cent of total state income is from oil.

Since the 1990s, Iran has gone through continuous and large-scale socio-economic and human development. Economic development has led to urbanisation (70 per cent), a greater rate of literacy (89 per cent in urban areas, 75 per cent in rural) and the emergence of a modern working class. The presence of a young, ethnically integrated and educated population with different levels of religiosity and secularity is clearly visible, with an increasing participation of women in public life. Such people are challenging the very state that has brought about these developments. The relative improvement in health, education and employment has raised people's socio-political consciousness and aspirations, and has led to the further development of women's, student and workers' organisations.

Grassroots democracy in Iran

In the 1990s, pressure from below led to the election of the reformist government of Mohammad Khatami (1997–2005). This was a period of expansion and of the empowerment of civil-society organisations, media and social movements. The more progressive elements within the reform movement called for a massive extension of democracy. The Islamist modernists or 'religious new thinkers' (roshanfekrane dini) are a vital part of this movement. They believe in a dialectical relationship between belief and knowledge and advocate the opening up of Islamic theology to contemporary philosophy. In the context of individualism, democracy and human rights, they propose the separation of religious values and secular realities.

At the economic level, all governments since the end of the Iran–Iraq war (1988) have embraced neoliberalism, privatisation and integration within the global economy, under the control of a strong state. The demise of the interventionist state structure since the mid-1990s has led to a rise in unemployment, a decline in quality of social services and a falling standard of living. In 2005, the conservative candidate Mahmoud Ahmadinejad stood on an anti-poverty and anti-corruption platform and was elected president. Since then, however, poverty and corruption have grown, and privatisation – under state control – has intensified. These economic problems together with political repression have exacerbated the grievances of a large part of the population, who have demonstrated their continued opposition in the post-June 2009 election uprisings.

The movement for democratic rights has enjoyed the support of a number of influential clergy. Grand Ayatollah Mottahari (1920–1979) and Grand Ayatollah Montazeri (1922–2009) both argued, following the 1979 revolution, that religious thinking and the religious community can be separated from politics and state authority. Subsequently, other dissident clerics, journalists and academics, self-styled 'religious new thinkers', have challenged the ruling orthodoxy. They have advocated a broadening of Islamic theology into the realm of contemporary philosophy – in effect, proposing the separation of religious values and secular realities. They believe it is possible to bring about a just Islamic governance, where justice and human rights are given particular importance. As is argued by Vali Nasr (2007: 172–8), the discourse of these clergy in Iran is similar to that of Grand Ayatollah Fadlallah, the spiritual leader of Hezbollah in Lebanon, and of Grand Ayatollah al-Sistani in Iraq. The thinking of these Shi'a Islamic ideologues is serving to revive the concept of *ijtihad* (a bridge between divine injunctions and requirements of any time and place), which is the key to an Islamic interpretation of modern developments and circumstances, and the force that is shaping the discourse of democracy in the Middle East.

The concept of democracy is problematic. In this book it means the struggle against authoritarianism and the establishment of democratic and individual rights. In the early twentieth century the diverse movements in Iran, comprising nationalists, communists, liberals and Islamists, debated the issue of democracy according to their different ideologies. Civil-society activism, however, which began in the mid-1990s, is a new phenomenon in Iran; it has played a crucial role in challenging the state, in sustaining the demand for democracy and in raising the issue of the compatibility of Islam with modernity and democracy (Rostami-Povey 2001, 2004). The majority of the Iranian population seeks a balance between the power of state institutions and civil society, in order to guarantee good governance, accountability, collective and individual freedoms, and the place of religion in politics. Most believe in the prevalence of modern ideological thinking in the context of Iran and Islam (Gheissari and Nasr 2006: 9–16). In this context they refuse to perceive 'modern/traditional' and 'West/Islam' as binary oppositions and are careful not to define their movement as the mere follower or imitator of 'Western culture'. Within this movement the secular left and nationalists have gone further, arguing that democracy should embrace a greater representation of Iran's social diversity.

Thus democracy is a powerful grassroots force in Iran. Despite Western governments' attempts to enforce 'regime change' through covert operations and funding for 'democracy Afghanistan and Iraq style', the democracy movement – under the umbrella of the 'Green Movement' since the June 2009 uprisings – is independent and will not be manipulated by foreign agents. The objectives of the 1979 revolution were independence, freedom and justice. For the majority, independence was achieved with the overthrow of the Shah's regime, which had kept Iran as a client state of the USA; under the Islamic Republic the struggle for democracy continues, with calls for political inclusion, and an increase in civil and individual liberties.

Perception of Iran's foreign policy in the Middle East

Since the 1979 revolution, despite the tension between Iranian and Arab nationalisms and the Shi'a and Sunni divide, as well as diverse forms of religiosity and secularity, Iran's foreign policy has been popular with the majority of the people in the Middle East. Often those who were interviewed for this book reminded me of the Arabic saying: *'Ana ou akhi ala ibn ami, ana ou ibn ami ala il ghareeb'* ('Me and my brother against my cousin, but me and my cousin against the outsider'). In examining the religio-political relationship between Iran and Lebanon, Iran and Iraq, Iran and Palestine, and Iran and Egypt, this book discusses the regional context of the Iranian religio-political state: why Iran is emerging as a power in this region, with the possibility in due course of influencing regional and global politics. The focus is on the complexities of nationalisms[1] and religions, in particular the historical and contemporary interpretations of the Sunni–Shi'a divide and the hybridity of Arab, Iranian, Muslim, Shi'a, Sunni, non-Muslim and secular identities.

People in the Middle East are not informed about the reality of Iran. The Arab world speaks one language, Arabic, while Iranians speak Farsi; hence there is very little communication between Iranians and Arabs. The intellectuals in the region may share the English language, but the ordinary people tend to communicate with each other through a mutual perception of the roles of Israel and the USA in the region. This book will demonstrate that in Lebanon, Palestine and Egypt, Iran is popular simply because it is the only country in the region that supports the Palestinians and the Lebanese, while opposing Zionism and Western – in particular US – policies in the region; this despite the fact that the mainstream Arab media and politicians portray Iran as a non-Arab, Shi'a threat to the Sunni Arab world. Of course the Shi'a and Sunni divide is a historical, cultural, theological and political reality. But, as I discuss in this book, Israel's attacks on the Palestinians and Lebanese have brought these communities closer to each other, and closer to Iran. They see Iran as Islamic modernism, an example of Islamic revolutionary practice; a model of Islamic state power, with a long legacy of popular anti-imperialist struggle.

In the case of Iraq, however, the majority of the people in the Middle East are critical of the role of Iran. They share the view of many Iraqis that the rise to power of an Iraqi Shi'a leadership is the direct result of US policy. In their judgement, the USA has destroyed Iraq as a functioning country and used it as a base to threaten Iran's sovereignty. Under these circumstances, they see Iran manoeuvring to find a presence in Iraq in order to counter the possible threat from the USA and Israel. As a result, Iraq has become a battleground for the USA and Iran to settle their differences, with Iraqis the victims of the contradictory relations of conflict and collaboration between the two powers.

Many are also debating the internal political repression in Iran. Despite strong support for Iran in Lebanon, Palestine and Egypt, the uprisings in Iran since June 2009 have raised questions for the secular left, nationalists and Islamists alike in these societies. Witnessing the brutality in the streets against the demonstrators, many sympathise with the movement and feel that they cannot trust a regime that is not accountable to its own people. Yet they also see the support of Western, Israeli and mainstream Arabic media for the democracy movement in Iran and therefore question whether this is an external attempt to destabilise the country. Thus the support of people across the Middle East for Iran's democracy movement is limited and ambiguous. The Iranian state has monopolised the anti-imperialist and anti-Zionist position and does not tolerate independent demonstrations and organisation. For this reason, the Iranian democracy movement, in its opposition to the Iranian state, has mistakenly expressed no support for the anti-Zionist movements in the Middle East and in some instances has shown hostility towards Palestinians and Lebanese. Sadly, the disunity between movements in the region will only strengthen the Iranian regime, the Arab regimes, as well as the West with its divide-and-rule policies.

Meanwhile, Iran's role in Iraq and internal political repression are overshadowing the positive perception of Iran in the region. As this book goes to press, in the eyes of many in the region, Turkey – a secular state, which supports the Palestinians – is replacing Iran as the alternative to those states that have lost all credibility for their passive stance against Zionism and imperialism.

The rise of Islamisms in the region

Analysis of the internal dynamics of Iran and of the religio-political relationships between Iran and Lebanon, Iran and Iraq, Iran and Palestine, and Iran and Egypt, raises the question as to why Islamists have become established as alternative in these societies. What is the nature of these political Islamists. Throughout 1950s, 1960s and even after the death of Gamal Abdel Nasser – the most important Arab nationalist leader of the time – the secular left and nationalists played a key role as opposition movements to the regimes in the region and as a rallying point against imperialist domination and Zionism. However, following the 1979 revolution in Iran, the growth of Islamisms became evident. By the end of the first decade of the twenty-first century, the Islamists are becoming the dominant oppositional force among the urban poor, professionals, students, women and workers. This growth in influence is not restricted to the establishment of the Islamic state in Iran, the rise of Hezbollah in Lebanon, Hamas in Palestine and the Muslim Brotherhood in Egypt. The entire region is witness to a range of other Islamic organisations, as well as to the growing influence of diverse Islamist writers, thinkers and preachers unaffiliated to any organisation.

The process in which resistance to US imperialism and Zionism has passed from the secular left and nationalists to Islamists is significant. Islamism is a socio-political phenomenon and as such must be understood through historical interpretation. Islamist ideologies and organisations need to be located within the political field and understood in the context of wider social forces nationally, regionally and globally (Harman 1994) to be understood. Using historical analysis, this books argue that two factors have determined the rise of Islamisms: first, the failure of the secular left and nationalists to achieve grassroots support; second, the support of the West for dictatorial regimes.

The left in the Middle East is diverse, offering different readings and interpretations of Marxism. Historically the dominant tendency slavishly adhered to Soviet 'communism' and the Stalinist tradition. The Iraqi Communist Party and, to a lesser extent, the Iranian Tudeh (Communist) Party, enjoyed a mass base and managed to develop successful alliances with nationalist movements. Nevertheless, the Stalinist tradition throughout the region failed to develop successful hegemonic projects in Iran, Lebanon, Iraq, Palestine and Egypt. For decades they were crippled either by their total subordination to groups that they identified as a 'progressive national bourgeoisie' or by abstaining from critical support for forces such as nationalists and Islamists which had mass support among the oppressed sections of society. They failed to grasp that such nationalists and Islamist forces have complex relations of collaboration and conflict with imperialism and capitalism. That is, their anti-capitalist and anti-imperialist stance is limited to mobilising mass support, in order to break down the obstacles created by global capitalism to prevent the creation of independent states and societies. As a result, the left failed to support these movements in the name of maintaining their political independence in order to win the grassroots to their ideologies. In Iran, following the 1979 revolution, they dissolved themselves within the state that they identified as anti-imperialist; and in Egypt, under Mubarak, they supported the regime's suppression of Islamists (Callinicos 2006; Harman 1994; Abdelrahman 2009).

With their collective memory of the colonial past and faced with continued aggressive Western domination, Zionism and the subordination of their regimes to the USA, the majority of the people across the Middle East have historically identified with anti-imperialist nationalism. The Soviet Union, however, had no concern for the objective conditions of these societies and so prevented the communists from building anti-imperialist alliances with nationalists. Consequently divisions appeared within the ranks of the Communist movements and splinter groups formed. Some survived to varying degrees but all were enormously weakened and disoriented (Ismael 2005). Furthermore, the Soviet Union was dominated by a wealthy and corrupt bureaucratic state elite, managing a very unequal society. This meant that 'Communism' had long abandoned its historical role as the champion of oppressed peoples everywhere, especially in societies subject to Western imperial power. This was especially true in the Middle East. Stalin's decision to recognise, and even help arm, Israel sabotaged the Communist movements throughout the region. This failure to understand Zionism as a creation of Western imperialism severely marginalised the Communist contribution to progress, development and change in the region.

Historically, nationalism and liberation from imperialism have been intertwined in the region. In the Arab World, in particular, nationalism and anti-imperialism promoted Arab unity. From the 1950s, Arab nationalism incorporated anti-Zionism, nation-building and pan-Arabism. Egypt was at the heart of Arab nationalism in the 1950s and 1960s. The 1967 war and the defeat of the Arab world by Israel were, therefore, considered a defeat for Arab nationalism. By the 1990s Egypt had completely abandoned the quest for Arab unity and the liberation of Palestine; and the USA and Israel succeeded in isolating Egypt from the Arab World. As is argued by Abu-Rabi (2004: 77–80), the intention of the USA was to keep the Arab world divided. The American–Israeli alliance and the co-opting of the majority of the Arab states and of the Iranian state of the pre-1979 revolution in support had a devastating affect on nationalisms in the region. Open-door economic policies, deteriorating economic conditions, widening inequalities, failure of secular nationalist regimes and the impact of the Iranian Revolution together led to the rise of Islamism and popular antagonism towards the rulers and their Western back-ers. The subsequent occupation of Iraq, in 2003, dealt another blow to Arab nationalism.

Western support for dictatorial regimes in the Middle East, along-side aggressive Western–Israeli policies, was, therefore, the second important factor that led to the demise of the secular left and the nationalists and the rise of marginal Islamist groups pledged to violence and extremism. However, as is argued by Naguib (2006, 2009), the historical development of Islamist movements, the socio-economic and political context, as well as regional and global factors all impacted on the organisations, changing their social composition and determining the nature of political Islam.

Change in political Islam

Political Islam takes many forms (Burgat 2003). Nevertheless, the dominant rhetoric of Western politicians, media and even some academics characterise it simply as 'anti-democratic', 'terrorist' and 'fundamentalist'. This view ignores the presence of contradiction and change, reducing all forms of Islamism to a reactionary identity politics. This book, through a critical approach, locates political Islam in Iran, Lebanon, Iraq, Palestine and Egypt within their historical and socio-political contexts. It argues that it is essential to distinguish between the different trends within Islamism, rather than conflating and dismissing them as fundamentalist, anti-democratic and terrorist. The depiction of the Muslim-majority Middle East as monolithic and static, with Islam portrayed as an immutable culture and religion, ignores the socio-economic and socio-political changes in these societies, in particular the movements which are struggling for reform. As this book demonstrates, it is socio-economic and political factors that determine the cultures of these societies rather than religion. To regard Islamism as rigidly dogmatic and violent compared to Western secularism is also to ignore the presence of these features in secular societies, and to deny the capacity of Islamists to interpret and reinterpret Islamic laws and regulations in response to socio-political and economic developments. In this context, the discourse of the 'clash of civilisations' – put forward by Samuel Huntington (1998) and Bernard Lewis (2003) and suggesting a clash between 'anti-modern' Islamism and Western modernity – is at best simplistic and at worst simply racist (Bayat 2009a: 225; Gunning 2007: 1–24; Dabashi 2007: 1–11).

Modernity is a process that occurs at different levels and is experienced unevenly (Appadurai 1996: 3–4). The notion of a plurality of modernity, or multiple modernities, suggests the existence of commonalities and differences among the variety of paths to modernity and challenges the assumptions that modernity is exclusive to the West and has an entirely Western origin (Sadria 2009; Salvatore 2009).[2] Modernity also implies capitalist development, the creation of the modern state, constitutional laws, and monopoly of power over people within the framework of the nation-state. It implies the creation of institutions such as the army, education, health, employment and media, as well as the coming into existence of different classes and patriarchal relations. In the Middle East the processes of socio-economic and political development took place as the result of the encounter of internal dynamics with colonialism and imperialism. This combination led to uneven socio-economic and political development, as a result of which states use repressive mechanisms and coercive measures in certain instances, while also promoting consensus and legitimacy.[3] The Iranian state, for example, clamps down on its opponents and yet builds consensus and support through a resolute policy of pan-Islamism, anti-imperialism and anti-Zionism. The Egyptian state, for its part, similarly suppresses opposition, whilst striving for legitimacy through its support for Egyptian and Arab nationalism.

As is discussed later in the book, in Iran in the 1980s thousands of political opponents of the regime were killed. In the 2009–10 street demonstrations, a number of people died; thousands were injured, imprisoned and tortured. This level of political repression constitutes the unacceptable face of modern political Islam. Nevertheless, it is important to note that such repression happened under the secular pro-West, pro-Israel state of the Shah before the 1979 revolution. It is also a feature of the pro-West conservative religious state of Saudi Arabia, and of the pro-West secular states in the region, including Egypt. In this context, we cannot dismiss modern Islamic politics as uniquely barbaric and violent, as suggested by the 'clash of civilisations' thesis. As is argued by Asef Bayat (2009b), the Islamic state in Iran is not in fact archaic or pre-modern; it is an authoritarian, patriarchal and ideologically exclusive system which exerts power through modern state institutions. Moreover, events show that the more the authoritarian state suppresses democracy, the greater is the demand.

Huntington and Lewis also see Islam as the primary factor shaping state formation and distorting civil society. This approach treats the Muslim-majority societies as unchanging and stagnant, and ignores the capacity of civil-society organisations and movements to challenge the status quo and confront conservative ideologies. As will be seen, the authoritarian states in Iran and Egypt are challenged by modern civil-society organisations such as trade unions, women's groups, students and, in particular, religious modernists. In Palestine and Lebanon, we witness how the growth of civil-society organisations and the diversity of their supporters, especially the young and educated activists, and women in particular, have challenged the policies of conservative leadership. They are struggling against universalism and the monopoly of religious power by conservative leaders, thereby shifting these political Islamist movements towards modernism, tolerance and democracy. In Iraq, resistance to the occupation and to the government supported by

Iran has been led by genuine civil-society organisations. They condemn terrorism and call for an end to the occupation and for unity among the people of Iraq. Women, in particular, play an important role in generating norms, networks and reciprocities which are essential for the survival of communities in the face of conflict and foreign occupation.

For many Islamists, Islam is compatible with the modern ideologies of liberalism, Marxism and postmodernism. Thus, for them, through reforms Islam is able to accommodate social change, progress and political freedoms. The Sorbonne-educated Iranian sociologist Ali Shariati, who used the Marxist concepts of class and anti-imperialism combined with Shi'a Islamic discourse, played a crucial role in the success of the 1979 revolution. He was one of many who contributed to modern Islamic thought during the revolutionary period in Iran by insisting that Islam and modernism are mutually compatible, and that Islamic concepts can be interpreted and re-interpreted according to time and place. It is in this context that the majority of the people in the Middle East view the 1979 revolution in Iran as the outcome of a successful modern mass movement rooted in urban areas. The majority of Shi'a communities throughout the Muslim world understood the revolution as a pan-Islamic revolution. Hence many Sunnis throughout the region saw, and still see, the Iranian Revolution and the country's anti-imperialist and anti-Zionist position as a positive force. Many hoped, and indeed are still hoping, for the closing of the Shi'a and Sunni divide and a move towards the democratisation of Muslim-majority societies. As is argued by Laleh Khalili (2007a, 2007b), in Lebanon, Hezbollah has also reinforced the revolutionary image of Shi'ism. Its sustained struggle against Israel led to victory against them, as a result of which both Hezbollah and Iran are now celebrated throughout the region, and the success of their strategy recognised by Hamas supporters.

Historically, the tradition of seeing compatibility between Islam and modernism has, of course, been a constant in Sunnism, as it has in Shi'ism (Bayat 2005: 36–7). Sayyid Jamal al-Din al-Afghani (1838–1897), who was born in Iran and received a Shi'a education, was a pioneer of Islamic modernism – transforming Islam from a merely religious faith into a religio-political ideology, with an emphasis against Western domination. Muhammad Abduh (1849–1905) and Rashid Rida (1865–1935), who were influenced by Afghani, pioneered an Islamic modernist school of thought, which became prominent from the late nineteenth century. These Islamist modernists, in different ways, asserted the compatibility of Islam with modernism – including the acquisition of modern science, gender equality and women's education. Hassan al-Banna, the leader of the Muslim Brotherhood, and Sayyid Qutb, an influential ideologue of the Muslim Brotherhood in Egypt, were also followers of Afghani and Abduh, and both played important roles against British colonialism in Egypt (Hourani 1962: 130–244; Rahnema 2005a).

Since the 11 September 2001 attacks in the USA, the Western notion of the 'threat of Islamic fundamentalism' has intensified, regenerating the racist ideology of Islamophobia. Edward Said (1978) and Leila Ahmed (1992) have famously and critically discussed Orientalism as a means of domination. In this context, this book contests the concept of 'Islamic fundamentalism', seeing it as homogenizing and essentialising the diversity of Islamisms, thus nurturing Orientalism and Islamophobia.

Today Islamisms range from neo-Wahabism (out of which al-Qaeda have arisen), to anti-communist jihadis (created and supported by the CIA to fight against the Soviet Union in the 1980s), followed by Talibanism, to the pan-Arabism and pan-Islamism of the Muslim Brotherhood and Hezbollah. The Muslim Brotherhood, Hezbollah and Hamas have shown their ability to present policies that offer a way forward for their societies at large, and for this reason they are popular with a large majority in the Middle East. The Taliban and al-Qaeda, however, are certainly incapable of sustaining such a project and derive their strength instead mainly from the invasion of Afghanistan, the occupation of Iraq and Zionism's crimes in Palestine. Therefore, this book discusses a contextually specific form of conservative Islam and, in opposition to conservative Islam, a contextually specific form of reformist, liberal and democratic Islam in Iran, Lebanon, Palestine and Egypt. It argues that socio-economic and political circumstances have constantly shifted the boundaries between conservative Islam and liberal-democratic Islam, both in Iran and in many other parts of the region.

This is an important observation. As is argued by Naguib (2006, 2009), many analysts, from Marxists to postmodernists and those writers who deploy the concept of populism (Amin 2001; Achcar 2006; Zubaide 1993), have also ignored the shifts in political Islam. By simplifying the diversity of Islamisms and the internal contra- dictions of Islamic movements, such writers ignore the dynamics of change within them. As this book argues, the Islamists in Iran and the organisations such as Hezbollah, Hamas and the Muslim Brother- hood are not only different from each other but also have their own inherent contradictions and internal conflicts. Their commonality, however, is that, in the absence of secular left and nationalists, they have been able to win the support of the majority of the people in the region and to mobilise against imperialism and Zionism. Their supporters are not just the 'disgruntled petty bourgeoisie' or 'mercantile capitalists'. They have support among the poor and the rich, workers and capitalists, women and students – all of whom have conflicting interests. In this book, the narratives of the Lebanese Hezbollah, Palestinian Hamas and Egyptian Muslim Brotherhood demonstrate that these organisations have changed over time, and show how such diverse groups of Islamists are in different ways seeking a compromise with democracy.

Asef Bayat (2009a: 78) calls these movements 'Social Islam', which seems a very useful concept as they contribute to social welfare – the provision of health and education and financial aid to the disadvan- taged. They are also involved in community development and social networking, through NGO activism. In this context such 'Social Islam' is also political:[4] the movements are not only engaged in the provision of resources but have won the support of a majority of their people by becoming political, cultural and economic alternatives to regimes committed to neoliberalism, authoritarianism, Zionism and imperialism. Hence they articulate the struggles of large sections of the oppressed urban people in their societies.

The participation of these groups in electoral politics, as modern political organisations, is also significant, and as such they have won the support of significant sections of their societies, especially women and young people. Since the 1970s, the Muslim Brotherhood has been challenging the Egyptian state through electoral politics and has won support in professional syndicates and local and national assemblies. Since the 1990s, Hezbollah has worked consistently and systematically to win the support of a majority among diverse communities in Lebanon, through parliamentary participation and integration into Lebanese politics. Hamas followed the example of the Muslim Brotherhood, and Hezbollah and has participated in electoral politics since 1992, winning the support of a majority of Palestinians across diverse communities.

However, as is argued in this book, the anti-imperialist and anti-Zionist stances of the Iranian regime, of Hezbollah of Lebanon, of the Muslim brotherhood in Egypt and of Hamas in Palestine, which have brought these diverse modern Islamists together, are likely to be short-lived as these organisations engage in complex relations of collaboration and conflict with the forces of neoliberalism and imperialism. In the absence of a secular left and a nationalist movement, they enjoy mass support, which they are mobilising to break down the obstacles created by the West and Zionism on their way to building independent states and societies within the terms of global capitalism. Despite its limitations, this trajectory is positive inasmuch as it opens the way for a process of democratisation that will provide the testing ground for different ideologies and political currents to prove their value and relevance.

Considering the suffering of the people in the region at the hands of authoritarian regimes, Israel and the West, the political success of Islamist movements has been to combine nationalist aspirations, anti-imperialism and modern interpretations of Islam. As argued by Asef Bayat, religions are neither inherently democratic nor inherently undemocratic. Whether or not Muslim societies become democratic depends upon the intellectual and political conviction and the will to struggle of the people in these societies, rather than the essence of Islam (Bayat 2005: xvii–5, 187–94). Indeed, this book argues that the majority of Islamists in Iran, Lebanon, Iraq, Palestine and Egypt, be they diverse individuals, groups or movements, have in fact embraced a democratic Islamic idea: they see Islam as an ideology to resist repression and authoritarian political domination.

The case of *roshanfekrane dini*, 'religious new thinkers', in Iran is particularly important, for they are far in advance of their counterparts in Lebanon, Palestine and Egypt. They believe that religion cannot impose on the will of the people. Instead its role in politics must be legitimised through popular support, which will open the way not only to reformist laws and regulations but also to the building of a social movement rooted in democracy. These new thinkers are both inside and outside the system, and are often willing to ally with secularists, democratic nationalists and the left. They have far broader grassroots support than other parts of the democracy movement.

However, arguably it is the Egyptian political opposition movement that has shown the way forward through joint political work and coordination with the left, nationalists and Islamists. Despite certain antagonisms between these diverse groups, an emergent younger generation is open to cooperation and is concretely planning for the democratisation of society by campaigning against Western domination and opposing political repression by their own regime. By their support for the Iraqis, Palestinians and Lebanese, they are demonstrating that only through the global weakening of relations of domination is it possible to create a space for democracy through mass struggle.

The authoritarian regimes of the Middle East have historically been resistant to political change. Nevertheless, contemporary movements in the region are changing their societies from within. The role of the West and Zionism has had a devastating impact on the democratic movements, leading to the strengthening of extremist Islamists such as al-Qaeda and the Taliban. The future of democracy in Iran and in the wider region depends on challenging not only local politics but also imperial domination, and on blurring the growing divide between the West and the Muslim world.

The organisation of this book

Chapter 1 discusses the historical causes and legacies of the 1979 revolution in Iran and looks at the major players – women, workers, Islamists, nationalists and the left. It argues that the support of the West, especially the USA and UK, for the dictatorial regime of the Shah, combined with a lack of coherent and locally determined ideas and strategies to win grassroots support, weakened both the secular left and the nationalists and was instrumental in the emergence of Islamic conservatism in the years after the 1979 revolution. Nevertheless, a dialogue and contest took place between those who wished to preserve traditional conservative Islam and those wishing to embrace a democratic modern model. The Iran–Iraq war (1980–88) increased the popularity of conservative Islam in Iran and across the Middle East. In consequence the domestic practice of internal repression and regionally popular foreign policy evolved.

Chapter 2 discusses the progress of Iranian society during the 1990s, and considers the challenge to Islamic conservatism that emerged. The chapter examines the socio-economic and political developments in this period; the emergence of the reform movement in the 1990s; and the continuing struggle of the democracy movement (trade unions, students, ethnic and religious minorities and women) under the conservative government of President Ahmadinejad since 2005 and the uprisings since the post-June 2009 presidential election. The chapter concludes that, notwithstanding the specific forms of ideological conservatism and political repression, these movements continue their struggle for democracy in Iran.

Chapter 3 discusses the Sunni–Shi'a divide historically and the change in the discourse of Shi'ism in Iran: from its rise to power between the sixteenth and the eighteenth centuries to the marginalisation of Shi'a clergy in the twentieth century, from the assumption of political and state power following the 1979 revolution to the 1990s when the 'religious new thinkers', as an important part of the democracy movement, challenged the rule of the conservative clergy. The aim is to analyse the implications of the internal socio-political dynamics of Iran for the region.

Chapter 4 looks at the historical background to the relationship between Iran and Lebanon. It suggests that the emergence of Hezbollah was the direct result of the Israeli invasion of Lebanon and Western support for Israel, which led to the weakening of the secular left and nationalist movements, and to the rise of Islamism. The chapter then discusses how since the early 1990s Hezbollah, supported by Iran, began to participate in electoral politics and to fulfil the function of the state through provision of resources and how it won the support not just of a majority among the Shi'a communities but also of Sunni Palestinians and sections of the Christian and Druze communities. In this context, the argument is made that, contrary to popular perception in the West, Hezbollah is not an extension of Iran. For a majority in Lebanon, the popularity of Hezbollah, which is supported by Iran, is a response to Israel's wars on Lebanon.

Chapter 5 examines the historical background of the relationship between Iran and Iraq, in particular the relations of continuity and change between their Shi'a communities. It is argued that, despite historical Shi'a ties between the two countries, the majority of Iraqi Shi'a communities have identified with Iraqi and Arab nationalisms rather than Iranian Shi'ism, and still do so today. The rise of a Shi'a leadership to political power in Iraq is the direct result of the US and allied policy of 'regime change' in Iraq. It is argued that the majority of Iraqis, including Shi'a communities, are critical of the role of Iran in Iraq. Iran, under threat of the USA and Israel, is using the situation in Iraq to divert attention from these attacks. As a result, Iraq has turned into a mosaic of warring factions where a great mass of people are being abused.

Chapter 6 discusses the relationship between Iran and Palestine. The historical background to the establishment of the Zionist state demonstrates the support of Iran for Zionism under the secular state of the Shah. In contrast, since the 1979 revolution Iran's policy has reversed. This chapter argues that the rise of Hamas to power is the direct result of Zionist and US policies in the region. By the mid-1990s Hamas, supported by Iran, emerged as a resistance movement. Like Hezbollah, Hamas participates in electoral politics and provides social welfare. Its electoral victory clearly demonstrates the support of diverse communities (secularists, Islamists and Christians) for the organisation. The relationship between Iran and Hamas is multidimensional – political, ideological and cultural. There are many criticisms of the role of Iran in Palestine, levelled in particular by Fatah supporters; there are also criticisms of the role of Iran in Iraq, and indeed of the political repression in Iran. However, for the majority, Iran is still the only country in the Middle East which stands against Zionism and American policy in the region.

Chapter 7 considers the historical background to the relationship between Iran and Egypt. It is argued that, as in Iran, capitalist development in Egypt has involved foreign domination. As a result, different actors – Islamists, nationalists, communists, women, workers and minorities – have engaged in anti-imperialist struggle. Also as in to Iran, Islamist modernist schools of thought have been influential in Egypt. From the early twentieth century until the 1979 revolution, the two countries' states cemented their relationship by means of their links to Western domination and the relationship with Israel. The opposition movements in the two countries have likewise cemented their relationships – against their rulers and their Western supporters; Nasser's and Mossadeq's nationalisms were popular forces in the region. The rise of Islamism in Egypt is the direct result of the inability of the secular left and nationalists to provide an alternative. Although the states and movements in Iran and Egypt are very different, political Islam in Egypt has now changed and the majority of the people identify with the democratic Islamists, as they do in Iran. Yet, unlike in Iran, the movement for democracy in Egypt is showing the way forward by opening up to the wider movements in the region.

In Chapter 8 I analyse the global context of the Iranian religious–political state and society. I argue that the West's hostility towards Iran is rooted in a desire to return the country to the status of a client state of the West, in order to ensure the latter's economic and political domination in the region, and to deny Iran independence. The constant threats of war, military intervention, sanctions, covert operations and funding for 'regime change' are undermining the democratic movement in Iran, which can only increase the Iranian regime's influence in the Middle East. Similarly, the West's hostility towards the modern Islamist movements will intensify political hostility against the West and their client states, thereby ultimately strengthening Islamic conservatism in the region and globally.

ONE

The legacy of a revolution

It is impossible to understand the experience of the 1979 revolution in Iran, or the subsequent Islamisation of state and society, without first seeing the roots of the changes in the nineteenth and twentieth centuries. Although the country was never colonised or formally ruled by a foreign power, capitalist development in Iran in the nineteenth century, though unique in some ways, shared many features of uneven economic development experienced by countries that were so colonised (Tabari 1983: 53; Poya 1999: 29). Fundamentally, the development derived from the need of the European capitalist market to import Iranian goods and to export European manufactured goods back to Iran.

An increase in Iran's trade with Russia and Britain led gradually to the transformation of a largely barter-based economy into a monetised one. The influence of Western capitalism served to increase trade and the import of foreign goods; this accelerated the growth of the urban population, of non-agricultural activities and of commercial agriculture. Participation in the global market changed pre-existing patterns of economic and social life through the reorganisation of labour into proletarians, semi-proletarians and petty commodity producers, sectors which broadly persist today.

During the second half of the nineteenth century, Britain and Russia imposed their banks upon Iran and began indirect exploitation by acquiring 'concessions' to collect taxes and to extract and market raw materials and agricultural products, in exchange for an often paltry sum paid to the Qajar Shah's dynasty. For example, in 1890 a British company obtained the monopoly over the production, sale and export of tobacco from Iran, a concession that produced a massive wave of popular discontent. Strikes and street demonstrations made the campaign against tobacco concession highly successful. This experience led to the Constitutional Revolution of 1906–11 and consequently to the fall of the Qajar dynasty (Algar 1969; Keddie 1966; Browne 1910; Abrahamian 1982). As is argued by Vanessa Martin (1989), the Constitutional Revolution formed part of a process of change and conflict between the old and the new order.

With the discovery of large quantities of oil in Iran in 1909 Britain established the Anglo-Iranian Oil Company to exploit the country's new-found natural wealth (Issawi 1971: 316–22). During the First World War, British and Russian troops occupied almost all of Iran, creating widespread popular opposition to the occupying powers. However, after the Russian Revolution, the Bolsheviks quickly abandoned tsarist privileges such as various concessions in Iran. This concentrated popular anger against Britain, which both controlled the oil and supported the governing autocratic regime in Iran. In this period the labour movement was associated with the Communist movements in Iran and in Russia and played an important role in the struggle against the Anglo-Iranian Oil Company (Zabih 1966: 1–35; Lajevardi 1985: 14; Rostami-Povey 2004, 2005).

In December 1925, Reza Pahlavi declared himself the Shah of the Pahlavi dynasty. Under the influence of the British he was committed to building a modern secular state, promoting nationalism, looking to pre-Islamic identities and curbing the role of the ulema (religious authorities). Iranian economic development in this period centred largely on infrastructure. This was linked to the Shah's desire to control the country effectively through the army, and to the desire of British capital to exploit the oil resources with greater ease, but it also laid the foundation for industrial development in this period. Peasant and nomad communities, which suffered as a consequence of the economic reconstruction, resisted the unjust social relations brought about by the landlords and the state (Cronin 2008: 141–70). Industrial development under Reza Shah began during the global depression of the 1930s, when the terms of trade were in Iran's favour, as oil was exported in return for imported capital goods. Rapid integration into the world economy meant that the landed aristocracy and the propertied middle class declined in terms of economic, social and political power, being replaced by a new bourgeoisie and professional salary-earners. The aim of Reza Shah's state-building was to centralise state power and to keep the clergy and religious institutions under strict control. Development was accompanied by massive repression of all political groups, from communists to liberals, protesting clergy, trade unions, women's organisations and ethnic minority groups (Najmabadi 1991: 52; Abrahamian 1982: 135–65; Cronin 2003).

Iran's population has always been only two-thirds Persian and Farsi-speaking (the official language); the remaining third comprises other ethnic groups (Azeri, Kurd, Arab, Baluch, Turkmen, Gilaki, Qashqai, Bakhtiari, Shahsevan, Lur). The official religion is Shi'a Islam, but there are other religious minorities – Sunni Muslims, Sufi Muslims, Jews, Armenians, Assyrians, Chaldians, Zoroastrians and Bahais (Sanasarian 2000; Abrahamian 1982: 12). Under Reza Shah's state these minorities were denied linguistic, cultural, religious and ethnic rights – this in addition to the denial of civil rights to the whole population. This repression produced a desire to fight the central state authority which, I argue, had become part of politics in Iran.

When the economic depression reached Iran, the imposition of low wages, long working hours and bad labour conditions caused widespread industrial discontent. Reza Shah's state increasingly faced opposition by women, by workers, as well as by ethnic and religious social groups. In 1941, Britain and Russia invaded Iran, fearing Reza Shah's support for Nazism. The occupying powers forced the Shah to abdicate in favour of his son Mohammad Reza Shah (hereafter referred to as 'the Shah') and to leave the country.

Throughout the 1940s, the political groups that had been suppressed by Reza Shah – liberal nationalists, communists and Islamists – organised and offered political alternatives (Abrahamian 1982: 135–65; Gheissari and Nasr 2006: 45–6; Poya 1999: 40, 36). In 1947, following World War II, Mohammad Mossadeq founded the National Front, demanding free elections, an improvement in economic conditions, press freedom and the right to political participation. In 1950, the National Front denounced the Anglo-Iranian Oil Company for paying inadequate royalties, bypassing local taxes, refusing to employ Iranian workers and interfering in the national sovereignty of Iran. The Tudeh (Communist) Party and the Islamists supported Mossadeq and the National Front and demanded the nationalisation of the oil company. In 1951, street demonstrations and an oil workers' strike led to the victory of Mossadeq's nationalist government and their policy of oil nationalisation. Mossadeq, with mass support, further challenged the position of the Shah and in so doing became an anti-imperialist icon in the Middle East, especially for Egyptians, who at the time were also experiencing British domination (see Chapter 7).

The Iranian oil nationalisation seemed to ride a wave of anti-imperialist movements throughout the colonial world, from India with Nehru, to Egypt with Gamal Abdel Nasser, and spreading throughout North Africa and Latin America. Britain's response to the nationalisation was to cut Iran out of the oil market by mobilising a global boycott of Iran's oil, which plunged the country into financial crisis. Under Winston Churchill and Dwight Eisenhower, MI6 and the CIA were instrumental in a successful coup in 1953 and the establishment of a dictatorial regime under the Shah. With the help of the two agencies, the Shah, who ruthlessly suppressed the National Front and the Tudeh Party, ruled without an organised opposition (Abrahamian 1982: 263–8; Lajevardi 1985: 50–70; Ansari 2003: 106–25, 233–54; Gheissari and Nasr 2006: 51–4; Katouzian 2009: 229–62).

The 1960s and 1970s under the Shah saw not only an oil-boom economy, but also American domination of the government. In this period Iran's economy and society transformed with unprecedented speed and intensity. The import-substitution industrialisation policy meant that the oil industry accumulated surplus wealth, obtained Western technology and financed industrialisation – the building of infrastructure and industrial plants based on product assembly as well as component manufacture. Hence it was that the state – now a rentier state – derived a substantial portion of its national revenue from its oil, by way of massive extraction and export to other countries (Nomani and Rahnema 1994: 145, 176; Katouzian 2009: 263–87).

The Shah's state, supported by the West and particularly by the USA, was the main agent of capital accumulation, but the state also determined and regulated social relations within production and reproduction. Under the influence of the state, capital and religion, access to material resources and political power varied according to social class, gender, and ethnic and religious grouping. During this period, whenever the power of the state weakened, the suppressed groups – workers, women, students, ethnic and religious minorities – organised and forced the state to reform. Reforms were introduced in relation to education, health, employment and the specific rights of workers, and of ethnic and religious minorities, and in gender relations. Despite this, the process of economic development in this period remained structurally and spatially uneven. Only a small minority truly benefited from secular education, and from reform of laws concerning and opportunities in the labour market (Poya 1999: 28–60).

Oil wealth raised expectations that the state was unable and unwilling to fulfil. Import substitution emphasising capital-intensive industries led to the neglect of small-scale production and the agricultural sector. This contributed to rapid urbanisation, income inequality, social dislocation and cultural alienation. The Shah, his extended family and those of his close allies in charge of the state and other institutions spent the oil money on wasteful grandiose projects such as the annual celebration of the Persian Empire.[1] Their corruption, speculative property and financial activities, as well as heavy investment on the military, secret police, nuclear power plants, and public enterprises of little economic value, all created large-scale social and political discontent. The Shah's regime accommodated headquarters of both the CIA and Mossad (the Israeli secret police), who helped to train the notorious Iranian secret police which terrorised the population. Meanwhile, poverty and political repression continued to impact on the lives of the majority of people, who were denied basic access to health, education and employment. As the repression intensified, so the protest movement grew in strength and the Shah's authoritarian state faced stronger opposition by women, workers, students, diverse ethnic groups, nationalists, communists and Islamists (Poya 1999: 43–60; Gheissari and Nasr 2006: 63).

Finally, in 1978–79, this growing anti-Shah movement produced the political and social revolution that overthrew the most brutal regime in the Middle East. The revolution took place in the context of major civil discontent, with growing social and economic disparities, as well as popular anger against political repression. The major players in the revolution were women, workers, Islamists, nationalists and the left. But the ideological tensions between these groups soon became apparent. Was this a revolution about democracy, anti-imperialism, Marxism, Islamism, nationalism, women's rights, workers rights or minority rights? Divisions also opened up within, as well as between, these groups (Poya 1999: 35–60; Gheissari and Nasr 2006: 55–60, 80; Katouzian 2009: 288–323).

Tensions within the revolutionary movement

WOMEN

In the 1960s and 1970s, despite economic development and reforms in women's education, employment, unveiling and desegregation, the majority of women benefited little from the changes and remained poor, although a minority did benefit and even came to occupy important positions. The secular state maintained its legitimacy by making concessions to conservative religious gender ideology and tradition; in consequence gender identity served to maintain sexual hierarchies, the sexual division of labour and, as a result, female subordination.

The relationship between pro-Western capitalist development and conservative religious ideology was particularly painful for traditional middle-class women. They had to endure Westernisation whilst observing the absolute Islamic values of segregation, including wearing the chador (full-length cover) as dictated by their families, especially male relatives, who regarded the Western culture of modernity as wholly inappropriate for their women. These women were torn between their families' traditional values and a society which promoted Western values, including wearing the latest Western fashions. Many tried to resolve this dilemma by accommodating both values. They left home veiled and took their veil off before entering school, university or the workplace. But many others, under family pressure, took a defensive position and wore the veil as a sign of protest at the uneven nature of economic, political and social change. In respecting these values and traditions, on the other hand, they paid the heavy price of being labelled as backward in schools, universities and workplaces. In the 1970s women's political participation increased markedly. Many women realised that as long as poverty and repression existed in Iran, women would continue to be regarded as inferior beings. They played an important role in the fight against the Shah's regime (Tabari and Yeganeh 1982: 9–10; Poya 1999: 28–60).

WORKERS

The process of industrialisation in the 1960s and the 1970s increased the number of industrial workers. As real wages rose, so did living standards, until late 1977/1978, when a recession set in. Unemployment grew and wages fell. Throughout the country, workers in industries such as electricity, water, health, textile, construction, machinery and car assembly went on strike, demanding higher wages and demonstrating against poor working conditions. In some parts of the country, workers cemented alliances with the local clergy. When the police shot dead a number of protestors, further demonstrations took place seven and then forty days after the deaths, according to the requirements of Islamic Shi'a culture in Iran;[2] hence the deaths of the demonstrators led to cycles of forty-day demonstrations. As a result, the Shah began to talk about reform and a degree of political freedom, but the workers' strikes continued and led to street clashes between ordinary people in working-class areas of the cities and the army. And the more people died in the street demonstrations, the more the majority of the population turned against the Shah (Abrahamian 1982: 510–25).

Trade unions, and oil workers in particular, had played an important role in the 1950s' nationalisation of oil. In the 1960s and 1970s the term 'trade union' was replaced by 'state-sponsored syndicate' by the regime. In many cases workers' representatives were affiliated to the state secret police, who spied on the workers and reported them to the authorities. Nevertheless, the syndicates increased exponentially in number, from 30 in the late 1960s to approximately 519 in 1972. Many workers remained militant and class-conscious about their economic demands. Despite operating under a dictatorship, some strikes were successful and the workers won rights to national insurance, guaranteed sick pay, and retirement and unemployment benefits (Lajevardi 1985: 240; Rostami-Povey 2004, 2005).

In September and October 1978, more workers, including oil workers, joined other blue- and white-collar workers' protest movement, also demanding political and economic reform. Banks, schools, railways, internal flights, post offices, newspapers, universities, offices, oil refineries, car factories and petrochemical plants – all ground to a halt. The strikes – especially the participation of 30,000 oil workers, 100,000 government employees and 5,000 bank clerks – inspired the rest of the population. In cities and villages across Iran, people demonstrated against the Shah's system and his notorious secret police.

The Shah responded by offering an olive branch, and freeing a number of imprisoned clergy and Tudeh Party members who had been in jail since the 1950s. But the strikes and street demonstrations continued, with strike committees replacing the syndicates and taking over factories and workplaces. The army rank and file, composed entirely of conscripts, stopped shooting the demonstrators and joined them (Abrahamian 1982: 522–3).

Finally, in February 1979, events culminated in a general strike, including the 70,000 strong oil workers strike, and the collapse of the monarchy. After the revolution the strike committees that had played such an integral part provided the core leadership of the new *shoras*, workers' councils (Bayat 1987: 77–81; Poya 1987: 135–41).

ISLAMISTS

In 1962–63 Ayatollah Khomeini denounced the Shah's regime as corrupt, undemocratic and heedless of the economic needs of the population; he further criticised it for granting the Capitulation Agreement to the USA, giving diplomatic immunity to American personnel in Iran. In response the Shah forced Khomeini into exile in Iraq. Following this action, the Islamists became increasingly militant. Throughout the 1960s and 1970s a number of Islamist modernists, notably Ayatollah Taleghani and Ayatollah Mottahari, argued that Islam was compatible with modernity and through reform could accommodate social change, progress and political freedoms (Martin 2000; Gheissari and Nasr 2006: 48–9; Abrahamian 1982: 425, 2004; Rahnema 2005a: lv; Moin 2005: 64–97).

The Islamists, even the conservatives, in Iran were interested in Western intellectual ideas, including Marxist thought. For example, Ayatollah Taleghani argued that Islamic social justice is consonant with the Marxist position on the distribution of property, wealth and other resources. Ali Shariati, the young Paris-educated sociologist, presented a more extensive mixture of Islam and Marxism. He argued that Islam's teachings on social justice support Marxist views on egalitarianism and the distribution of surplus value and private property. The Mujahideen Khalq Organisation (MKO) also advocated a blend of Marxism and Islamism. These ideas were popular with the majority of the Iranian population, who at the time were attracted to

Marxism but had ties to Shi'a culture. Shariati died in 1977; however, his ideas helped mobilise many Iranians in the struggle against the Pahlavi state. The revolutionary ideology based on Marxism and Shi'ism as formulated by Shariati and Taleghani brought together the vast majority of Iranians, across the diversity of secular and religious groups. This pro-intellectual stance allowed the Islamists to mobilise far larger sections of the society than the secular left and the nationalists, who failed to attract the majority of the population to their ideas (Gheissari and Nasr 2006: 66–83; Abrahamian 1982: 450–530; Rahnema 1998: 363–8).

Ayatollah Khomeini, a conservative and traditionalist Islamist, in the 1960s opposed women's right to vote. But after the 1979 revolution, aware of the importance of women's contribution to the revolutionary movement, he changed his position and recognised this right. Similarly, prior to 1979, although he did not agree with Shariati's mix of Islamism and Marxism, he argued that an Islamic ideology and state would bring about social justice – empowering the poor and freeing Iran from imperialist exploitation (Gheissari and Nasr 2006: 84; Rahnema 2005a: lv; Martin 2000: 100–124). Khomeini discussed *Fiqh Poya* (dynamic Islamic jurisprudence) and distinguished between 'American Islam and Muhammadan Islam'. By American Islam he meant the pro-US, pro-Israel regimes in the region. He also challenged the 'backward' (*motehajer*) conservative Islamists under the Shah. He criticised the conservative way of looking at family planning and the banking system. In his view it was possible to equate the sharia (Islamic law) with modernity. In this context and according to his idea of *Velayat-e faqih* (Guardianship of the jurist, or recognising the most knowledgeable *mujtahid* – Muslim scholar – capable of interpreting the sacred texts as the ruler) he justified the concept of an Islamic state based on Islamic law, ruled by the *ulema*. Khomeini's political theory of *Velayate-e faqih*, which he formulated in exile in Najaf during the late 1960s, was in stark contrast to the view held by the nineteenth-century Shi'a *ulema*. According to the *ulema*, although they had ultimate political authority they could exercise it only when the government grossly transgressed the sharia and thereby endangered the Islamic community. In Khomeini's view the pro-Western secularism and authoritarianism of the Pahlavi shahs proved that the historical relationship between the shahs and the ulema[3] that had existed since Iran became a Shi'a kingdom in 1501 had ended because the Pahlavi shahs had weakened Shi'ism. This historical shift increased the political authority of the ulema (Abrahamian 1982: 476; Gheissari and Nasr 2006: 87).

NATIONALISTS

Following the CIA/MI6 coup in 1953, the anti-colonial and anti-imperialist nationalism of the Mossadeq era had faced severe censorship and been brutally suppressed by the Shah. Iran was transformed into a major non-Arab, Muslim, pro-Western – in particular pro-US – state. Between 1960 and 1963, however, control was relaxed somewhat. The National Front, drawing on the legacy of Mossadeq's nationalism, revived itself and recruited students, academics, workers and bazaar merchants. They organised strikes and sizable demonstrations, some mobilising up to 100,000 people. But in 1963 control was again tightened; the Shah outlawed the National Front and arrested its leaders.

The National Front was an umbrella organisation encompassing both individuals and diverse groups, such as the Liberation Movement, led by Islamist modernists. For example, Ayatollah Taleghani and Mehdi Bazargan (a liberal nationalist with good credentials from his association with Mossadeq's era of oil nationalisation) established close links with Ayatollah Khomeini and constructed a reformist Islamist platform to lead opposition to the Shah's regime. Despite political repression this organisation continued its activities abroad and in secret inside Iran. The Iran Party, also affiliated to the National Front, concentrated its activities among the Confederation of Iranian Students outside Iran. Likewise, the Socialist Society, whose base of support was among Iranian students in Europe and America (Abrahamian 1982: 457–73).

Just before the fall of the Shah, some members of the National Front opened negotiations with him regarding the introduction of democracy. But the revolutionary movement was no longer interested in political reform. As the movement grew, the Shah appointed Shahpour Bakhtiar, a leading member of the National Front, as prime minister. However, Bakhtiar was neither able to save the Shah nor to prevent the revolution. Others from the nationalist camp, including Karim Sanjabi, a liberal political leader and one of the founders of the National Front, and Mehdi Bazargan of the Liberation Movement, joined Khomeini's leadership; they were themselves politically too weak to form an alternative rallying-point. After the revolution, Mehdi Bazargan was appointed prime minister of the transitional government. However, he was not a strong enough leader to offer a secular liberal alternative (Gheissari and Nasr 2006: 81), and, as will be discussed later in this chapter, Khomeini's influence within the revolutionary movement began to hold sway.

THE LEFT

Communist and socialist groups also participated in the movement and contributed to the success of 1979 revolution. The Tudeh Party had been active since the 1920s and played an important role during the oil nationalisation. Also involved were other organisations such as Marxist–Leninists, Trotskyites, Stalinists and Maoists and the Fadayeen-e Khalq guerrilla group, along with the many women, workers, intellectuals and students sympathetic to Marxist ideas without having a formal attachment to any organisation. Arguably, a communist and socialist movement able to offer proper leadership could have given full expression to these peoples' demands for equality, the abolition of poverty, and the proper use of Iran's immense natural resources to develop the country. However, the left concentrated on criticising the Shah's developmentalist policies, for, whilst in the eyes of many working people the process of industrialisation in itself was relatively positive, it was the uneven nature of development that prevented them benefiting fully from socio-economic development. The left also ignored the important issue of democracy, which people were denied under the Pahlavi shahs. In consequence, the left failed to mobilise the working class, who, though beneficiaries of industrialisation, were hit hard by the economic crisis. The left did manage to influence the modern middle class, but not sectors with more religious values (Abrahamian 1982: 326–75; Cronin 2004: 1–16; Rahnema 2004; Gheissari and Nasr 2006: 67–8).

Most Iranian communists and socialists were directly or indirectly influenced by the policies of Stalin's Soviet Communism – a system which, it transpired, was close to exhausting itself. This decisively undermined their role in the revolution. 'Communism' had already failed the peoples of the Middle East, including Iran. The old Soviet Union was dominated by a wealthy and corrupt bureaucratic state elite, managing a very unequal society. This surely should have signified that 'Communism' had abandoned its historical role as the champion of oppressed peoples everywhere, especially in the colonies and former colonies of the Western imperial powers, including the Middle East. The failure to understand Zionism as a creation of Western imperialism, and Stalin's decision to recognise and even help arm Israel, sabotaged and severely marginalised the Communist movement throughout the region. To the astonishment of most of the world, the great old religion of Islam stepped into the resulting political vacuum. Thus it was that the mosques, rather than the factories and oilfields, gave direction to the revolution.[4]

The revolutionary period, 1979–80

Between 1978 and 1979, the working class and the traditional middle classes cemented their alliance with the Islamists. The majority of the population could not identify with the secular opposition;[5] the messages of the Islamists expressed the feelings and aspirations of the urban poor more effectively than did the liberal and left political groups. The Islamic opposition took the form of nationalism, independent of the Shah's repressive regime and its ally America. The secular left and nationalists failed to preserve their autonomy within the revolutionary movement and to build an alternative to the process of Islamisation. The resultant pressures produced a mass revolutionary movement, informed by both revolutionary Marxism and Shi'ism, and organised by the Islamists, which overthrew the hated dictatorship of the Shah.

The Islamic Republic rose from the ashes of the Iranian Revolution of 1979, arguably one of the most democratic yet least understood events of the twentieth century. Notwithstanding the limitations on democratic rights in the Islamic Republic, it was born out of a huge mass popular protest movement. The movement demanded democracy, a break with imperialism, the ending of poverty and access to resources. This basic explanation of the drivers behind the 1979 revolution is straightforward but often misunderstood. The majority saw the revolution as a first step towards liberation from the uneven economic and political developments of the Pahlavi state. The re-emergence of diverse women's, workers', ethnic and religious organisations struggling for their rights was an expression of people's desire for change in manifold ways. The failure of the left and liberal nationalists to establish a viable alternative meant that when, in a referendum in April 1979, the people were asked to vote for or against an Islamic Republic, the majority were in support.

However, once established, the new Islamic state began to ignore the diverse groups' struggles for their rights. Women were the first to bear the brunt of state repression. The Islamic state isolated secular women and favoured the participation of only religious women, in the interests of the patriarchal state. Material opportunities were provided for religious women and men to exercise a degree of power, in contrast to their marginalised status under the secular state of the Pahlavis. By determining that there should be a rigid sexual division of labour, the state deemed that women's place was in the home, thereby reinforcing patriarchal structures. Sex segregation and Islamic hijab (Islamic cover) were imposed on women. Motherhood and wifehood were considered the most important roles for women, while breadwinning was the responsibility of men. The public behaviour of women became a central issue. A large number of women were fired from their jobs because they did not comply with Islamic dress and behavioural codes. Many others were pushed into early retirement and redundancy. The state's policies on women's employment were reinforced by a strengthening of patriarchal relations in education and marriage through laws and regulations based on a traditional interpretation of sharia. The minimal advances women had made under the Shah were reversed. The exclusive right to divorce and the right of men to take four permanent and an unlimited number of temporary wives (sighe)[6] without the first wife's permission were reintroduced. Islamic legislation on the family was ratified. This included: a husband's right to forbid his wife to take employment; the requirement that a woman obtain permission from her male kin to work, travel, study and change her place of residence; in the case of divorce, a father had the right to custody of female children over 7 and male children over 2, which passes to his relatives in the case of his death; contraceptives and abortion were banned. This was a serious affront to the millions of women who had supported the revolution, including those religiously inclined. It exposed the distorted and contradictory ideals that motivated the revolution. However, as is discussed in the next section, these women continued their struggle for their rights. Women's political activities in the revolutionary period and their paid and unpaid work in the 1980s gave them a sense of collective consciousness set against their limited role in the home (Poya 1999: 62–73, 130–38).

At the economic level, the working class and the poor also suffered. The Islamic state advocated an Islamic command economy. It expanded the public sector and isolated the private sector. An international ban on trade with Iran isolated the country from the global economy, leading to an economic depression from which all sectors of the economy suffered and the result of which was declining output and rising unemployment. The ensuing collapse of the Iranian currency in the world market undermined Iran's foreign trade, creating shortages and inflation. Under pressure from the workers' shoras, wages had increased. As a result of inflation, however, real wages fell, so the increases did not help many poorer families. Unemployment and inflation drastically reduced purchasing power (Poya 1999: 61–7).

In this period, a policy of domestic repression coincided with a regionally popular foreign policy. As is discussed in forthcoming chapters, at a political level Iran's stance against cultural imperialism and American hegemony during this period and since has been popular with various movements in the Middle East. Iran's revolution inspired and organised Shi'a revolutionary organisations in Afghanistan, Pakistan, the Persian Gulf, the Emirates, Saudi Arabia, Iraq and Lebanon. In Lebanon the Hezbollah subsequently became a notable regional force. Tehran challenged the pro-Western authoritarian regimes in the region, and opposition movements throughout the region and beyond were inspired by the success of the Iranian Revolution and looked to Tehran for support. Politically, Iran thrived as the result of global Islamic activism while the West felt threatened by Iran's popularity in the region. Under these circumstances, in November 1979 a group of students led by militant clerics occupied the American Embassy in Tehran and held its personnel hostage, demanding that the United States extradite the Shah to Iran and apologise to the Iranian people for its involvement in the 1953 coup against Mossadeq and for supporting the Pahlavi monarchy. The memory of the CIA coup in 1953 greatly influenced this event, which was also a warning against possible American action in Iran. The event further consolidated the Islamic regime (Gheissari and Nasr 2006: 78–94; Rahnema 2005a: x–xiii).

Following the occupation of the US embassy, internal political repression intensified. The Tudeh Party, the nationalists, the liberal intellectuals and some other left groups followed the Islamic regime on the grounds that the action was anti-imperialist, but once the regime had asserted its power many of these groups' members found themselves persecuted. At this stage, the Mujahideen Khalq Organisation responded by resorting to an assassination and bombing campaign against the Islamic state authorities. Faced with these attacks, the state ruthlessly crushed all opposition; thousands were tortured and executed, and thousands more fled the country (Gheissari and Nasr 2006: 95; Abrahamian 2008: 181–2).

Despite political repression and social restrictions, the state pressed ahead with a genuine redistribution of wealth and sought ways to involve the poor and the Islamists in social, economic and political institutions. As Chapter 2 details, slums were abolished and absolute poverty virtually eliminated; literacy rates began to rise within a generation. Access to health and education raised personal expectations, which led to further pressure for democracy, an important aspect of the revolution fast becoming neglected by the state.

The Iran–Iraq war, 1980–88

The 1979 revolution in Iran threatened the economic and strategic interests of the USA and its allies in the region. After the revolution Iran withdrew from military and commercial alliance with the West in the region, distancing itself in particular from the oil-producing states in the Persian Gulf, which had lucrative economic relations with the West. The revolution was popular with the people of the region, many of whom had been suffering economically and politically for decades at the hands of the pro-Western regimes, which cared little about their poverty, unemployment, lack of basic human rights, access to education and health care, let alone the democratic right to political participation.

Ayatollah Khomeini argued that the revolution was not exclusive to Iran; it was for all the oppressed people of the world. But he emphasised that it could only spread if people in other countries were themselves convinced of the need to overthrow the other pro-Western regimes. Thus it was that the West perceived the revolution in Iran as a challenge to the other pro-Western autocracies in the region.

Iran's anti-imperialist foreign policy was particularly threatening to Saddam Hussein, who took the presidency of Iraq in 1979. He decided to invade the Iranian oil-rich province of Khuzestan, home to an Iranian Arab ethnic minority. The American administration, which at this time was engaged with the hostage crisis in Iran (November 1979–January 1981), was ambivalent about Saddam's move and did nothing to discourage him. Iranian monarchists, with their close ties to the American administration, encouraged the Iraqis to occupy Khuzestan by invoking the long history of Arab ethnic grievance against the central government. As is argued by Adib Moghadam (2008: 83–122), Saddam Hussein invented the myth of endemic Persian–Arab enmity, and under the slogan of 'liberating the oppressed Arab people of Iran' in September 1980 attacked the country (Ansari 2003: 229–39).

Iraq's invasion of Iran was generally regarded by the West as a means to weaken the revolution and to replace the Islamic state with a more amenable regime. During the early phase of the ensuing Iran–Iraq war, Iran was on the defensive. But by 1982 Iran had recaptured Khuzestan and Iraqi troops were forced to retreat to the border. Although Iran was not receiving any military help from external sources, while Iraq was being assisted with weapons, finance and military personnel by regional and international allies, it committed to continuing the war in order to oust Saddam Hussein. As is discussed in Chapter 5, Western states' support for Saddam Hussein at this time was based on the assumption that the war would weaken Iran and diminish its ability to spread 'Islamic fundamentalism' (Tripp 2008: 231). Thus the West remained silent when Saddam used chemical weapons against Iranian soldiers, and when he destroyed the entire Kurdish town of Halabja. It wasn't until Saddam's invasion of Kuwait in 1990 that events at Halabja were openly discussed in the West. As Shirin Ebadi (winner of the 2003 Nobel Peace Prize) has written:

> Saddam dispensed of nerve gas quickly and switched to what became his favourite chemical weapon, the blister agent known as mustard gas. Unlike nerve gas mustard carries a distinct scent – oddly enough, of garlic – but it has no antidote and kills with excruciating slowness. Shortly after the soldiers on the front caught its first whiff, their vision blurred and they began coughing uncontrollably, often vomiting at the same time. As the hours crept by, their skin began to blister, darkening first to a deep purple. Next, whole patches of skin fell off, and their armpits and groins turned black with lesions. Those who survived were hospitalised for a few days to a few weeks, depending on the severity of their exposure. If they regained functionality, they were sent back to the front. (2006: 76–7)

The UN called for a ceasefire and a withdrawal of forces to pre-war borders. But it was only several years later that it condemned Saddam's invasion of Iran and his use of chemical weapons, after UN monitors had acknowledged their use. Years later it not only emerged that the US intelligence agencies knew that Iraq was using chemical weapons but that the Reagan administration had provided Saddam with satellite images of Iranian troop deployment (Ebadi 2006: 77). And there was other evidence of US support for Saddam. In 1987 an Iraqi pilot had accidentally attacked the USS *Stark* and killed thirty Americans, whereupon President Reagan blamed the incident on 'barbarian Iranians'. In July 1988 a US warship in the Persian Gulf shot down an Iranian civilian airline, killing 290 passengers. Many in Iran and in the region could not accept that the US military, armed with sophisticated equipment, was unable to distinguish between a large passenger aircraft and a small military plane. Not only did Reagan not condemn this criminal act; the USA awarded the captain of the vessel a special medal. Such actions inevitably contributed to increased hostility towards the USA from Iran and the wider region (Ebadi 2006: 85; Ansari 2003: 235–9).

Between 1983 and 1986 the Mujahideen Khalq Organisation, which had been persecuted in post-revolutionary Iran, moved its headquarters and leadership to Iraq and fought alongside Saddam Hussein against Iran. In 1988 its fighters launched an attack on Kermanshah province in Iran. Their aim was to help Saddam to effect 'regime change' in Iran. They believed – and indeed still believe – that by fighting the regime in Iran they would bring down the Islamic regime by fomenting an uprising (Ebadi 2006: 86).

During the Iraq–Iran war, the USA and Israel (both of which had lost a valuable regional ally to the revolution) became even closer allies. As is discussed later, the Islamic Republic did not recognise the State of Israel, adopting the slogan 'liberating Baghdad from Saddam Hussein, liberating Palestine from the Zionists and ultimately confronting the US as the "Great Satan"'. This foreign policy, notwithstanding internal political repression, proved popular with the majority of the population of Iran and the region.

In response to Iran's popularity, the US and European governments continued to impose sanctions and supported the Iranian opposition, especially the monarchists and the MKO in their pledge to carry out 'regime change'. US policy on Islamist groups is inconsistent: they had supported the Taliban and al-Qaeda in Afghanistan against the Soviet Union but in the same period denounced the regime in Iran (Ansari 2006: 100–101). However, the more the West attacked Iran through its media and policies, the more popular Iran became with its neighbours. The Iraq–Iran war ended in 1988 after Iran's siege of Basra collapsed; in the end it was unwinnable. In the eight years of war, an estimated 1 million Iranians and half a million Iraqis had been maimed or killed.

The nature of the Islamic state

Since the start of the twentieth century, the boundaries between conservative and liberal-democratic Islam in Iran and beyond have been in a state of constant flux, buffeted by social, political and economic winds. The Iranian Revolution was a modern urban revolution, but the new Islamic state became repressive in order to survive when it faced challenges internally and externally, especially after Saddam Hussein's war. However, it is important to understand that the modern secular state under the Shah had been in many ways more repressive and patriarchal than the Islamic state. Since the 1979 revolution, the essence of the concept of hokomate mardomi (people's governance) has remained strong in Iran. Of course mardom (people) have in some historical periods embraced conservative Islam and in other periods democratic Islam.

In the 1980s, the concepts Mote'ahed (committed) and Motekhases (specialist)[7] became popular in Iran. The conservatives argued that those exhibiting ideological commitment to the system are good citizens. The liberal reformers, for their part, argued that it is the role of good citizens to specialise in scientific subjects (Motekhases). The dynamic of this debate led to the adoption of both terms by the state and other institutions – the idea that good citizens have to be both *Mote'ahed* and *Motekhases*. In this context, if we define conservatism in terms of preserving traditional values, then since the 1979 revolution the state has bridged the conservative–liberal divide more successfully than is commonly assumed. What is significant, however, is that the Iraq–Iran war created a state of emergency which led to a far more centralised and authoritarian state, which in turn imposed further Islamisation, involving repression of women, workers, ethnic and religious minorities, the left and the nationalists. These war years led to the decline of Iranian nationalism in favour of an intensified level of religiosity by the culture of *jihad* (striving against evil)[8] martyrdom. Thus war produced a strong state, shaping both its nature and its national and foreign policies, thereby allowing the more conservative faction of the Islamists to consolidate their power.

During the war period the state ruthlessly suppressed the secular movements: independent workers' *shoras* were replaced by Islamic associations; secular women's and students organisations were replaced by state-sponsored Islamic versions. The regime launched a reign of terror against the MKO and members and sympathisers of other political groups. In 1980, a bomb blast at the headquarters of the Islamic Republican Party killed seventy-two Islamist leaders. In response the state imprisoned and executed thousands of members of political groups. Such actions were not widely supported. Furthermore, a number of clergy objected to these manipulations of the political environment by the conservatives and in particular the human rights abuses in prisons. Ayatollah Montazeri, who remained an opponent of the authoritarianism of the state until his death in December 2009, in particular, protested in the strongest terms to Ayatollah Khomeini about executions and torture in the prison system. He was immediately isolated by the conservatives (Ansari 2003: 241–2; Abrahamian 2008: 182; Katouzian 2009: 350–51).

Of course this level of political repression constitutes the unacceptable face of modern political Islam. Nevertheless, it could have happened under a secular state. We cannot dismiss modern Islamic politics simply as a step backwards to totalitarianism and barbarism, as is often claimed in the West by academics and activists as well as by the media and politicians. Tragically, all the great successful revolutions of modern times, like the French Revolution of 1789 and the Russian Revolution of 1917, have used institutionalised terror to consolidate the power of the revolutionary leadership and to stabilise the immediate post-revolutionary period. In this respect, though such behaviour is inexcusable, Iran is in many ways not very different.[9]

Talibanism and Saudi-style conservatism have never existed in Iran. The Islamic Republic from its inception has been engaged in a battle between conservative and democratic Islam, because the majority of the people believe in Fiqh Poya (dynamic jurisprudence), the idea that Islam is compatible with modernism. The conservatism of the state and institutions in Iran is based on the promotion of patriarchal attitudes on gender issues and the limiting of democratic rights and citizens' access to public spaces. In this context the state in the 1980s gradually became dominated by conservative clergy; those clergy who believed in Fiqh Poya, such as Ayatollah Saanei and Mossavi Ardebili, lost their power.

The theory of Velayat-e Faqih became the political philosophy of the new regime. This was incorporated with the modern political philosophy of the separation of state institutions — parliament, government executive and judiciary. In this context, particular importance was assigned to elections and the vote of the people. The Shoraye Negahban (Council of Guardians), based on the model of the French constitution, was established, consisting of a number of clergy empowered to supervise all elections except for local councils. This institution supervises parliamentary and presidential elections and assesses the eligibility of the candidates; it also oversees the election of the Majlis Khebregan (Assembly of Experts), consisting of eighty-six senior clergy, which in turn chooses the leader of the Islamic Republic (to date, Khomeini 1970–89; Khamenei 1989–). These two institutions subsequently became extremely powerful, as no position could be secured without the approval of their members. The formation of Majma'e Tashkhise Maslehat (Assembly to Discern the Interests of the System, known as the Expediency Council) was to give the members of this council authority to mediate conflicts between parliament and the Council of Guardians. Therefore the process of electing leaders, members of parliament and the president involves both Islamic elites and the people's participation in elections. The Islamic elites are conservative, but the system involves not just religion and the state but the practices of both theocracy and democracy (Ghouchani 2004; Mir-Hosseini and Tapper 2006: 1–29).

Thus the reality is that the process of Islamisation in Iran has mass support. The leaders too enjoy grassroots support, as we will see in the next chapter. Khatami, Ahmadinejad and Mir-Hossein Mousavi (prime minister 1981–89; defeated presidential candidate in 2009), very different figures with distinct political views, have through the electoral process won the support of a majority of the population. Therefore the state and society in Iran are not so much 'fundamentalist' as in many ways modern and legitimate, based on dialogue and competition between those who wish to preserve traditional conservative Islam and those who wish to embrace democratic modern Islam. As Chapter 3 discusses, in Iran Shi'a Islam has historically been the site of contestation between conservative and liberal-democratic traditions; and yet both tendencies have achieved their goals through political process.

At the economic level, during the Iran–Iraq war, despite political repression and a war economy – producing, mobilising and allocating resources to sustain the war effort – the Islamic state set about genuinely improving the lives of millions of ordinary Iranians. In the 1980s, many Islamic foundations (Bonyad) – such as Mostazafeen (Downtrodden); Janbazan (Self-sacrificing People), comprising soldiers and their families engaged in the Iran–Iraq war; Bonyad Shahid (Foundation of the Martyred), comprising those who died in the Iran–Iraq war; Baseej (Mobilisation of Irregulars for the Iran–Iraq war); Komiteh Imam Khomeini (Ayatollah Khomeini Committee), pledged to help the poor; Nehzate Savad Amouzi (Adult Literacy Corps); Jahad Sazandegi (Reconstruction Crusade) – were set up. These organisations were funded by the state and provided social services to millions of the urban and rural working classes (Bayat 1997: 35–108).

In consequence, many religious women and men, and working-class women and men, benefited materially from the process of Islamisation, which duly galvanised their support for the Islamic state and society. In this period the state nationalised banks, insurance companies and major industries, and expropriated smaller industries and businesses. It distributed wealth by confiscating the property of the Pahlavi Shah and his allies – private domestic owners of capital and their counterparts who had fled the country after the 1979 revolution (Rahnema and Nomani 1990: 235–42; Poya 1999: 62–7). Shanty towns were demolished and their populations housed in confiscated properties. The religious middle class, the urban poor and the working class who supported the Islamic state were given priority in employment and education. Many Islamists had been alienated and marginalised by the processes of development in the 1960s and 1970s, under the Shah's secular regime. The Islamic state gave them access to material and ideological resources and a space to exercise power. Islamism was born out of material circumstances.

In the post-war era, three main political factions emerged: the pragmatists, who believed in stabilising economic relations at local and global levels; the conservatives, who were committed to traditional Islamic ideology and the right to private property; and the radicals, who believed in exporting the revolution by supporting revolutionary activism across the Middle East (Gheissari and Nasr 2006: 98–101). In this period, the state gradually changed its economic policy of self-sufficiency and ended its attempt to operate in isolation from a world economy dominated by the West; instead, it instigated a return to import-substitution industrialisation of the pre-1979 period and reconstruction began. Subsequent chapters examine the dynamic changes these processes brought in their wake.

The reformers, the conservatives and the struggle for democracy

In the 1990s, the restructuring of the Iranian economy was a move towards further integration into the global economy. Despite the emphasis on Islamic moral, ethical and financial laws, the uneven economic development in Iran rapidly adapted to world capitalism. In contrast to the first phase of Islamisation, economic laws and regulations were modified to allow the operation of a capitalist mode of production with an Islamic flavour, based on state and private ownership. Oil money had helped to generate funds; the Gulf War of 1991 and the American destruction of Iraq's economy pushed oil prices up, and Iran benefited. Yet the economy continued to depend heavily on oil revenues. As a result Iran's economic growth has now fallen behind Turkey, South Korea and Malaysia, whose diversified economies have allowed them to perform better (Karshenas and Hackimian 2008: 194–216).

Under President Ali Akbar Hashemi-Rafsanjani (1989–1997), Mohammad Hossein Adeli, the governor of the Central Bank of Iran (1989–94), pioneered an economic reform package which was crucial for the reconstruction of the country following the Iran–Iraq war. Foreign exchange and monetary policy were sustained; free-trade zones were created in the south of Iran on the Kish islands in the Persian Gulf; the deregulation of foreign exchange encouraged privatisation and higher imports; and increased taxes led to increased revenue. Development planning included investment in industries such as oil, petrochemicals, pharmaceuticals, food, car manufacturing, electricity, construction and agriculture. New dams, subways and airports were built. These measures resulted in a period of relative economic growth and rising consumption levels, which led to relative prosperity, expansion of the middle class, greater levels of education and longer life expectancy. However, extensive privatisation took place through heavy borrowing from international markets. The World Bank's loans in 1991 and 1994 were followed by adjustment policies, removing price controls and cutting subsidies, which saw further rises in inflation and unemployment. Many workers protested against delayed and non-payment of wages, health-and-safety issues, and redundancies resulting from subcontracting (Poya 1999: 96–8; Gheissari and Nasr 2006: 119–24; Abrahamian 2008: 184–6).

In the second term of his presidency, Rafsanjani offered the USA large-scale investment in Iran's oil and gas sector. However, the Clinton administration rejected his offer and instead imposed sanctions. In response, Iran deepened its trade ties to Europe, China, Russia and India (Mafinezam and Mehrabi 2008: 49–54). By the late 1990s, Iran was following the major proponents of free-market economics by curtailing the role of state social welfare and encouraging privatisation under state control. This trend continues today.

The Bonyads Islamic social welfare organisations that were set up in the 1980s, funded by the state, providing social services to millions of the urban and rural working classes, enjoyed grassroots support. In the 1990s these institutions were encouraged to become private enterprises in order to be independent of the state. Thus they gradually turned into capitalist organisations through holding companies and charities. They now own and control construction businesses, gas and oil export–import, and telecommunications. They are also engaged in the money and property markets. With their strong links to the state, they have become vehicles for self-enrichment rather than public service providers (Adelkhah 1998: 76–7; Maloney 2000: 83–112; Bayat 2005: 125, 2009).

Contrary to Western perceptions of Islamic 'fundamentalism', during this period Iran embraced neoliberal economic policies and the government and parliament encouraged both privatisation and NGOisation as the precondition for transition to a market-oriented regime, including domestic economic liberalisation and a more open approach to the international economy (UNDP 2000). Although Iran's economic policy changed in line with global economic policy, the Iranian state as a rentier state – depending on its oil revenue for economic development – under political pressure from various civil-society organisations continued its interventionist policies. The notion of the interventionist state revolves around the idea that it is embedded in civil society, and subject to political pressures exerted by civil-society organisations (Evans 1995).

Under pressure from the activism of women, youth, students and workers, the state invested in public services which benefited low-income families in both rural and urban areas. Using the usual indicators, conditions can be seen to have improved:

- 93 per cent of the population benefiting from improved drinking water;
- 84 per cent have adequate sanitation facilities;
- 99 per cent of children are immunised;
- the HIV prevalence rate among adults is 0.1 per cent (the lowest in the region);
- the urbanised population is 70 per cent;
- female life expectancy is 71, male life expectancy is 70;
- contraceptive use is 77 per cent (the highest in the region);
- literacy rates have risen from 22 per cent in the 1960s to 85 per cent in 2007 (89 per cent in urban and 75 per cent in rural areas);
- 65 per cent of university students are women;
- child mortality is 39 per 1,000 live births;
- communication has improved 400 per cent (providing people with telephones and the Internet);
- average population growth is 1.6 per cent (compared with 3 per

cent in the 1960s and 1970s), as the result of effective family planning since the 1990s;

- the average age of marriage for men is 26 and for women 23 (in 1966 the average age of marriage for women was 18 and for men 26) (Rahimi 2003; Abrahamian 2008: 180–82; Machini 2008a; Sreberny and Khiabany 2009; Iran Statistical Yearbook 2006–7; Britannica World Data 2005, 2006, 2007, 2008).

As is argued above, one important impact of the Islamic welfare state was the provision of education to the majority of the population. In particular, priority was given to the education of Islamists and the working classes in both urban and rural areas, in order to promote greater prosperity. This is very significant, for under the rule of the Shah in the 1960s and 1970s the state served to enrich only a small elite and did little to develop the rest of the country. In 2006–07 there were 14.5 million school students in Iran, and 93 per cent of schools are state run; this is an increase of 60 per cent compared to the level before the revolution. In the same year there were 2.8 million students in higher education, 68 per cent of whom were undergraduates, 6 per cent postgraduates and the rest school-leavers (Abdollahi 2008).

During this period, the culture of education changed. Having a high-school diploma was no longer considered enough. Even families in rural areas could send their sons and daughters to towns and cities to benefit from further and higher education. Most towns and cities have two or three campuses of various universities. Yet every year the demand for further and higher education exceeds supply. Students criss-cross the country, commuting from the capital Tehran to small towns and vice versa, in order to access the appropriate institutions. Higher education is no longer the preserve of the middle and upper classes of the urban centres. This opening up has increased class and cultural diversity throughout the country. As is argued by Khosrokhavar (2009: 211–46), significant advances have been achieved in terms of scientific research and activity. Most participants are the new generation, who have in effect created a scientific community in Iran where one did not formerly exist.

The proportion of female students in higher education now stands at 65 per cent. Nevertheless there are more male graduates in most subjects than female graduates, though it is expected that in some areas this will be reversed in the near future. This will in turn affect the labour market. For this reason, in 2007–08 the state attempted to impose a quota system, by offering 60 per cent of places to males and 40 per cent to females, even if female students' grades are higher. Female students and their families are challenging this discriminatory practice by campaigning and lobbying their members of parliament.

Statistics on the labour market also suggest a greater level of economic development now in comparison with the 1960s and 1970s. In 1973, the number of large industries employing more than ten workers was 3,973; in 2007, this had increased to 16,018, employing more than a million workers. Some 96 per cent of these industries are in the private sector, the rest being publicly owned and controlled. Of these, 25 per cent employed 10–49 workers, 12 per cent employed 50–100 workers, and 63 per cent employed 100 or more workers. In all, 22 per cent of the population work in agriculture, 27 per cent in industry, and 49 per cent in services. Some 2.3 million people (66 per cent men and 34 per cent women) work in state institutions. In all, 81 per cent are employed by private enterprises and 19 per cent by state-sponsored institutions (Iran Statistical Yearbook 2006–7; Britannica World Data 2005, 2006, 2007, 2008).

Together these enterprises can be categorised as the formal sector of the economy. Within this, 39 per cent of specialists are women (30 per cent of women who are employed in the formal sector are specialists in their field). In addition, thousands of women write books, make films and play high-level sport. Over 2,000 women are members of city and rural councils (Machini 2008). The majority of journalists who attend parliament and cover parliamentary news are women, and women blog intensively, contributing to increasingly feminised media (Shahidi 2002; Farhadpour 2006).

There are also hundreds of thousands of small-scale industries in the informal sector employing fewer than ten workers. In addition to the officially recognised formal and informal sectors, a large number of women (including homemakers) and men contribute to the economy in other ways; these hundreds of thousands of workers are invisible in the statistics. This is because obtaining a licence and/or registering as a small-scale workplace or NGO takes a long time due to Iranian bureaucracy. Each year a million skilled workers join the economy, and yet only two-thirds can readily be absorbed. In the increasing number of modern coffee shops in the large urban centres, for example, young male and female university graduates who are not part of the formal economy earn a living. Many are in favour of young women working in these coffee shops because the presence of a waitress makes it easier for young women to frequent them without being harassed by men; so the character of these traditional institutions is changing (Zanan 2004).

Many writers on Iran advocate further liberalisation of the economy, particularly the majority of state institutions that are in the control of the conservatives (Karshenas and Hackimian 2008; Ansari 2006). Yet continued economic development and improved Human Development Indicators seem to indicate an important role for the state provision of resources and contribute to the increasingly high expectations of a young and educated population. Like many other developing countries, following the demise of the interventionist state, unemployment has risen, social services have declined and the standard of living has fallen for a significant proportion of people, which has led to civil discontent. In the wake of the 1979 revolution and the distribution of wealth, improved health care, education and employment raised people's socio-political consciousness and in turn led to the development of civil society, broader media and the growth of women's, students' and workers' organisations. Together, they created the reform movement that led to Khatami's presidency.

The reform movement

Since the mid-1990s, workers, women and students have been demanding political and social change. After years of repression in the 1980s, in the early 1990s Islamic political parties and organisations expressed differing opinions on economic, political, social and foreign affairs. Under President Rafsanjani the press grew bold. Within strict Islamic confines, universal suffrage and freedoms of speech, the press and assembly were achieved. Many people felt that they were participating in political life, and eagerly followed debates in the Majlis (parliament), the workings of the judicial system and government through the media. This form of Islamic pluralism and parliamentary rule was very different from the workings of the autocratic secular state of the Pahlavi Shah. The Islamic state had no choice but to accommodate this limited pluralist system.

The political participation of workers, women and students led to Mohammad Khatami winning a landslide victory with 85 per cent of the votes in the 1997 presidential election. The 1999 parliamentary election likewise saw the defeat of the conservatives and a landslide victory for the reformers in parliament. The reformers were also victorious in the local council elections. Although secular national- ists and the left had been prevented from forming political parties, following these elections, for the first time since the establishment of the Islamic state, many people identifying themselves as secular left, liberal and nationalist joined the reform movement. A number of clergy supported the movement. Islamist women in particular, such as Azam Taleghani (daughter of Ayatollah Taleghani), Fatemeh and Faeze Hashemi (daughters of Ayatollah Hashemi Rafsanjani) and Shahla Habibi (daughter of Ayatollah Habibi), became involved in the reform movement. The reformist government of President Khatami attempted seriously to confront the problems of modernity, polarised between a conservative wing and a reformist wing. The more demo- cratic element within the reform movement reflected the unfinished business of the Iranian Revolution. It called for a massive extension of democracy. The constant demands of the majority of the popula- tion strengthened the democracy movement. Art, cinema, theatre, literature, music, diverse Islamic dress codes, journals, magazines and newspapers all began to blossom with a new sense of possibility. The reform movement made quiet overtures to the secular left and liberal groups. It supported embryonic independent trade unions, students' organisations and women's organisations. By 2000, there were hundreds of new publications – newspapers, magazines, intellectual journals. The works of foreign intellectuals like Karl Popper, Hannah Arendt, Edward Said, Tony Cliff, Alex Callinicos, Noam Chomsky, Arundhati Roy, Jürgen Habermas, Anthony Giddens, Pierre Bourdieu, as well as those of Marx, Lenin, Trotsky, Stalin and Mao, circulated freely. Even secular Iranian activists had a voice.

Throughout 2000–04 the process of NGOisation was encouraged by the government and parliament. They viewed this process as a way to transfer the state's responsibility to provide basic care for its citizens to NGOs. Women, students and youth grabbed this opportunity and established their NGOs, which became an important component of the democracy movement, although they were constantly under attack by the conservative-dominated judiciary. This was a period of bitter power struggle between the conservatives, who were rapidly losing popular support, and the reformers. As a result, some of the flourishing acts of freedom met with tragic consequences. Eighty secular and religious writers, poets and political activists were killed under mysterious circumstances. Between February and May 2000, the conservatives, who controlled the judiciary, closed down reformist newspapers, journals and magazines, arresting hundreds of editors, journalists, writers and activists. Nevertheless, the democracy movement continued its struggle, and as a result the arrested were released and banned publications reappeared (Bayat 2005: 113–18; Gheissari and Nasr 2006: 136–42).

Some reformists have subsequently swung radically away from Islam as an organising principle in public life; others are religious and politically more moderate; many are somewhere in between. Since the late 1990s, many Muslim reformists who have the support of sections of the working class, women, students and youth have suffered unrelenting persecution at the hands of the conservative-controlled judiciary. In fact, since the 1980s when the left-wing and nationalist oppositions were ruthlessly crushed, the conservatives have concentrated their attack on Muslim reformers. Despite persecutions, the reform movement continued the struggle for change and challenged the institutional power of the conservatives, achieving the reform of some laws and regulations in the interests of women, workers and students.

In 2002, the German philosopher Jürgen Habermas visited Iran at the invitation of the Centre for Dialogue between Civilisations, created by President Khatami. Attaollah Mohajerani, former culture minister and an ally of Khatami who fought hard to liberalise the media while in office, hosted Habermas's visit. Habermas observed 'how in an informal manner philosophers, sociologists, journalists and artists officially and unofficially challenged the country's theocracy'. He debated and engaged with students about secularism in the West at the University of Tehran, historically a symbolic location for the students' protest movement and since 1979 a location where the official Friday prayer ceremony takes place. Habermas argued that 'The picture of a centrally administered, silent society in the grip of the secret police just doesn't fit, at least not from the impressions I received from my encounters with intellectuals and citizens of an uninhibited, spontaneous and self-confident urban population.' He found young people well informed and able to discuss political issues openly. Habermas was challenged to debate the relationship between state, society, religion and secularism, during which he commented that 'discussions in Iran sometimes give the impression that participants have returned to the Reformation' (Hoffmann 2002).

However, in this period many within the democracy movement became disappointed with the low level of support in parliament and in the government for the continuation of reform. A boycott of the 2003 local elections demonstrated the degree of demoralisation, which led to many reformers losing their seats. The parliamentary election of 2004 produced the most serious crisis facing Iran's theocratic rulers since the revolution in 1979. The Council of Guardians, the unelected constitutional watchdog consisting of conservative clergy, disqualified reformist candidates, including eighty reformist members of parliament (fourteen of them women). These MPs, led by women, in particular Elaheh Koolaee, protested by organising sit-ins and resignations. They tried to delay the election in order to negotiate further, but the conservatives refused. As a result, the reformist parties, with the support of the democracy movement, called for a boycott of the parliamentary election. They argued that the election was not fair or free, as it was to be enforced by the military and the police. The students and reformist parties planned a number of protest rallies, but they were refused permission. Nevertheless, they protested by writing articles on their websites and in reformist newspapers.

As a result, in the spring of 2004, parliament fell into the hands of the conservatives, who also control Iranian television and radio, the army and the police. Many grassroots activists were disillusioned with the reformist leadership's conciliatory approach, believing that President Khatami should have fought the conservatives when they had previously vetoed further reforms, or when the judiciary closed down newspapers and journals and arrested students, workers, women and journalists, or when the reform of laws was delayed or dropped. In consequence, people increasingly came to regard the reformist leaders as apologists for the theocratic regime.

In 2005, the conservative candidate Mahmoud Ahmadinejad became president of the Islamic Republic of Iran, with 62 per cent of the population participating in the election. A minority of intellectuals, including women activists such as Shirin Ebadi, winner of the 2003 Nobel Peace Prize, boycotted the election on the grounds that it lacked legitimacy because the Council of Guardians had rejected women candidates. Yet a large number of young people and women did participate in the election, especially in the second round. The majority of the population voted for Ahmadinejad not on religious grounds but for economic reasons. He did not call for greater Islamisation; he stood for resolving economic problems, poverty and corruption. The leadership of the reform movement had failed to engage with these issues, which were affecting a large number of working people. As is argued by Gheissari and Sanandaji (2009: 275–98), the conservatives, especially the pragmatists, had a much more coherent agenda for economic reform than the reformists. The vote was in part a protest by some of the poorer sections of the population against a reformist government that had moved to a free-market economy and attempted to shrink the Islamic social welfare system. On the political level, the result of this presidential election highlighted the limitations of the leadership of the reform movement, who suffered defeat, but it did not mark the defeat of the democracy movement itself. This was demonstrated by the parliamentary election in 2008, when, although many of their candidates were disqualified by the conservative leadership, the reformists won 30 per cent of seats.

The limitations and contradictions of the Islamic state and its institutions – politically repressive but committed to looking after the poor – have seemed to politicise the majority of workers, women, students, and ethnic and religious minorities, especially those who supported the Islamisation of society. They have been struggling against inequality and to increase their participation in all arenas. Moreover, the support of the majority for reform played an important role in eroding the legitimacy of authoritarian rule and promoting democratic issues. The informal associations of workers, women, students and minorities are deeply involved in the process of democratisation and are the cause of the split between the reformers and the conservatives and the emergence of a group of 'pragmatic conservatives' from the latter camp. Some are non-clerical veterans of the Iran–Iraq war who are influenced more by nationalism and economic imperatives more than by revolutionary Islamic ideology.

It is therefore misleading and ill-informed, even racist, to label the Iranian state a 'theocratic state dominated by medieval mullahs'. The Iranian state as a capitalist Islamic state is repressive and has systematically undermined the autonomous spheres of social activity. However, it has also provided education and health to the majority of the population: young working-class men and women in urban and rural areas are now enrolling in higher education in unprecedented numbers. They have high expectations: the desire for equality before the law; equal political participation; the right to health, education and employment; and women's right to choose whether or not to wear the Islamic hijab. This process has led to an increase in class, gender and ethnic consciousness, especially among the new generation. As is discussed further below, in spite of all the perils of confronting state power, the various social groups who formed the democracy movement have since the mid-1990s been engaged in campaigns for class, gender and ethnic equality. They have achieved many more reforms in family law, education and employment than have been seen in the majority of US-backed regimes across the Middle East. Furthermore, in their own way, they have been bravely challenging the theocratic nature of the state.

The democracy movement

TRADE UNIONISTS

Trade unions are an important centre of power in civil society. The history of trade unions in Iran demonstrates that they have not been homogenous institutions; some have enjoyed grassroots support and some have been agents of the state. They have survived long periods under authoritarian regimes and at different periods their actions have confirmed a profound reactivation of civil society.

The history of the Iranian labour movement begins in the early twentieth century. Through strikes, factory occupations and demonstrations they achieved a minimum standard of safety, hygiene and sick pay, a 48-hour week, paid holiday for Fridays (the weekend) and the fundamental right of workers to form unions. Women workers won specific demands such as maternity leave and the right of mothers of new-born babies to take paid time off to breastfeed in the factory during working hours (Rostami-Povey 2004: 254–66; Lajevardi 1985: 1–28).

Such rights were enshrined in Iranian labour law. In 1951, the oil workers' strike led to the victory of Mossadeq's nationalist government and oil nationalisation. This period ended with the 1953 CIA coup. 'Trade unions' were replaced with 'syndicates'. The new autocratic monarchy controlled the trade-union movement, along with other social movements. During the 1979 revolution strikes were organised by strike committees, which had replaced the syndicates. After the revolution the strike committees provided the core leadership of the new *shoras*. In this period, campaigning by unemployed workers forced the government to reopen some of the closed factories; in other cases they opened them under their own control (Bayat 2008: 91–115). Pre-1979, cultural restrictions affected women's mobility; many families did not allow their daughters and female family members to join syndicates. But during and after the 1979 revolution more women became active *shora* members, including many in the pharmaceuticals, food and textiles industries. They struggled to set up workplace nurseries and literacy classes for women workers and to establish better health and safety conditions. Women's activities served to raise gender consciousness. For the first time women were engaged in trade-union activities as women. This was significant in a number of ways: the *shoras* were under attack; both women and men were battling to save them, but male workers were against female representation. Women believed that they should be represented in the *shoras* as women workers, because they had specific demands. In 1998 the Women Journalists Trade Association was established. Their newspaper, *Women's Voice*, discussed issues such as gender wage differentials among media workers, women's long working hours, their absence at management level and the impact of the closure of media in 2000–2002 on women's employment (Farhadpour 2006). Thereafter, the Women Publishers' Trade Association, the Women Teachers' Trade Association, the Women Nurses' Trade Association and the Women Lawyers' Trade Association were all established. The establishment of these trade associations demonstrated that Iranian women workers find it difficult to create the conditions for men and women to define and pursue their democratic rights. So in their own way they were, and indeed still are, challenging the male-dominated trade unions themselves. This may lead to the formation of more women's trade unions, or women workers may force male-dominated institutions to recognise them as members.

In the early 1980s Islamic *shoras* and associations replaced the independent *shoras*, but militancy and strikes continued. Workers' organisations are state-sponsored under the Islamic state, yet in their own way they have been challenging its theocratic nature. A number of activists now argue that the term 'Islamic' applied to workers organisations leads to the exclusion and alienation of some workers, thus weakening the *shoras*. They therefore argue for the re-establishment of independent workers' organisations (Rostami-Povey 2004, 2005).

Throughout the 1990s workers protested against late and non-payment of wages, and over health and safety issues, and resisted redundancies due to privatisation and subcontracting. In 2001, there were 303 workers' actions throughout the country, most in Tehran. The majority of these protests took place in health and education and in the textiles, shoes, metal, car, clothes, oil, petrochemicals and carpet industries. They took the form of strikes and demonstrations at the workplace or outside the relevant ministries or parliament and also involved petitions. The teachers' protests were particularly impressive, as throughout the country thousands went on strike, 400 schools were closed down, tens of thousands marched in Tehran and assembled outside parliament and the prime minister's office. Many were arrested and later released (Maljo 2008; Abdollahi 2008).

Under Khatami's government, the more open political environment led to a greater number of strikes and protests. Tehran's bus workers' union, which was banned in the 1980s, re-established itself in 2004. Under the conservative government of Ahmadinejad, in December 2005 police arrested twelve of the union's leaders who were campaigning for the right to organise and fight for better pay and working conditions through collective bargaining. A few days later, more union members were arrested for staging a bus strike calling for the release of their colleagues. The government released all the arrested union members except the leader, Mansoor Ossanlou. So the union called another strike, demanding his release from solitary confinement, and more workers were arrested. The workers then called for a general strike and organised more protests. Their demands included the immediate release of their leaders and colleagues, the introduction of collectively negotiated contracts, and recognition of the syndicate. In response to the new actions the government arrested more union members, as well as family members of the arrested workers, along with students and activists who had supported the strikers.

In 2009, 1,700 employees of Wagon Press Company, one of the largest manufacturers of railway wagons and vehicles in Iran, went on strike, demanding unpaid wages.[1] Some 400 workers at the Iranian Aluminum Company also went on strike for the same reason. Similarly, in various industries in different parts of the country – including Ahwaz Pipe Mill, Mahyaman Factory, Govah Heavy Machinery, Iran Telecommunications Industries, Haft Tape Sugar Cane Factory – workers took strike action in 2009. Many workers were beaten and tortured, though the government dared not execute them, as would almost certainly have happened under the Shah. As Eisa Saharkhiz told me in an interview:

> In the 1990s, a space was created for political debate within the trade unions and workers' syndicates. As a result even under the conservative government of Ahmadinejad and despite arrests and imprisonments, workers continue their demands. For example, Iran Labour News Agency [ILNA], which as a workers media was connecting workers with each other, was closed down, but two newspapers *Kar* [Work] and *Kargar* [Workers] have replaced it. The workers are fully aware of the secret of their success – unity and solidarity. On this basis they try to do networking through their independent unions and syndicates. Although the establishment of workers' organisations has faced oppression, they have connected their movement with other movements and as a result have the support of large sections of society. It is important to realise that, despite the arrest and imprisonment of activists, it is not possible for the authorities to totally exclude or eliminate syndicates, trade unionists and their leaders. However, pressure from outside, such as the constant threat of sanctions and war, strengthens the position of conservatives and weakens the position of the workers and trade unionists.

Workers and trade unionists engage in lobbying members of parliament. A number of MPs have a base within the trade unions, in particular Sohaila Jelodarzadeh, the reformist female MP who won her seat back in the parliamentary election of 2004 through the votes of workers and unions. She worked as a leading member of the Workers House (Khane Kargar). Under Khatami this institution oversaw the gathering together of different workers' organisations and acted as the centre for distribution of workers' bonuses. Under Ahmadinejad, though, the role of the centre has been weakened. Nevertheless, Jelodarzadeh established a women's section which provided education and training for women workers.[2] Reform of certain laws, such as the recognition of female-headed households, and the making available to women of loans and pensions, have improved their standard of living. The journalists' trade union was set up in the 1990s with 1,500 members. By 2009, despite political repression, its membership had risen to 4,500. Mashallah Shamsolvaezin, a journalist and spokesperson for the Association of Press Freedom, explained to me:

> When they close down newspapers we object and write letters of protest and stage sit-ins and demonstrations. We give financial support to the families of journalists who are in jail. We continue to demand a free press, security of employment, justice and fare trials for the journalists who are in jail. We also work on human rights issues and gender equality issues. We feel that gradually we will succeed in standing strong and push the boundaries to force the government to behave in a responsible manner.

STUDENTS

Before the 1979 revolution the student movement was dominated by left-wing students, but thereafter it was dominated by the Islamists. The Tahkime Vahdat (To Foster Unity) student organisation played an important role in the American embassy occupation of November 1979–January 1981. Since the 1990s the student movement has gone through significant changes. It is a diverse movement that includes both religious and secular students. While some believe in concentrating on the sectional interest of students, others wish to extend the movement's scope to embrace political issues. Some belong to Islamic societies; others are left wing or liberal. In some cases, Islamic societies changed their names to become student societies. During

Khatami's presidency, Tahkime Vahdat became the identity of radical students and the organising centre of student activities, meetings and conferences. Under the pressure of female students, it established a women's section. Since 2007 a number of the centres have closed down. When students have tried to reopen them, there have been clashes between conservatives and reformists. Other centres have been taken over by conservative students with the support of the state and other institutions.

Some Islamic societies engaged in political activities have become radical whilst keeping their Islamic identity. Advare Tahkime Vahdat (Alumni Organisation) has been set up for postgraduate students who have completed their studies but who want to remain active within the student movement. Some have extended their engagement to the women's movement and the trade unions, utilising two websites, through which they network.[3]

The student movement has in most cases moved beyond its sectional interest. The objectives of campaigns range from better classrooms and accommodation to campaigning in elections and for the release of students and teachers who have been arrested. Sometimes a sectional interest or a student issue will turn into a political demand. The movement has organised demonstrations and meetings both inside and outside universities, as well as engaging in lobbying and advocacy work. In 2004, students campaigned for the release of Hashem Aghajari, a history professor and disabled hero of the war with Iraq, who was sentenced to death for a speech in which he advocated an Islam that wasn't dependent upon the clerics. The death sentence provided the university students with an opportunity to unleash their anger upon the regime. They continued their struggle until the death sentence was lifted and the professor was released. In some cases, then, the student movement has played an important role in opening up the space for political activities in society.

Many female students argue that the student movement has historically been male-dominated; there are very few women in the leadership. For this reason women activists often engage with both the students and the women's movement. The role of women within the student movement has made itself apparent in the way the dress of female students has changed: whereas in the late 1980s and early 1990s they had to wear the black chador, the Islamic dress code is now more diverse. It is true that some have been arrested for pushing the envelope too far, but they have bravely continued to challenge the authorities in order to demonstrate that the hijab represents a woman's right to choose. In this the female students have the support of many of their male peers, who tend to see women's rights as integral to the struggle for democracy. In 2008, as we have seen, female students campaigned against the quota system in universities which gives priority to male students and discriminates against female students by limiting their choice and restricting them to local universities. They argue that this discriminatory regulation is intended to control the movement of women and restrict social mobility. Again, the support of the women's movement and of many male students has been crucial here.[4]

Following the disputed June 2009 presidential election and subsequent uprising, students played an important role throughout the academic year, demonstrating inside their universities to demand democracy and an end to political repression. Their views are diverse. Some believe in the separation of religion and state. Some believe in breaking the chains of religion that imprison the country. Others believe in cautious reform and see Islam as an important part of people's lives which cannot be ignored by the state. They are not all against Western culture per se, but most young Iranian people across classes and cultures prefer 'world music' – a mixture of Arabic, rap, rock and Iranian music. Often, though, this music is deeply political, advocating women's rights, as well as an end to conflict, poverty, hunger, political repression and conservatism. A minority of young people do glorify the West, and the USA in particular; indeed some have left Iran, those with money settling in Los Angeles. In exile, they have made musical links between the two worlds – 'Tehrangeles' music (a mixture of Western and Iranian music) – through the Internet. To gain a foothold in Iran, the Tehrangeles musicians have had to adapt to the authentic rhythm of the Tehran street. Despite a mushrooming of Internet cafés, not everyone has access to the Internet; nevertheless Tehrangeles music has spread like wildfire. The majority of students and youth reject the idea that modern, progressive attitudes are exclusive to the West. They also oppose the rigid traditional rules and regulations set by the conservative clergy in Iran. They are actively trying to construct emancipatory models that derive from their own experiences, models that are inclusive of Western, Eastern, Islamic and Iranian culture – like Tehrangeles music.

These young people are puzzled by the US wars in Iraq and Afghanistan. At the same time they are angry that anti-imperialist sentiment is the monopoly of the state, and that this and other institutions impose restrictions on them while their values are under constant attack by the conservatives. Nevertheless the voices of young women and men can be found in Internet chat rooms, websites and student meetings. They say: 'We are the real victims of conservatism, be it Islamic or American. We have struggled to achieve a reformist government but our demands have not been met. We demand civil rights, the right to participate in economic, political, social and cultural arenas; the right to choose what to wear, the right to love and enjoy life.'

ETHNIC AND RELIGIOUS MINORITIES

About 99 per cent of Iran's population is Muslim, the Shi'a communities comprising 89 per cent and Sunnis 10 per cent. The remaining 1 per cent non-Muslim religious minorities are Armenians, Assyrians, Chaldeans, Jews, Zoroastrians, Bahais and Iranian Christian converts (Sanasarian 2000: vii). The ethnic composition of Iran is 35 per cent Persian, 16 per cent Azeri, 13 per cent Kurd, 10 per cent Gilaki/Mazadarani, 7 per cent Lur, 3 per cent Arab, 2 per cent Baluch, 14 per cent other ethnic groups and nationalities, including Qashqai, Bakhtiari and people of Afghan and other Arab origins (*Iran Statistical Yearbook* 2007–8; Britannica World Data 2004–08). Farsi is the official language and is spoken by the majority of the population. Other languages spoken are Turkish, Kurdish, Baluchi, Luri, Arabic, Gilaki, Assirian and Armenian, a linguistic plurality which continues to grow. As Lois Beck has argued, historically tribal people in Iran invented and reinvented their identities according to changing socio-economic and socio-political conditions. Each tribe was composed of diverse ethno-linguistic and ethno-religious origins. Throughout history, communities have survived by mixing with others and constantly transferring their political, social and cultural benefits (Beck 1990: 189).

Today Shi'ism in Iran is diverse, comprising the majority of Persian-speaking Iranians, Arabs and Turkish-speaking Azeris. So the majority Shi'a are not all Persian. The majority of Kurds and Baluchs, for their part, are Sunnis. The Sunni minority is well aware of its distinctiveness from the Shi'a. Historically there has never been a united Sunni front against the Shi'a, as each group is divided along lines of class, ethnicity, gender, geography and language, as well as religion. Ethnically and linguistically, Turkic-speaking people are the largest minority in Iran; they are divided among Shi'a and Sunni sub-ethnic groups. The majority, in particular the Azeris, have assimilated into the Persian milieu. Kurds are concentrated in the west of Iran, in the border area with Iraq. Baluchs are concentrated in the south-east of Iran, in the border area with Pakistan. These two communities have shown less interest in 'Persianisation' than the others. Arabs are concentrated in the south-west of Iran, in the oil-rich area close to the Persian Gulf and in the border areas with Iraq, Saudi Arabia and Kuwait. These three groups have a history of separatist movements. But Sunni Turkmens and Shi'a Azeris have not been particularly separatist (Sanasarian 2000: 8–14).

The history of Iran demonstrates that those social movements that were indigenous and had an anti-colonial and anti-imperialist character (such as the Tobacco Protest in 1890–92, the Constitutional Revolution of 1906–11, Oil Nationalisation in 1951 and the 1979 revolution) were successful due mainly to grassroots support. This is in contrast to nationalist/ethnic separatist movements in the twentieth century, which have not been successful.[5] A number of factors have contributed to the failure of these movements. First the nationalist separatist movements of Azerbaijan and Kurdistan in the 1940s had the support of the Communist Tudeh Party and the Soviet Union and were able to exploit existing socio-economic disparities.

But the Soviet Union withdrew its support from these movements once it reached agreement with the Shah's state. As a result, many people rejected ethnic separatism based on foreign encroachment. First, these movements failed because they did not enjoy popular support (Abrahamian 1982: 174–6; Gheissari and Nasr 2006: 52; Ansari 2003: 88–98; Moulodi n.d.). Second, given the option of joining Iraq, in the case of the Kurds, or moving to Kuwait or Saudi Arabia for the Arabs, or living in Pakistan for the Baluchs, or for any of these communities to set up their own country, they have all preferred to remain within Iran. This is because, despite political repression, these communities have greater access to resources such as education, health and employment in Iran than they would have in any of these bordering countries (Sanasarian 2000: 14). Third, under both the Pahlavi regime and the Islamic Republic all attempts by separatist movements have been brutally crushed. Therefore the struggle of national and ethic minorities has continued in the context of the politics of rights and identity (Vali 2002: 82–94).

During the period of Reza Shah's rule (1925–41), the process of Persianisation was imposed on different ethnic groups as part of the drive to strengthen the state and to encourage industrialisation and Westernisation. Mandatory teaching of the Persian language, the renaming of both the country, Iran instead of Persia, and a number of regions (Lurestan became Kermanshah, Arabestan became Khuzestan), aimed at the de-ethnicisation of Iran, and at creating a unified nation-state. Ethnic communities were forced to comply with new rules and regulations. Mohammad Reza Shah (1941–79) followed the same policy. The 1960s' land reform policy further reduced the authority of ethnic and religious groups. The state controlled and co-opted a number of ethnic and religious opposition leaders into state and other institutions. The teaching and publication of the Kurdish, Turkish and Baluchi languages and their literatures were banned, although a diversity of ethnic and religious groups continued to speak their languages and dialects. Learning and teaching in Farsi did not result in widespread Persianisation (Abrahamian 1982: 102–281; Ansari 2003: 40–74; Sanasarian 2000: 14–17).

The Islamic Republic has advocated a transnational Islam to create an Islamic identity; any attempt at separatism has been repressed with brute force. Nevertheless, ethnic minorities have continued their struggle for inclusion in the socio-economic life of Iran. At the same time, the state has included minorities in its formal policymaking institutions such as parliament and local councils, and it recognises the Zoroastrian, Jewish and Christian religious minorities (predecessors of Islam). They are politically represented and practise their religion, with rules and restrictions; that is, they have the right to observe their religious services, ceremonies and holidays (Sanasarian 2000: 19–24). The Bahais, however, are not recognised as a religion and are persecuted.[6]

The minorities' political representatives in state institutions lack direct political authority. But they are able to voice their opposition and debate their communities' needs and demands. For example, during the provisional government of Mehdi Bazargan in February 1979, when the new constitution was written and ratified, Article 12 declared that the official religion of Iran was Twelver Shi'a. In a heated debate in the Assembly of Experts, *Majlis Khebregan*, the Sunni deputies objected, but in a majority vote (52 for, 2 against, 3 abstentions) Twelver Shi'a was duly confirmed as the official religion. Sunni deputies from different regions also objected to Article 14, which recognises Zoroastrians, Jews, and Christians as religious minorities in Iran, but fails to mention Sunnism. The chair of the assembly responded by declaring that the recognition of Shi'a as the official religion did not mean that Sunni communities are not recognised, but rather that they are acknowledged as part of the Muslim majority. However, the minority deputies insisted on the principle of religious diversity and respect for each religion's ethnic and regional specifities. They also raised their voices against the discrimination imposed on them by the state and other institutions – such as not being allowed to serve as president, prime minister, ambassador or chief of the armed forces. These debates over ethnicity, religion and language demonstrate how each group in Iran highlights its historical roots in coexistence with Muslims. The Zoroastrians, Jews and Christians, for example, argue that they have lived in Iran for over 2,000 years; as such they challenge the concept of minority, having lived in the country long before Iran became a Muslim society (Sanasarian 2000: 14–17, 60–64).

The minority MPs in parliament forcefully defend their communities' interests. In 2006, the Jewish MP Maurice Motamed challenged President Ahmadinejad for his Holocaust denial comment.[7] Debate within the Iranian parliament, notwithstanding all of its limitations, represents a radical departure from the past. The Shah's regime emphasised homogenisation, and open political debate between different groups never existed. Despite discrimination, the post-revolutionary political climate created an opportunity for minority MPs to air their issues. This clearly represents a movement towards democracy and the reality of a diverse Iranian society, which the Islamic state will be unable to ignore (Sanasarian 2000: 64).

Abdolaziz Moloudy, an Iranian Kurdish Sunni sociologist, documents that the situation of Kurds in Iran today has improved in comparison with that before the revolution. However, with the fall of the Shah in Iran, and later of Saddam Hussein in Iraq, the expectations of the majority of Kurds, both Sunni and Shi'a, for local independence grew and they now demand inclusion in the socio-economic and political life of Iran as equal citizens (Moloudy n.d.). Nayereh Tohidi (2009: 299–323) also argues that the grievances of ethnic minorities have their roots in the uneven distribution of power and resources.

Despite improvement, discrimination against minorities persists. As Mohsen Kadivar confirmed to me in an interview, a particular form of discrimination is practised against Sunnis:

> According to the constitution recognised religious minorities have the right to exercise their religion and have their own place of worship. In some ways they have more rights in Iran than in many other countries in the region and around the world. However, the Sunni communities are in some ways deprived of the same rights that have been secured for others, although their numbers are greater than other religious minorities. By law they are entitled to have their place of worship to pray according to their own culture.

They have their own mosques in Sunni-majority cities and regions, but not in Shi'a-majority cities and regions. This is despite the fact that in these big cities there are churches, synagogues and Zoroastrian temples. For Shi'a communities attendance at Friday prayers is optional, but for Sunni communities it is an obligation. Therefore in not having their own mosques they are unable to perform an important religious duty. Hence many go to the Pakistan embassy in Tehran to perform this task, which is a disgrace. They have their representatives in the Majlis but too few in terms of their population. The Sunnis are a bigger minority than the Jews, Armenians and Zoroastrians, and they should have a greater number of MPs, but they don't. The Sufis are also discriminated against. They have their place of worship, the khaneghah, but in some cases these have been destroyed. Of course we must recognise that the Shi'a communities in Saudi Arabia and Muslims in Israel are much more oppressed than the Sunnis and other minorities in Iran.

The degree of inclusion of religious and ethnic minorities in the political decision-making institutions is also under state control. In parliament, there are two seats for the Armenians, one seat for the Assyrians, one for the Jews and one for the Zoroastrians; the Sunni communities have many more seats, as a minority religion and representing the Sunni-majority provinces. The religious minorities participate in parliamentary elections through a competitive and open process of candidate registration. Elections involve campaigning and the distribution of leaflets throughout all the cities. Candidates speak at meetings in order to win the vote of the community. Individuals can simply nominate themselves, but they have to do this through the agency of the government rather than through their religious or ethnic centres. In this sense the state controls the process. The ethno-religious groups show discontent with Tehran's institutional domination of policy formation. Both Sunni and Shi'a ethnic groups' representatives discuss in the media the concept of self-determination of Azeris, Baluchs and Arabs. They argue that the ethnic movements in Iran have never been separatist, but rather all demand equality within the system (Sanasarian 2000: 8–14). For example, Mohammad, an Arab Shi'a activist, told me:

We as the Arab minority in Iran demand equal rights with the majority Persians. Our demands are about citizenship rights, in terms of language, culture and the removal of economic, social and political discriminations. That is why in different parts of the country there is unrest. We don't want separation from Iran, we want equal rights. During the Iran–Iraq war 12,000 Arabs died in the war with Iraq. This demonstrates that Iranian nationalism is strong among Iranians no matter what ethnicity or religion they identify with. There are many political prisoners, from different ethno-religious groups, speaking and writing about their grievances. In Khuzestan 80 per cent of the population is Arab and they live in poverty. The minority Sunni Arabs are the poorest of the poor. The Arabic language is recognised as the second language in the constitution. We speak our language but we want to be able to teach it to our children. We don't want to replace our language with Farsi. We want both. Foreigners exploit our situation to attack Iran. They have their own agenda. If we resolve our issues ourselves we will be empowered and will not allow foreign intervention to abuse our issues at our expense. The problem of the minorities is not just to do with the state's and other institutions' policies. The racist discourses of anti-national minorities come from our intellectuals. There is a racist Farsi literature which portrays Arabs and Turks as inferior beings. In both Khatami's and Ahmadinejad's governments there have been only a few members of minorities. But they don't challenge ethno-religious oppression. We need more minorities in positions of power at local, regional and national levels to deal genuinely with our grievances.

The Sunni–Shi'a divide in Iran has to be contextualised within ethno-religious identities and the wider struggles of differing ethnic and religious minorities who are challenging the state and other institutions with legitimate claims to equal citizenship rights. Attempts at Persianisation or pan-Islamism by the Iranian state and society have not weakened ethno-religious and linguistic diversity. In this context the ethno-religious minorities argue for the decentralisation of the state as a way of strengthening the nation. For the minorities, the whole of Iran is not greater than the sum of its parts; rather, each community is essential to the country's composition and strength. Therefore they constitute a part of the larger democracy movement struggling to build a responsible state that treats all citizens equally. Mashallah Shamsolvaezin explained to me:

> Throughout the history of Islam we have had reform movements in both Shi'a and Sunni traditions. Today the reform movement in Iran is playing a particularly important role as it is systematically arguing for the separation of religion from politics and the state. If we succeed the gap in the Shi'a and Sunni divide will be reduced, which will be a historical victory for democratic Islam as against conservative Islam. We can succeed in bringing democracy to Iran and the region.

WOMEN

There is a wealth of literature on the role of women in the post-1979 revolution era in Iran.[8] As discussed above, in the 1990s women played an important role within the reform movement. In 1997, prior to the presidential election, Azam Taleghani, the founder of the Islamic Society of Women in Iran, challenged the constitution on the ground that it does not allow women to be president of the Islamic state, and duly declared herself a candidate for the presidential election. Since then, women have raised this issue at every presidential election, staging sit-ins and demonstrations to project their voices. They have argued that theirs is a diverse movement, politically and religiously, but one which is united in attempting to force candidates to acknowledge their demands for women's rights and their integral role within democracy. Their struggles have led to debates at every presidential election. Even the conservative-dominated parliament and media have been forced to debate the issue, and new pro-democracy journals, newspapers, websites and weblogs have sprung up, challenging candidates on their past history and their future promises. Shahla Sherkat, publisher and editor of the monthly journal *Zanan* (Women) played an important part in creating a platform for women's rights issues. The journal was closed down in 2007. New coalitions have been built between religious and secular nationalists and reformers. Women's political struggles have forced a number of candidates, both conservatives and reformists, to discuss democracy issues.

Jamileh Kadivar, a political scientist and gender and Islam specialist, argued that 'there is no evidence in the Quran to suggest that
women cannot be judges'. She said to me:

> Issues such as the right of women to become president and judges,
> the reform of family law, equality between men and women in
> dieh law (blood money), and so on, are issues which are discussed
> by a number of clergy such as Saanei and Janati. These are positive
> steps forward, despite the fact that conservative institutions are real
> obstacles in the way of reforming laws and regulations. The unity
> between women is also important, whether they are religious new
> thinkers, secular, housewives or employed. The problem today is
> the large gap between elite women and ordinary women. We need
> to reach ordinary women and men. The problem is not just male
> domination as such but that many women accept male domination
> as the norm.

Successful pressure for the reform of family laws and regulations
has resulted in significant changes. Women judicial advisers, with
judicial status, are consulted by the head of the court before a final
ruling on divorce is issued. Marriage contracts for girls younger than
13, and for boys younger than 15, are now subject to parental consent; the process of raising the official age of puberty for girls from
9 to 13 is under way. A new clause in marriage law gives women
the right to divorce, the custody of children, and the right to forbid
the husband to marry a second wife (subject to these rights being
written into the marriage certificate). Female-headed households
receive a pension and are eligible to receive loans. All government
departments have women's committees and all newspapers and
journals have women's pages. Under certain circumstances, abortion is approved. The number of seats in the Iranian parliament
held by women is now the same as in Turkey, and the number of
female professionals is similar to the position in South Korea. In
Ahmadinejad's government (2009–) the health minister is a woman,
Dr Marzieh Vahid Dastjerdi.

In the first decade of the twenty-first century a number of
campaigns – among them the One Million Signature Campaign, the

Campaign Against Stoning to Death, and the Campaign of Mothers for Peace – were relatively successful and enjoyed the support of a number of clergy. In 2007, through a successful campaign, women managed to change the law to allow Iranian women who have married foreign men to pass on their Iranian nationality and citizenship rights to their children, if the children were born in Iran and have lived in Iran for eighteen years or more. Women have also challenged the discriminatory law that forbids women access to sport grounds alongside men. There is a VIP section in the Tehran football stadium for women, but even those with VIP cards are demonstrating and demanding to enter as equal citizens (Rostami-Povey 2007a).

In September 2008 a number of women activists who had been campaigning against the new Family Protection Bill lobbied members of parliament and managed to stop it. They argued that the bill was against the rights of women in marriage and divorce. They won changes to two important clauses: a husband may no longer marry a second wife without his first wife's permission; the removal of tax from mahr (bride price), as this would have discriminated against poorer women.

For many women's rights activists, the reform of laws and regulations is only half the issue. Equally important, women's rights must be sustained and institutionalised. This task can only be achieved by tackling poverty and providing opportunities for women to have access to employment.

Elaheh Koolaee, professor of politics and international studies at the University of Tehran, was an MP 1996–2000. In this period, due to the efforts of women MPs, a number of family laws were changed in favour of women. For example, women were given the right to custody of both girls and boys up to 7 years old. Before this date, women had the custody of boys for up to 2 and girls for up to 9 years old. In some cases, men were willing to agree to the woman having custody so that they could freely marry another woman. But many mothers could not accept the custody of their children because of poverty.

The reformed law gave custody of children to their mothers if the father was a drug addict. However, many men ignored the new law, refusing to hand over the children. As a result family violence has increased. There are men who have killed their wives, and women who have killed their husbands, over the custody of their children. Implementation of the reformed laws requires a change in the culture of male domination and more equal gender relations, as well as poverty reduction, so that both women and men can be empowered materially and ideologically. Since 2001, under the pressure of conservatives in parliament, the reform of family laws has slowed down (Koolaee forthcoming).

A number of women's rights activists are engaged in poverty-reduction strategies and female employment. Fakhrolsadat Mohta-shamipour is the executive manager of the Association of Women Entrepreneurs. She organises workshops, seminars and conferences on women and work, aimed at providing access to employment for women. As was discussed earlier, there are a large number of educated women who have not been absorbed into the labour market. Through the Association of Women Entrepreneurs many gain access to resources and are able to set up their small to medium-size enterprises and employ other women workers. The organisation also endeavours to make women visible and to show the social utility of women's work for the family and the community.

Fakhrolsadat Mohtashamipour is also the chair of the board of directors of the Association of History and Women Researchers. In this organisation, women historians and their associates work to produce a feminist reading of Iranian history. They challenge conservative male readings of Islam and Islamic texts which dis-criminate against women, organising seminars and conferences throughout the country, which are popular with young women students. These young researchers eagerly participate in making women visible in the history of Islam and of Iran – that is, women who have made valuable contributions to the political, cultural and social life of the country. Female researchers thereby gain confi-dence in using historical examples to challenge those conservative

Islamists who use Islam to exclude women. Such lived experiences demonstrate these women's daily confrontation and engagement with the state, patriarchy, religion and other social, economic and political structures, and their own struggle to change patriarchal gender relations.

Prior to the June 2009 presidential election a 'coalition of women' formed to declare women's demands. Through these activities they managed to put women's rights issues at the centre of electoral campaigns. Elaheh Koolaee played an important role in Mir Hossein Mousavi's pre-election campaign; Jamileh Kadivar did likewise for Mehdi Karoubi. Zahra Rahnavard, an academic, who is married to Mir Hossein Mousavi, played a decisive role in representing the grievances of women in his pre-election campaign. Although, as a result of political repression, leading members of various campaigns left the country, women continued their struggle for gender rights and democracy. In the disputed post-election events of 2009 the presence of women was clearly visible, as they participated in rallies in their millions.

Despite political repression, there is a greater degree of gender consciousness in Iran today and more reformed laws and regulations on women's issues than ever before. Today women in Iran enjoy more rights than they do in most countries in the Middle East.

The 2009–10 uprisings and the Green Movement

In the June 2009 election, President Ahmadinejad was re-elected for a second term. Millions of protesters throughout the country challenged the election result (Ansari 2009a). They wore green – 'the colour of Islam' – in support of Mir Hossein Mousavi, the defeated candidate. Pro-government media and politicians accused Mousavi, who became the de facto opposition leader, and his supporters[9] of attempting to overthrow Iran's Islamic system. Mousavi and Karoubi (a founding member of the Association of Combatant Clerics), along with the other defeated candidates, supported by former president Khatami, labelled the new government illegitimate and called for protests to continue. In the ensuing street demonstrations a number of people died, and thousands were injured and imprisoned. Leading members of the movement were tortured and forced to confess that they were conspiring with foreign powers; Western support for the movement, expressing a growing global Islamophobia, fuelled the Iranian government's fear of 'regime change'.

In fact the democracy movement resolutely regards Iran's independence as a hard-earned reality, achieved at great sacrifice in the 1979 revolution. As is argued by Adib-Moghadam, foreign agents will not be allowed to manipulate the movement.[10] Indeed, many protesters displayed pictures of former prime minister Mohammad Mossadeq, arguing that they would not let history repeat itself. In other words, they wanted democracy but no foreign intervention, such as the 1953 British and US coup that overthrew the Mossadeq government. Contrary to much speculation in the West, the protest movement is not based on an 'urban modern secular middle class', represented by Mousavi, which is pitted against 'rural traditional religious working classes', represented by the government. The democratic opposition and pro-government forces alike derive their support from both constituencies. Many people on both sides of the struggle have benefited from state subsidies, state investments and the proceeds from oil income. But the majority are opposed to political repression and corruption. And they are supported by a number of influential reformist politicians and clergy.

The Friday prayer sermons have been a platform for the political viewpoints of different clergy. The former Iranian president Hashemi Rafsanjani, the head of the Expediency Council and of the Assembly of Experts, at a Friday prayer sermon on 17 July 2009 stated his support for the democracy movement, criticising political repression and calling for national unity. Subsequently he refused to give further sermons in order to avoid likely clashes between rival groups and between the democracy movement and the police. On Friday, 18 September 2009 the Friday prayer coincided with 'Al

Quds Day' ('Jerusalem Day Rally') at the end of Ramadan. After the 1979 revolution this day became an annual day of support for Palestinians and, according to Ayatollah Khomeini, also a day to oppose all injustice and oppression. Rafsanjani, who had traditionally led this sermon since 1979, was replaced by a pro-government cleric. During the sermon, protesters demonstrated against political repression.

Mehdi Karroubi, the other defeated presidential candidate, criticised the government for allowing the torture (including rape and sexual assault) of the protesters and demanded the prosecution of those involved in violence against the demonstrators.[11] Ali Larijani, the parliamentary speaker (who was fired by Ahmadinejad as the chief negotiator on nuclear issues with the West in 2007); Mohammad Baqer Qalibaf, the Tehran mayor; and Mohsen Rezai, former commander of the Revolutionary Guards,[12] and the third defeated presidential candidate, were also critical of the repression against the protesters. In November 2009, Mahmoud Vahidnia, the 25-year-old well-known mathematician, at a meeting between Ayatollah Khamenei and the country's elite scientists, which was broadcast live by state television, criticised the brutal post-election political repression, denounced the state media for biased coverage, and asked why leaders of the Islamic Republic should be above criticism. As a result, a parliamentary committee was set up to examine the post-election violence, and a number of officials who were responsible for the rape, torture and death of political prisoners were arrested.[13]

The protests continued throughout 2009 and into 2010. In December 2009, Grand Ayatollah Montazeri, an outspoken critic of the government, died. Hundreds of thousands of protesters turned out for his funeral. A week later, on the day of the Shi'a mourning ceremony of Ashoura, which is symbolically about justice (see Chapter 3), protesters experienced another day of brutal suppression when a number of people were killed in a clash with the security forces, and hundreds more were injured or imprisoned. The next demonstration was organised for the thirty-first anniversary of the 1979 revolution, on 11 February 2010. Prior to the demonstrations, the authorities had arrested hundreds more, including student leaders, women's rights activists, journalists and bloggers. Furthermore, heavy security, intimidation and a media blackout, including the blocking of text messaging and Internet censorship, gave the authorities the upper hand. A lack of leadership in the movement, which saw people ask 'What should we do?' 'Which direction shall we go in?', meant that the protestors were heavily outmanoeuvred by a pro-government demonstration.[14]

It was demonstrated that the state is capable of asserting its power through violence, intimidation and political repression. However, the ruling elite are deeply divided: some are in favour of opening up to the global economy and global culture; others exploit the constant threat of war and sanctions against Iran in order to silence the democracy activists. The Islamic institutions are also deeply divided. As was discussed above, they were established after the 1979 revolution to safeguard the interests of the people, and yet later turned into essentially capitalist enterprises. Some within these institutions are holding to the principles of the 1979 revolution and the idea of working for the interests of the people; others use the religious ideology to safeguard their own interests. In this context, the armed forces and the security agencies are also divided. After the 1979 revolution they were formed to defend the revolution and the country, and yet over time have became increasingly involved in commercial and material interests (Ansari 2009b). The ongoing demonstrations since June 2009 have opened up a new space of radical politics in the historical consciousness of Iranians. Thus the democracy activists are self-confident and see their movement as the continuation of the Constitutional Revolution of 1906–07, the oil nationalisation of 1951, and the 1979 revolution. They believe that they have achieved two of the three demands of the 1979 revolution, independence and an end to monarchy, and they are now struggling for the third demand, freedom from state oppression (Adib-Moghadam 2010).

For many democracy activists, the reform movement marks the end of their coexistence with the conservatives. They argue that they are facing a narrow-based conservative regime which has forced democracy activists into permanent opposition. In this context, their organisation, the 'Green Path of Hope', could turn into a civil society movement and struggle for democracy.[15] The strength of the Green Movement inside Iran has demonstrated that the ideological ties binding people to the existing state are breaking. Nevertheless, the degree of support for the ruling order also demonstrates that large sections of the society are not free from the ideas that blind them to the reality of the existing oppressive order. Different parts of society have different conceptions of their state and system, and the Green Movement has been unable to translate the post-June 2009 presidential election crisis into a unifying issue. The leadership has not shown its ability to lead the movement and instead has sought to compromise with the conservatives.[16]

The democracy movement in Iran since the 1979 revolution, with its strengths and weaknesses, will register in history as one of the most important movements in the world in the late-twentieth and early twenty-first centuries. Its activities have been undermined by political repression from an authoritarian and patriarchal social order. Nevertheless, it has boldly challenged institutional power and influence, and has achieved substantive goals. It is recognised as a social group with common interests and a legitimate claim on society.

THREE

Islamist modernists

The Sunni–Shi'a divide

The history of Shi'ism in Iran is one of both continuity and change. In the early period, around the seventh century, the Shi'a communities, as oppressed minorities, challenged the legitimacy and authority of the dynasty of the Caliphs. During the Safavid dynasty in Iran (sixteenth–eighteenth centuries), the Shi'a clergy accepted the Safavid monarchy as the protector and promoter of Shi'ism. After the 1979 revolution when the Shi'a clergy came to power, they challenged unjust rulers in the region and globally. However, today the rule of the Shi'a clergy in power is being challenged by Islamist modernists, 'religious new thinkers', who are struggling for the separation of religion from politics and the state. This chapter looks at these historical developments and argues that Iran's strong foreign policy, admired in the Middle East region, has its roots in a dynamic interpretation of Shi'a philosophy regarding the right to challenge tyrannical rulers.

There are 1.3 billion Muslims in the world: 15 per cent are Shi'a, 85 per cent Sunni. Shi'a communities are mainly concentrated in the Middle East – from Lebanon to Pakistan – where there are equal numbers of Shi'a and Sunni. The Shi'a communities around the Persian Gulf constitute 80 per cent of the population (Nasr 2007: 34).

The first month of the Islamic lunar calendar is the month of Muharram. On the tenth day of this month, the Shi'a communities commemorate the anniversary of the death (the martyrdom) of Imam (leader) Hussein, the grandson of Prophet Muhammad in 680 CE in Karbala in Iraq. This day is called *Ashoura* (the Arabic Word for 'tenth'). They also commemorate the fortieth day (*Arbaeen*) after the martyrdom of Imam Hussein, who in their view died resisting tyranny. As is described by Nasr (2007: 20), these events are passionate communal gatherings, symbolising opposition to the oppressive rulers of today, because in many parts of Muslim-majority societies, from North Africa to the Middle East, to Central Asia and South Asia, the Shi'a communities are in the minority (except in Iran and Iraq). Throughout their history, as marginalised communities, they have kept alive the tradition of commemoration of these events, not just as an old conflict but as a demonstration of defiance against unjust authoritarian rulers and foreign aggression. At times, they have not been allowed by their governments to commemorate these events as such celebrations are seen as a challenge to the ruling regime.

Many examples illustrate this powerful sentiment. The role of the Pahlavi shahs was challenged in Iran leading up to the 1979 revolution. The role of Saddam Hussein in Iraq was questioned, as was that of Israel in both Lebanon and Palestine. When Saddam Hussein's regime fell in spring 2003, 2 million people identifying themselves as Shi'a in the Iraqi city of Karbala commemorated the Arbaeen. Saddam Hussein had banned these gatherings for years. They demonstrated to show the religio-political identity that had been denied them by Saddam Hussein. Tens of thousands of Iranians, many poor and elderly with nothing more than a bundle of food, walked across the Iran–Iraq border to visit the shrine of the Shi'a Imams in Iraq, from which Saddam had banned them. The shrines of Shi'a Imams in Iraq, Damascus and elsewhere, with their golden domes, green and blue tiles, mirror walls, chandeliers and carpets, were the gifts of Iranian kings, including the Pahlavi shahs, and Iranian merchants. The vast kitchens of these shrines have fed the poor throughout Muslim-majority societies (Nasr 2007: 18, 31–7, 56, 79; Ghouchani 2004; Kadivar 2000: 45–99).

The origins of the Sunni–Shi'a divide go back to early Islam, with each strand claiming itself as the original orthodoxy (Hourani 1991: 22–62). This is a divide not just about theological disagreements, but about different readings of history, political power, domination, subordination and the uniqueness of identity (Shariati 2000: 109–61; Nasr 2007: 31–62). Following the death of Prophet Muhammad in 632 CE most Muslims followed the tribal tradition of the head of the Islamic community (umma) being selected by a council of respected senior elders. The council chose Abu-Bakr, the Prophet's close friend and father-in-law as the Prophet Successor, or caliph. A small group of the Prophet's companions believed that his cousin and son-in-law, Ali, was more qualified to lead the Muslim community. Through consensus, Abu-Bakr became the leader and Ali accepted the consensus. After Abu-Bakr, Omar and Othman were chosen and Ali became the fourth caliph. The Shi'a (the followers of Ali), however, continued to challenge the leadership, and to this day argue that the rightful leaders of Islam could come only from the descendents of Ali and Fatima, the Prophet's daughter, and their sons Hassan and Hussein. They maintain that when the Prophet was returning from Mecca to Medina in his last pilgrimage, at Ghadir Khum he declared Ali as his successor. Therefore for them Ali is the first leader, and following Ali the leadership is strictly limited to his eleven descendants (Rahnema and Nomani 1990: 19–20).

Since then, Muslims have been divided into two groups: the Sunni (ahl al-sybbag wa'll-jama'ah, people of tradition and consensus) communities, who saw the caliphate regime as the continuation of Nabovat (the Prophet's mission); and the Shi'a communities (the followers of Ali), who saw Imamate ('leadership', the institution of the rule of the Imams as vicegerents of the Prophet) as the continuation of the Prophet's mission (Shariati 2000: 179–86). As is argued by Mohammad Ghouchani (2004) and Jamileh Kadivar (2000: 445–83), the political discourse of Shi'ism as a religio-political party questioned not only who should have succeeded the

Prophet, but also the issue of leadership and the legitimacy of the rulers of Muslim nations.

In the period 632 to 661 CE, when Abu-Bakr was succeeded by Omar, Othman and finally Ali, the conflict between the two sects intensified. Omar was killed by an Iranian prisoner of war; Othman was killed by mutinous Muslim soldiers. Ali was challenged by Abu-Bakr, then Aisha (the Prophet's wife), Muawiay (Othman's cousin, who was the governor of Damascus), and finally assassinated.

After Ali's death, under the Omayyad dynasty (661–750), the caliphate system was transformed from an interrelationship between religion, politics and leadership into a separation of religion from politics; and governments, as the leadership, delegated the religious scholars to perform religious duties. The majority Sunnis accepted the new regime. But the minority who identified themselves as Shi'a continued to challenge the Omayyad regime. Hussein (Ali's son) and the people of Kufa, a city near Najaf, rose against the Omayyad rulers. At the battle of Karbala in 680 CE, Hussein, his brother Hassan and their army fought the Syrian army for six days and were defeated by the Omayyad general. Hussein's sister, Zaynab, accompanied her brother's head to Damascus, where she successfully defended the life of Hussein's son (Ali ibn Hussein), who succeeded his father as the fourth Shi'a Imam. Zaynab, with her success in this war, ensured the continuity of Shi'ism. She is buried in Damascus and her shrine is a popular place for Shi'a Pilgrims to visit (Nasr 2007: 40–43).

The Omayyad caliphs, who ruled from Damascus, and the Abbasids, who ruled from Baghdad (750–1258), imprisoned and killed Shi'a Imams. Shi'a mosques, were attacked during Ashoura and Arbaeen commemorations. The Shi'a communities and their leaders escaped to Iran, Pakistan, Afghanistan and India, and as a result many Shi'a shrines emerged to serve the Shi'a communities throughout the region (Shariati 2000: 215–19).

The Shi'a communities ruled over the Sunnis for short periods: Persian Buyids ruled Baghdad in the middle of the tenth century and Ismaili Fatimid ruled over Egypt for two centuries. However, these periods were relatively brief, and the Shi'a communities lived predominantly as a minority under Sunni rule. The Shi'a communities therefore continued to challenge the legitimacy of the Omayyad and Abbasid rulers in Damascus and Baghdad. They argued that the line of leadership continued until 874 CE when the Twelfth Imam Mahdi was withdrawn by God into a miraculous state of occultation at the age of 9. In this context, for these Shi'a communities the return of Imam Mahdi, or the Hidden Imam, would bring the end of time and the advent of perfect divine justice. This messianic view, similar to that of the Jews, Christians and Zoroastrians, became the new dominant discourse of Shi'ism in Iran (Nasr 2007: 67; Kadivar 2000: 45–83).

The Sunni Schools of law include Hanafi, Maliki, Shafii and Hanbali. The Shi'a school include the Twelvers Imam (mainly in Iran), the Ismailis, Alavis (mainly in Syria) and Zaidi. Sufism emerged in the eleventh and twelfth centuries in Iraq and Egypt; in some ways it resembles aspects of Shi'ism. Both the Shi'a Imams and the Sufi leaders are regarded as mediators between human beings and God. Sufi love of Ali is stronger than Shi'a love of Ali. The influence of Sufism has generated interest in Shi'ism in many Sunni societies, as the hard-line Sunnis reject both Sufism and Shi'ism, and Sufi communities are as much under attack as the Shi'a. In Syria there is harmony between the Shi'a and Sunni communities. The Syrian government, dominated by Shi'a Ismaili Alavi, has been challenged by the Sunni Muslim Brotherhood, but it has relied on Sufism for its legitimacy (Nasr 2007: 59–61).

Despite the historical conflict, these communities are not monolithic. The followers of each sect are divided by language, ethnicity, class, gender, geography, politics and different levels of religiosity and secularity. They are Arab, Persian, Afghan, North African, Asian, South Asian and Southeast Asian, all with their own distinct national and cultural identities. They have experienced conflicts, but they have also lived in harmony and have experienced friendship through intermarriage and mixed communities, especially in Iraq. As will be discussed in Chapter 5, they have fought each other, but they have also fought the common enemy. The hostility between these two communities does not run as deep as that between Protestants and Catholics (Vali Nasr 2007: 20–26).

For Sunnis, the Quran, the Hadith and Sunna (tradition) are important sources to be followed. In this context, religion is separated from the state, a principle respected by important Islamic religious centres such as Al Azhar in Cairo. Governments and states in Muslim-majority societies are considered representatives of the religion and the followers of the Prophet. Therefore the role of the clergy is to deal with religious matters and not political matters. For the Shi'a communities, beside the Quran and the Hadith, the concepts of *aql* (reason) and *ijtihad* (application of human reason and rationality) are also important (Shariati 2000: 242–4; Rahnema 2005a: 7–9). These concepts allow new interpretations and readings of the original sources by the *mujtahids* (learned religious scholars) according to time and place. This allows them to understand the specific meaning of the Quran through commentaries and its implicit meaning through interpretation. As is argued by Ali Rahnema (2005a: 8), the concept of *ijtihad* 'constitutes a bridge between eternally valid divine injunctions and time-specific requirements of any age'. Since the thirteenth century, or, according to others, the tenth century, Sunni leadership closed the door of *ijtihad*. However, to the present day, there has been a debate between the Sunni clergy and scholars over the relevance of applicability of *ijtihad*.[1] For the Shi'a clergy the concepts of *aql* and *ijtihad* allow them to interpret socio-political and socio-economic matters in democratic, in conservative, in autocratic and in theocratic ways. In some cases, the Sunni clergy have rejected these interpretations and in other cases they have accepted them. For example, Mohammad Hossein Adeli, the governor of the Central Bank of Iran between 1989 and 1994, explained to me how his interpretation of sharia enabled him to reform the banking system in Iran to operate according to the needs of today's world, a reform that some Sunni majority societies have also accepted:

> we created *Oraghe Mosharekat* [an Islamic banking bond]. We discussed this issue with Muslim economists in Iran and in the Muslim-majority societies, as well as with the clergy and Islamic

scholars. Some accepted it and some rejected it. But it became the norm in Iran and was successful. Since then in some Sunni Muslim-majority societies this system is accepted and is used.

In Shi'ism, the most senior clergy are to be emulated (*marja' al-Taqlid*). Religious contributions by community members help the clergy to perform charitable duties and to educate seminary students. For example, Shi'a communities across the Middle East and beyond contribute to grand ayatollahs such as al-Sistani in Iraq, Fadlallah in Lebanon and a number of ayatollahs in Iran. Historically the senior clergy have resided in Najaf in Iraq and in Qom in Iran; there have been strong links between the clergy and the merchants of the bazaars.

Although most aspects of everyday worship are very similar for Shi'a and Sunni Muslims, there are small differences. Those who identify themselves as Shi'a hold their hands at their sides when praying, while the Sunnis clasp them. But the most important distinction is the importance of visual imagery in Shi'ism. Popular Shi'a artworks are similar to those in certain branches of Christianity and can include the human figure. But such representation is frowned upon and condemned by Sunnis as a form of deviance from Islam, as an expression of idol worship. The Shi'a communities in Iran also differ from Sunnis over the concept of impurity, which exists in Zoroastrianism, the pre-Islamic religion of Persia, and in Hinduism in India. Zoroastrian doctrine believes that non-Zoroastrians are unclean. Hence conversion to religion is considered the way to purification (Sanasarian 2000: 23–4). Within the Shi'a communities there is a belief that martyrdom will strengthen Shi'ism, as with Imam Hussein. Sunnis have historically frowned upon martyrdom, but in recent years Sunni extremists have embraced a version of it in the form of suicide bombing (Nasr 2007: 57).

Iran and the Islamic empire

At the time of the rise of Islam, the Byzantine and the Sassanid empires were the two major powers in the area. Judaism, Christianity and Zoroastrianism were the prevailing religions in these empires. Islam explicitly yet discreetly affiliated itself with the traditions already established in the region. According to Islam, Muhammad was a prophet in the Judeo-Christian tradition, and the Quran incorporated many stories to be found in the Bible. As a consequence, the assimilation of the social traditions of Christian and Jewish populations into Islamic life and thought occurred easily. Converts to Islam from Christianity, Judaism and Zoroastrianism brought their traditions and customs with them. Social values and practices such as the veil, virginity and the harem came from ancient Persia and the Zoroastrian tradition. Women in Christian communities in the Middle East also practised the wearing of the veil. The concept of marriage was similar to that of the Judaic and Zoroastrian religions. Family and family-based community were among the many institutions inherited and continued by Islam (Ahmed 1992: 11–123).

At the time of the Prophet Muhammad, Arab communities lived in the Arabian Peninsula, Iraq and the region of greater Syria, including Syria and Palestine. Islam was an urban religion. Within a generation after the death of the Prophet Muhammad, Islamic Arabs had conquered Iran. Arab Muslim armies defeated the Persian and Egyptian superpowers and forced out the Byzantines from the Near East. They conquered countries from North Africa to Western Europe. Soon the Islamic Empire stretched from India and Central Asia to the West. Egypt and Iraq became Islamic Arab countries in the period of the making of the Arab empire. Iran was not Arabised but Islamised. The gradual process of conversion to Islam did not exhaust Iranian cultural energy. A new and distinct Iranian identity within the Islamic world was created – a great cultural renaissance that included the poetry of Ferdowsi, Nezami, Sa'di and Hafez (Yarshatar 2009). A combination of the political and the social survival of an old Iranian elite and the possession of cultural self-confidence lay at the heart of the survival of Iranian national identity. The administrative legacy of the Sassanid kings, the economic advance of Iran, its tax system, and the urban centres were attractive to the Muslim conquerors. These, together with the adherence of the kings of the Sassanid Empire

(224–651 CE) to Iranian cultural values, led to the preservation of a distinct Iranian identity – the Persian language, a non-Arabic and non-Semitic language survived. The Arab conquest, which took place over centuries, allowed the survival of local power structures, and the Iranian elite, who adopted and adapted Islam, maintained the old cultural and political traditions. However, the history of pre-Islamic Iran was integrated into the classical Arabic tradition (Bullieet 2009; Kennedy 2009; Bosworth 2009; Hillenbrand 2009).

When the Sassanid dynasty collapsed, Zoroastrianisn survived as the religion of the elite and the upper classes. Local rulers for a long time continued to rule according to Sassanid tradition, especially in the Caspian Sea area. The conversion of people to Islam was mainly through attraction, in a process that took place over centuries. There was no imposition of Arab Muslim laws on the Iranians. In the ninth century Zoroastrians who were still practising their own religion and were in positions of power within the administration translated Persian literature into Arabic. The contributions of scientists such as Razi and Avicenna (Abu Ali Ibn Sina) to the field of science and medicine, and Iran's role in the dissemination of their contribution to Europe through the Arabic language, were also important (Richter-Bernburg 2009).

The Shi'a rise to power

In the tenth and eleventh centuries, Shi'ism was strong in North Africa and southern Syria, while Iran was the centre of Sunni theology. Nevertheless, Iran provided refuge for the Shi'a communities escaping persecution from Baghdad and Damascus. As Shi'ism declined in North Africa and Syria, Iran became the centre of Shi'ism. The eighth Shi'a Imam Reza is buried in Mashhad and his sister Massoumeh is buried in Qom. Both these shrines and other Shi'a shrines in Iran are visited by millions of Shi'a visitors every year from Iran and the region and beyond. Twelver Shi'ism came to Iran during the Safavid period. In 1501, Ismail Safavi defeated the Mughals and established the Safavid dynasty. The Ottomans and the Safavids competed with each other for domination of the Muslim world. The wars between the two empires gave distinct religious identities to Iranians, Turks and Arabs. Finally the Safavids, originally a Sunni Sufi order, established Shi'ism as the state religion in Iran as a means to differentiate themselves from their main politico-military rivals, the Ottomans (Keddie 1981: 21–36). They became the Shi'a empire; the Ottomans ruled over Arab lands and made Istanbul the centre of Sunni'ism in 1517. The difference between these two superpowers was not just over religious matters, but concerned the political issue of who should rule the Muslim world. Many Shi'a communities in majority Sunni areas were forced into exile and some were killed. This created more conflict between the two religions – the Ottomans saw themselves as the caliphs of the Islamic world and were threatened by the powerful Shi'a government in Iran (Nasr 2007: 65–7).

In this context the Safavid shahs sought unity with the Shi'a scholars and the Shi'a scholars needed the support of the Safavid shahs. Their survival and prosperity depended on each other. In this period the political discourse of Shi'ism changed. Shi'ism became the official religion, so Shi'a scholars had relative power. They ceased being an oppressed minority and became a considerable majority integrated within the political system. At this time, at the heart of the discourse of Shi'ism was the relationship between political leadership and Shi'a scholars, rather than conflicts as in the previous period. The nature of the debate therefore changed. The Shi'a communities considered the Safavids a legitimate government until the Twelfth Imam arrived to establish a truly legitimate Islamic regime (Kadivar 2000: 99–162).

Under the Safavids, Iranian/Shi'a artistic activities flourished. Shah Abbas, who came to power in 1587, created a modern version of the ancient Iranian cultural identity, and Shi'ism was instrumental in the formation of a distinctive national identity. Intriguingly, this paralleled early modern nation-state developments in Western Europe. Abbas chose the ancient city of Isfahan as the capital city, which was called Isfahan Nisf-i Jahan (Isfahan, half of the world). Monumental architecture, the magnificent blue mosque being just one example, new styles in painting, and calligraphic art forms flourished. Maidan-i Naghsh-i Jahan ('The Piazza as Portrait of the World'), with its two magnificent mosque compounds and unparalleled ceramic tile work, and bazaar, flourished and became the centre of international culture and commerce (Canby 2009). The Safavids brought Shi'a clergy and scholars from Lebanon, the Arabian Peninsula and Bahrain to deepen the roots of Shi'ism. These scholars and clergy were patronised by the Safavids and established the foundation of Shi'a scholarship, seminaries, libraries and mosques in Iran. So, since this time, Shi'ism has had close ties with Iran – the relationship between Iran, South Lebanon and Iraq goes back centuries. Hence the fact that influential clerics have Iranian roots. For example, Ayatollah al-Sistani of Iraq is of Iranian origin (see Chapter 5).

From the fall of the Safavids (1501–1722) until the Qajar period (1794–1925) the power of Shi'a scholars declined. However, during the Qajar period the shahs, who ruled through military power and political repression, could not ignore the power of the clergy. Lack of state administration and the inability of the Qajar shahs to meet the economic, social, political and cultural needs of the population led to the public popularity of the clergy and their active participation in socio-economic and political issues. In this period, Sayyid Jamal al-Din Asadabadi (known as 'Afghani') (1838–1897), an Iranian and Shi'a Islamist scholar, was a pioneer of Islamic modernism and anti-imperialist activism, rejecting both Islamic conservatism and blind imitation of the West. He extolled justice and the rule of law in the context of anti-colonialism and anti-state authoritarianism. He initiated what would become a growing trend to change Islam from a religious faith into a politico-religious ideology. As is discussed in Chapter 7, Muhammad Abduh, a pioneer of Islamic reform in Egypt, was drawn to Afghani's ideas when they met in Al-Azhar in Cairo. Together they made an enormous contribution to modern Islamic thought. This tradition continued into the late nineteenth and early twentieth centuries. In the late nineteenth century, the Iranian ulema played an important role in the tobacco protest movement against the British and in the Constitutional Revolution of 1905–06, and in the Jangali (Jungle) movement (1914–20) against the Qajar monarchy (Martin 1989; Rahnema and Nomani 1990: 19–21; Bayat 2005: 25; Keddie 2005: 11–29; Haddad 2005: 30–63; Kadivar 2000: 185–353).

The marginalisation of Shi'a clergy in the twentieth century

During the Pahlavi shahs' leadership (1925–79) Shi'ism as a political religious movement once again played an oppositional role (Ghouchani 2004). As was discussed in Chapter 1, under the influence of the British and later the USA, Reza Shah's and Mohammad Reza Shah's socio-economic developments led to the marginalisation of large sections of the population, including the clergy. Ayatollah Kashani supported the nationalist movement of Mossadeq, and in the 1960s Ayatollah Khomeini emerged as an important politico-religious figure (Bayat 2005: 24). Nevertheless, the majority of the Iranian clergy agreed to legitimise the monarchy as long as the monarch defended Shi'a identity. Even Ayatollah Khomeini believed in the separation of religion from politics, although, as was discussed in Chapter 1, at the end of the Shah's period, under the pressure of political circumstance, he changed his position and argued that religion had to play a political role in order to end the Shah's rule, and on this basis he argued for the implementation of *Velayat-e faqih* (Guardianship of the jurist), though he emphasised that religious practices must be compatible with the current period (Kadivar 2000: 353–61). This was at a time when the majority of the people objected not only to the domestic policy of the Pahlavi era but also to its foreign policy, in particular the Shah's relationship with Israel. In this context a contemporary reading of the Shi'a tradition of rising up against unjust governments and rulers was revived. As was discussed in Chapter 1, it is in this period that Ali Shariati criticised the clergy for not being engaged with the political situation and involved in the 1979 revolutionary movement. Many clergy duly criticised Shariati, as their position was unchanged: to await the return of the Twelfth Imam to bring justice to the world. Shariati's reply to them was: 'The Shi'a communities should not merely await the Twelfth Imam in a passive state but instead should feel themselves called upon actively to work for the hastening of this return' (Nasr 2007: 129).

For Shariati, religion can become worldly through a culture of criticism. Therefore religion can be informed by all ideologies including Marxism, Freud, Sartre, the Latin American liberation theology of the 1970s, postmodernism and liberalism. He used the class analysis of Marxism and socialism, but he criticised Soviet Communism. He also criticised liberalism and existentialism. Shariati argued that freedom and egalitarianism could be achieved by liberating 'God and his love from the monopoly of religion, freedom from the monopoly of capitalism and egalitarianism from the monopoly of Marxism' (Rahnema 1998: 160). For Shariati, colonialism and imperialism constituted Islam's main enemy; Marxism was a rival and competing ideology; and Shi'ism stood for defending the poor and the marginalised, and the pursuit of justice. He presented a popular, modernist and militant view of Islam that influenced the thought of a wide spectrum of people in Iran and across the Middle East (Nasr 2007: 129). Many clergy, including the Islamic modernists such as Ayatollah Mottahari, opposed Shariati as an extremist. Despite the many criticisms he faced, Shariati gave many lectures in the Hosseiniyeh Ershad, a centre of modernist Islamic discourse in Tehran. There he argued that 'Islam is an ideology and a social revolution which intended to construct a classless and free society on the basis of equality and justice and in which would live enlightened, responsible and free people' (Rahnema 1998: 236). He articulated a new language which penetrated the minds of his audience, who in their thousands filled his lectures in Hosseiniyeh Ershad. His mission was to revolutionise and modernise the understanding of Islam. He detested the persistence of outmoded traditions, customs and institutions and believed that change was inevitable, and in doing so gave birth to a social movement[2] which ultimately led to the 1979 revolution (Rahnema 1998: 350–70; 2005: 208–50).

The Shi'a world welcomed the Iranian Revolution with great pride. Iran became a model for the Shi'a communities in the region to fight for their rights. Shi'a demonstrations, riots, clashes with ruling regimes occurred across the Middle East. For example, uprisings in Bahrain and Kuwait caused alarm, especially for the Saudis as their oil workers are predominantly Shi'a, and 1979–80 saw political riots in the oil-rich eastern provinces, in reaction to which the Saudis immediately clamped down on pro-Iranian activists among the oil workers (Nasr 2007: 138–9). As is discussed in forthcoming chapters, many Sunni communities in the region also viewed the revolution in Iran positively, not least in relation to the role of the country in the region, and its shift in policy from a pro-Israel to a pro-Palestinian stance, and from being a friend of pro-US governments to supporting the poor and marginalised people in the region. The left groups also looked at Islam with great interest. For in Iran, Islam as an ideology of resistance had succeeded in engaging with the poor and working classes, and through mass mobilisation had overthrown one of the strongest states in the region.

'Religious new thinkers' and the challenge to the rule of clergy

Before the 1979 revolution, the concept of 'religious new thinkers' was associated with the work of Ali Shariati and Ayatollah Taleghani. After the revolution, a number of politicians and clergy followed the same path and laid the foundations for reform. With the establishment of the Islamic Republic, the Iranian Shi'a movement was transformed into a Shi'a government. From the early days of the Islamic Republic Grand Ayatollah Mottahari argued that the theory of *Velayat-e faqih* is ideological, and should not lead to the involvement of clergy in politics and government; the role of the clergy is supervisory and should prevent practices which may be against sharia law (Ghouchani 2004). But, as was discussed in Chapter 1, soon after the 1979 revolution internal and external factors led to an increased role and influence on the part of the conservative clergy in state and other institutions. Following Ayatollah Mottahari, Ayatollah Montazeri became the leading voice in challenging Iran's theocratic constitution. Until his death in December 2009 he remained critical of and openly discussed the supervisory role of the clergy, challenging the implementation of Velayat-e faqih. As a result of his criticisms of the leadership, he was replaced as the annointed successor to Ayatollah Khomeini by the current supreme leader, Ayatollah Khamenei, and in 1997 was placed under house arrest.[3]

The criticisms of Velayat-e faqih are pitched at different levels. Some argue that from one perspective the theory of Velayat-e faqih was the expression of the times in which it was produced; in the late-1970s' revolutionary period the clergy had to participate in politics to ensure the victory of the revolution. But now there is a need for the separation of religion and politics. Others argue that certain interpretations of Velayat-e faqih are creating a reaction in society that could lead to the decline of religion, whilst others are against the theory of Velayat-e faqih from a secularist point of view. Some also claim that the clergy should not be involved in politics, but that they should ensure that religion is preserved. Generally these explicit criticisms have moved Iran towards secularism.

In 1993, Khatami also used the term 'religious new thinkers' and argued that a new form of intellectualism is needed to appreciate religion and human rights. His argument was that the West does not stand only for colonialism and imperialism; it also fostered the ideas of Marx, Goethe and Hegel – representing modernity, freedom and democracy. Abdulkarim Soroush, an Islamist thinker, also argued that this form of intellectualism 'can learn from the west without being its slave' (Bayat 2005: 84–8).

In this context, many 'religious new thinkers', such as clergy, academics, journalists and intellectuals, collaborated with Khatami's administration, while others took a more critical stance in relation to religious conservatism. The term 'religious new thinkers', therefore, has been used to describe those Islamists in Iran who argue that Islam and modernism are mutually compatible, as it is possible to interpret and reinterpret Islamic concepts according to time and place. Some within this trend are liberal, others are neoliberal, while some are more left wing and believe in social democracy. At the heart of their analysis is the view that conservative political leaders strengthen popular religion to mobilise the mass of the population for their own interests. This popular Islam was successful both during the revolution and later for the mobilisation of the masses for the war with Iraq. The analogy with early Islam and Shi'ism in particular is a powerful instrument with which to mobilise people. For these 'religious new thinkers' the notion of popular religion has weakened, as religious ideological issues are not the answer to the grievances of the mass of the people, which today concern more material issues.[4] The Islam of the 1980s was ideologically determined, and now people's perceptions and identities have changed. The provision of education, health and employment to the poor and the marginalised in the 1980s and 1990s raised people's expectations. The failure of both the reformist government of Khatami and the conservative government of Ahmadinejad to meet the expectations of the young and educated population has intensified the demand for more satisfactory levels of education, employment, social welfare and democracy.

As a result, many 'religious new thinkers' have criticised the role of clergy who exercise their power through state and other institutions. Some critical clergy have even been imprisoned for their views. In 1998, Mohsen Kadivar (1999 and 2002) was jailed for drawing a critical parallel between the discourse of Shi'ism and tyranny and absolutism. He argued that

> The track-record of the revolution is not that glorious if seen in terms of people's demands and the promise articulated in the slogan that became the revolution's motif: Independence, Freedom, Islamic Republic ... elimination of monarchical oppression and the establishment of Islamic justice. The revolution's balance sheet is positive only with respect to the first slogan, as Iran today is relatively independent of foreign powers. But the revolution only succeeded in transforming the face of monarchy in Iran; autocratic rule and monarchical relations have remained intact, and are reproduced in the form of the absolute vali-ye faqih [leader]. Not only are the people unable to choose the vali-ye faqih directly, they have no control over his style or governance and cannot dismiss him if he goes against their will. Like an absolute monarch, the

vali-ye faqih occupies his position for life and is above the law. As for freedom the revolution has failed Iranians. One of the prerequisites of freedom is freedom of opposition, that is, the degree to which those who oppose the government or the ways of its rulers can be active in society and can air their views.[5]

Another cleric, Yusef Eshkevari, was arrested in 2000 after returning from a conference in Berlin at which he discussed Islam and democracy. In his speech he acknowledged that, 'even if Khatami should be defeated in his work this time not only has democracy become the first priority, but there is an unprecedented consensus among the intellectuals and the political elites that the historical time of despotism is over in Iran' (Farhadpour 2000; Mir-Hosseini and Tapper 2006: 108). Similarly, other dissident clerics, journalists and academics, such as Mohammad Shabestari, Abdulkarim Soroush, Said Hajarian, Habibollah Peyman and Mashallah Shamsolvaezin, are challenging state and other institutions and discussing to what extent religious theory and the religious community can be separated from politics and state authority. Their objective is to progress democracy step by step and in doing so learn from the process. These 'religious new thinkers' argue that it is possible to bring about a just Islamic governance similar to the regime in early Islam, when justice and human rights were given particular importance.

As Shi'a intellectual Islamists, these thinkers place emphasis on the *Hokomate Ali* (Imam Ali's governance in early Islam). In an interview with me Habibollah Peyman argued:

> Ali recognised the rights of everyone, even those with whom
> he disagreed, even those who were non-believers; he tolerated
> diversity and recognised their rights. Democracy is about recognizing
> that societies consist of diverse groups and diverse religions.
> Individuals and groups have rights which have to be recognised by
> other individuals and by governments. In this democracy everyone
> has to be treated equally by the law. People should have the right
> to participate in decision-making. As is stated in the Quran, *Imamate*
> [leadership] requires *edalat* [justice], that is to say leaders should be
> just leaders to implement justice. Governance has to be based on
> consultative democracy.

Mohammad Mojtahed Shabestari, a highly influential philosopher and theologian, also challenges the ruling orthodoxy; he believes in a dialectical relationship between belief and knowledge and suggests the opening up of Islamic theology to contemporary philosophy. In the context of individualism, democracy and human rights he proposes a separation of religious values and secular realities, as he believes that religious absolutism is unworkable (Shabestari 2000).

Ayatollah Saanei, a supporter of reform of family law in favour of women, has argued that religious laws and regulations should be interpreted according to time and place.[6] His support has been important for women's activities and their struggle for the reform of discriminatory laws and regulations. Throughout the 1990s, the minority women's NGOs, together with other women's NGOs, had campaigned for the reform of the Islamic law of *dieh* or 'blood money' (when a person kills another, they must pay blood money to the family of the victim, in addition to civil punishment). According to Article 881 and Articles 10 and 59 of civil law, only one-twelfth of the *dieh* was liable in the case of religious minorities; that is, if a Muslim accidentally killed a member of a religious minority, he or she only paid one-twelfth of *dieh* to the family of the dead person. Also, according to this law, the blood money for women is half of that of men, a provision which therefore discriminates particularly against women from religious minorities. In 2002, religious minority (Zoroastrian, Jewish and Armenian) women's NGOs succeeded in reforming this law and changing it in favour of minorities. Following this victory, women's NGOs, in collaboration with women's lawyers and female members of the Majlis, began to press for equal blood money for men and women. This has represented a major challenge by women across ethnic and religious identities to the traditional Islamic laws in Iran. In 2008, as a result of the women's campaigns, it was agreed that, on health grounds, *dieh* for women and men should be equal. Marzieh Mortazi explained:

> First we argued that if women and men have blood-related diseases their *dieh* should be equal. With the support of a number

of ayatollahs, this was agreed. We then continued pressurising the authorities to extend this equality to those who are killed in accidents. The Council of Guardians may reject this equality because the conservative clergy may interpret this reform as being in contradiction with sharia law. In which case our plan is to refer our demand to the Expediency Council and argue that it should be accepted as it is according to the present needs of society. We are confident that it will be accepted.

According to Farideh Machini (2008b), another women's rights activist, 'there are 2.5 million female-headed households. We need to change the regulations to suit the needs of the time. In Islam religion can be involved in politics but only with people's consent.' She provides a convincing argument by challenging the conservative leaders who have changed the laws and regulations governing the Islamic banking system in order to make the Iranian economy compatible with the global system, but who refuse to change family law in favour of women. In this context she argues that

> there are those in Iran who see gender equality as a Western ideology and an intervention that will weaken Islam. Western demonisation of Iran and Islam strengthen this position in Iran. In opposition to this position there are those who see the roots of women's oppression as being in Islam. Today we have a movement between these two views, which are a world apart. The discourse of religious new thinking and intellectualism as a new movement emphasises the importance of Islam in Iran. We believe that Islamic laws and regulations historically have been interpreted by men in the interests of male-dominated society, and in the name of religion have perpetuated women's subordination. We challenge the male reading of Islam. The growing participation of women in the public sphere of life is challenging patriarchal attitudes. These women want to have a different interpretation of religion according to the demands of today's world, as this is the only way to preserve religion.

These 'religious new thinkers' believe that religion cannot impose on the will of the people; instead its role in politics must be legitimised through popular support. They challenge the leadership when it moves away from the interests of ordinary people. As was discussed in Chapter 2, political repression, controls on the media, and restrictions imposed by the state on the operation of a free press, the right to free assembly and freedom of speech create obstacles on the path of democracy activists working to develop a dynamic connection with ordinary people. The internal and external pressures have impacted on the democracy movement, inasmuch as gaps are appearing between the elite and the grassroots. Nevertheless, the 'religious new thinkers' are strongly rooted in their society, as they work within the Islamic context and tradition. Therefore they are successful in gaining popular support.

Following the presidential election and the uprising in the summer of 2009, Grand Ayatollah Montazeri supported the democracy movement and invited people to continue their protest. He argued that

> In 1979 the Shi'a clergy stood on the side of the people. Today it is divided. One side is holding on to political power with any means necessary and the other continues to stand on the side of the people and places a greater importance on the rights of the people than the rights of the regime. Therefore, the Shi'a clergy is facing a historical choice, to become the ideological agent of a dictatorial regime or to stand on the side of the people and return to the Shi'a culture of protest.[7]

He warned the state authorities by arguing that if people cannot raise their voices about their legitimate rights, and if their demonstrations are suppressed, complexities will develop that could uproot the foundation of the government. As is argued by Bager Moin, 'his political opposition to injustice represented an important act of defiance. He attempted to change the basis of Shi'a jurisprudence from protecting the right of the faithful to protecting the right of the citizen.' He was the only cleric who issued a fatwa (religious ruling) calling for respect for the rights of Bahais in Iran. In this context, 'he extended the boundaries of Shi'a jurisprudence into the realm of human rights'.[8] Mohsen Kadivar argues that according to the constitution, citizens have the right to protest:

Our protest is non-violence and we are for a truly democratic Islamic state that respects human rights, women's rights and allows the people to freely elect their religious and secular leaders. In such a society, religious leaders do not have the right to determine how the country is led in opposition to the majority of the people. In the long run the regime cannot oppose millions of peaceful demonstrators, unless it opts for a massacre and, in doing so, completely loses its legitimacy.[9]

My analysis of the internal political dynamics of Iran, as a religio-political state since the 1979 revolution, demonstrates that the contradictions inherent in the Islamic state are shifting the boundaries of conservative Islam, leading to the emergence of an important democracy movement. As is argued in forthcoming chapters, Iran is popular with the majority of the people in Lebanon, Palestine and Egypt simply because it is the only country in the region which opposes Zionism and imperialism.

However, the support of the people across the Middle East for Iran's democracy movement is limited and uncertain because Western politicians and media also support it. For many, Iran's repressive domestic policy is in contradiction with its anti-Zionist and anti-imperialist regional policy. They have embraced a democratic Islamic idea and see Islam as an ideology to resist repression and authoritarian political domination. It is in this context that the position of the reformist clergy in Iran – which is comparable to that of Ayatollah Fadlallah, a prominent Shi'a leader in Lebanon, and of Ayatollah al-Sistani in Iraq – is shaping the future of democracy in the Middle East.

The relationship between Iran, Lebanon and Hezbollah

The relationship between Iran and Lebanon dates back to antiquity, when the Persian Achaemenid Empire ruled the Phoenician coast between 539 and 332 BCE. After the defeat of the Persian Empire by Alexander the Great, Lebanon became part of the Hellenistic Seleuid Kingdom, and in the first century BCE Lebanon became part of the Roman province of Syria. Later, in 614 CE, Sassanid rulers captured Jerusalem (Chehabi and Mneimneh 2006: 2–3). In the seventh century BCE Lebanon fell under Arab conquest and Islamic influence (Salibi 2005:5). The early Twelver Shi'a communities had lived in the Jabal Amil region of South Lebanon and in the Beqaa Valley since the ninth century, and during the period of the Crusaders' rule in Syria (1099–1291) the Islamic Druze emerged in different parts of Syria, including the southern Mount Lebanon (Salibi 2005: 12–13). The historical relationship between Iran and the Shi'a communities in Lebanon significantly increased in the sixteenth century when the Safavids invited Lebanese Shi'a scholars to deepen the roots of Shi'ism in Iran (Hourani 2006: 51–61).

Throughout this complex history there have been conflicts, harmonies and alliances between different communities. Family alliances across religious lines have been particularly widespread. As is argued by Ussama Makdisi (2000: 7), sectarianism as a 'modern knowledge' was created by European colonial hegemony through the Ottoman Empire. The Maronite and Druze leaders gave recognition to the European powers as the protectors of their communities rather than the local Lebanese rulers. This intensified the process of political sectarian identity.

The present state of Lebanon emerged in 1920, when the French exploited the League of Nations and carved out a part of Syria to create 'Greater Lebanon'. The existing borders of the Lebanese nation-state were established according to this mandate, combining the majority-Christian Ottoman province of Mount Lebanon (the historical home of the Maronites) with surrounding areas, including the Beqaa Valley and the South (Norton 2007: 11).

Between 1920 and 1975, the Maronites dominated the Lebanese state and its politics, and defined Lebanon's identity according to their own cultural and class interests. The Sunni elites also participated in state affairs. The formation of a National Pact laid the foundations for a sectarian political system that ensured Shi'a under-representation; the cabinet was divided equally between Christian Maronite and Sunni members and the Shi'as received 10 seats in the 55-member parliament.

In 1943 independence was achieved, and since then the president has always been a Maronite, the prime minister a Sunni, and a relatively powerless speaker of parliament a Shi'a, even though the Shi'a communities constitute a greater share of the population. (As we will see, the emergence of Hezbollah as a political party changed this balance of power.) The Maronites and urban Sunnis benefited from the socio-economic structure, while the population of South Lebanon, the majority of whom are Shi'a, had no hospitals, no schools and no irrigation systems. In 1958, under the Shihab presidency, some roads and schools were built in the South and cash crops were introduced in rural areas. The military and the civil service also provided some employment to Shi'as. This encouraged migration to south Beirut; however, poverty and unemployment persisted and the area became known as the 'misery belt', wherein the Shi'a communities and Palestinian communities (predominantly Sunnis) worked as day labourers, lived in poverty, and were totally excluded from the rest of society (Deeb 2006a: 72–3; Harik 2005: 20–21; Shaery-Eisenlohr 2008: 21–2).

The Shi'a landlords nominally supported their communities but at the same time protected their own material and class interests and migrated to Europe, the USA, Latin America, West Africa, as well as to other countries in the region. The majority of the Shi'as constituted a 'community-class' as they were the poorest of the poor. The Israeli occupations of South Lebanon intensified the low educational, occupational and economic status of the Shi'a communities, and as slum dwellers in the 'belt of misery' they constituted the most disadvantaged segment of Lebanese society. Earlier, in the 1950s and early 1960s, many Shi'as became affiliated to pro-Nasser parties, such as the Ba'ath Party, the Syrian Social Nationalist Party (SSNP), the Communist Party of Lebanon and other Arab nationalist and left-wing parties. Whilst they lived in poverty and suffered from socio-political marginalisation, they became radicalised and politicised by Arab nationalism, and by socialist and communist ideologies and organisations. After the 'black September' of 1970, when King Hussein of Jordan crushed the Palestine Liberation Organisation (PLO), many Palestinians escaped to Lebanon. Others, the majority of whom were Sunni, moved to South Lebanon[1] following the 1973 Arab–Israeli war. The extreme lack of discipline among PLO fighters in Shi'a neighbourhoods led to Shi'a lands and farms being taken over for the creation of refugee camps, causing tension between the Shi'as and the Palestinians (Khalili 2007a: 47–54). Nevertheless, the Shi'as, like other Lebanese people, joined with the PLO and the Popular Front for the Liberation of Palestine (PFLP) in opposing Israel's invasions of Lebanon, which were supported by the West. Their collaboration with these organisations was also an indication of their opposition to the corruption and backwardness of the Shi'a clergy, who supported the elite Shi'a landowning class (Saad-Ghorayeb 2002: 14–15; Deeb 2006a: 78; Nasr 2007: 110–11).

Since 1948, a number of Shi'a charity organisations have been established in Lebanon. In 1959, Sayyid Imam Musa al-Sadr, an

Iranian Shi'a cleric with Lebanese family ties, went to Lebanon to replace the Shi'a clerical leader in the southern Lebanese city of Tyre. He was helped by various religious groups in Iran, who founded a number of charitable institutions in South Lebanon to help the Shi'a communities. He presented them with an alternative ideology to that of the left and the nationalist parties and attempted to build a viable communal Islamic identity. He used the religious commemoration of Ashoura to build solidarity and develop political consciousness (Norton 1987: 41). In 1963 al-Sadr became more established in Beirut and Tyre, and in 1978 Muhammed Hussein Fadlallah established the al-Mabarrat Charitable Association, which later expanded to incorporate hospitals, schools, orphanages and cultural centres. The funding for these institutions came from wealthy Shi'as in the region and in West Africa, from khums and zakat (religious taxes),[2] and from fundraising events – which still raise millions of dollars every year (Harik 2005: 61; Deeb 2006a: 89–90).

In 1969 al-Sadr and Fadlallah helped to establish the Supreme Islamic Shi'a Council, and in 1970 they led a general strike demanding assistance for those displaced by the Israeli attacks in the South. In 1974 they established Harakat al-Mahrumin (the Movement of the Deprived) and demanded the reform of the Lebanese system. When civil war broke out in 1975, a militia branch of the organisation, the Battalions of the Lebanese Resistance (afwai al-muqawamat al-lun-baniyya – AMAL), was founded. In the 1970s, AMAL camps trained Iraqi, Iranian, Saudi and other Shi'a activists from the region.

In 1975, the Shi'as suffered the highest number of casualties at the hands of the Maronite militias, and in 1976 100,000 Shi'as from Nab'a were displaced and resettled in the overpopulated South, which further radicalised the community. In 1978 Israel invaded Lebanon; hundreds of thousands were killed or displaced. This war, and the 1975 civil war, drastically weakened the ability of the secular left and nationalists to defend the socio-economic rights of the poor in this area. Under these circumstances, AMAL's activities expanded and religion emerged as a mobilising factor for Lebanese Shi'a.[3] The 1979 Iranian Revolution was viewed by Islamists, in particular the Shi'as in Lebanon, as a powerful counter-narrative to Western modernity (Saad-Ghorayeb 2002: 8–15; Deeb 2006a: 75–80; Harik 2005: 18–22).

Before the revolution Shi'a communities in the Middle East related most strongly to the clerics in Iran. After the revolution this relationship shifted to one between these communities and the state in Iran. Hence the revolution in Iran was an important event for Shi'as throughout the world and especially for those in Lebanon. As academic Mona Harb explains:

> Iran is important for the Shi'as, because Iran's revolution made them important in history. It is not all about the religious relationship; it is about a political relationship. With the institutionalisation of the Lebanon Shi'a Islamic Movement in the 1980s, the history books included Shi'a heroes and Jabal Amil heroes. Before that, we never talked about them because the Shi'as were a marginal and oppressed section of society.

The revolution in Iran was viewed by Shi'a communities throughout the Muslim world as a pan-Islamic revolution. Many Sunnis in the Middle East also saw the Iranian Revolution and its consequences as a positive phenomenon.

The emergence of Hezbollah

The emergence of Hezbollah has been the direct result of the Israeli invasions of Lebanon in 1978 and 1982 and of Western support for Israel. The 1978 and 1982 invasions of Lebanon were highly destructive, brutal and, according to the United Nations Security Council (UNSC), illegal.[4] In the 1982 invasion, which was several times greater in magnitude than the 1978 invasion, Israel systematically and indiscriminately bombed towns, cities, villages, refugee camps, schools and hospitals, and placed Beirut under siege for three months. It was directly responsible for the Sabra and Shatila massacres. Beside deaths and injuries, once again a large number of refugees moved to the 'belt of misery' (Saad-Ghorayeb 2002: 13; Deeb 2006a: 81).

These invasions also led to the fragmentation of the Communist and Palestinian movements that opposed US and Israeli policies. The absence of coherent and locally determined ideologies, and of the military and political discipline required to win and maintain the support of the grassroots, weakened the PLO, the secular left and the nationalists. However, the impact of Israel's political and military interventions, supported by the West (the USA's foreign aid budget to Israel during the siege of Beirut increased to half its total foreign aid budget) was instrumental in weakening these organisations. The 1982 Israeli invasion of Lebanon destroyed the PLO, which subsequently was forced to recognise the State of Israel in 1988. When the PLO left Lebanon in 1982, the situation worsened for the refugees as the PLO had been providing them with education, health and employment (Khalili 2007a: 48–54).

In June 1982, Nabih Berri, the leader of AMAL, joined the National Salvation Committee, established by Lebanon's president Elias Sarkis. The aim of the Committee, which included Bashir al-Gemayel, the pro-Israeli Maronite leader of the Lebanese Forces Militia, was to replace the PLO in West Beirut with the Lebanese army. Berri cooperated with the Maronite Christian establishment and opposed the PLO in South Lebanon. His stance was not acceptable to the majority of Palestinian and Lebanese people. A number of AMAL officials split from AMAL and formed Hezbollah (Saad-Ghorayeb 2003, 2002: 13–15; Deeb 2006a: 55).

In September 1982, Bashir al-Gemayel, a senior member of the Lebanese Phalange party and the president elect, was killed in an explosion. His death was avenged by the Christian phalanges, who massacred the populations of the Sabra and Shatila refugee camps. Under the Israeli military and Defence Minister Ariel Sharon, the Lebanese Phalange militia raped, maimed and killed thousands of civilian refugees. The Sabra and Shatila massacre victimised not only Palestinians, but also the Shi'a refugees, who constituted close to one-quarter of those killed.

Following this, from 1985 to 1988, AMAL attacked and placed under siege the Rashidiyya camp in the South, as well as Sabra,

Shatila and Bourj al Barajneh, where Palestinians had already been massacred by the Israeli and Christian militias. This led to the decline of AMAL and a rise in the popularity of Hezbollah, who had demonstrated commitment to support the Palestinians rather than just empowering the Shi'as in Lebanon (Harik 2005: 35–6 and 65; Deeb 2006a: 81; Khalili 2007a: 53–4, 2006: 57–67; Nasr 2007: 113–15).

Hezbollah's sustained struggle against Israel, between 1982 and 1985, led to the withdrawal of Israel from Beirut. This paved the way for Hezbollah, supported by Iran, to become heroes throughout the region from the late 1980s onwards. Their strategy and their struggle against Israel in the Palestinian territories became popular with Hamas supporters. Clashes over political and territorial power between AMAL and Hezbollah took place in 1984, and Hezbollah declared itself an Islamic Resistance Movement (al-muqawama al-islamiyya). In 1987, Syrian troops clashed with Hezbollah fighters in west Beirut when Hezbollah refused to hand over their bases to Syrian forces. In 1988, in the 'War for Supremacy in the South' between AMAL (supported by Syria) and Hezbollah, Syria expelled Hezbollah from the South. Later that year Hezbollah relaunched its offensive against AMAL. But, following Iran's intervention, the war between the two rival Shi'a groups ended and Hezbollah surrendered its position to the Syrian forces, although it was permitted to continue its military operations against Israel from the South. This demonstrated the authority of Syria in Lebanon, although Hezbollah dominated the resistance movement in the South. It also forced Hezbollah and Syria to come to the understanding that Hezbollah would only be allowed to retain its arms in the South in order to continue its resistance against Israel, which was to Syria's advantage. The Taif Accord recognised Syria's dominant relationship with Lebanon. Iran also found Syria's hegemonic position in Lebanon to its advantage. Between 1985 and 1988 AMAL waged a brutal war against the Palestinian refugees, and in 1988 and 1989 Hezbollah and AMAL clashed once again for political control of South Lebanon. These conflicts undermined AMAL's political presence in the crowded Shi'a suburbs, and finally this intra-Shi'a fighting ended with an agreement between Syria and

Iran in 1989 (Harik 2005: 50–56; Saad-Ghorayeb 2002: 52–3; Deeb 2006a: 83; Khalili 2007a: 54).

Hezbollah's cooperation with the secular state of Syria demonstrated not only their common stance against Israel but also the pragmatism of the organisation. Moreover, the PLO's secularism did not prevent Hezbollah from condemning AMAL's 'War of the Camps' or from actively intervening on behalf of the Sunni Palestinian refugees. Hezbollah also sympathised with the activities of international left-wing, secular and Marxist groups, such as Fidel Castro's preservation of Cuba's independence from the USA. They supported Nelson Mandela and his activities against the apartheid system in South Africa and currently support Hamas and the Muslim Brotherhood (mainly Sunnis) in Palestine, Egypt and Jordan. This policy has made Hezbollah popular in the Middle East; they have supporters in Syria, Palestine, Jordan and Iraq, and their television station, Al-Manar (Lighthouse), is the most popular in the region after Al Jazeera (Saad-Ghorayeb 2002: 20–21; Nasr 2007: 115).

Hezbollah's participation in electoral politics

It is widely documented that the USA and Israel blame Hezbollah for the 1983 bombings of the US embassy, Marine barracks and French military headquarters in Beirut; the 1985 hijacking of a TWA flight to Beirut; and bomb attacks against Israeli targets in Argentina in the early 1990s (Norton 2007: 69–93). Nevertheless, Hezbollah has denied any association with Islamic Jihad, which was responsible in the 1980s for bombings in Lebanon which killed several hundred people, and claims that it has intervened to secure the release of the hostages the organisation has taken (Saad-Ghorayeb 2002: 96; Deeb 2006a: 83; Harik 2005: 36–8; Harb and Leenders 2005: 173–97).

From the 1990s, Hezbollah worked consistently and systematically to earn the support of the majority of Lebanon's diverse communities through its parliamentary participation and integration into the Lebanese political system. This allowed the organisation to move away from being a narrow resistance movement to assuming the status of a social movement with relative grassroots support. In the 1992 parliamentary election Hezbollah won 12 seats and allocated 4 of them to non-Shi'a allies. In the 1996 election the party won 9 seats. Hezbollah was able to gain these seats in the South without AMAL, but agreed to Syria's request that it join AMAL's electoral list in the 1996 election, because its political survival depended on the unity of the Shi'a community (Saad-Ghorayeb 2002: 54–5; Harik 2005: 100–101; Rahnema 2005a; 1xxi–1xxiv).

After the 1992 parliamentary election, Hezbollah decided to establish dialogue with the Christian community, which became known as infitah (opening). Al-Sayyid Abbas al-Musawi, the second secretary-general,[5] led the party into participation in the secular, democratic political system. He was assassinated by Israeli forces in February 1992. His successor, Sayyid Hassan Nasrallah, continued along the same path, and notably initiated cooperation with the Christian communities (Saad-Ghorayeb 2002: 2–3).

In 1993 and 1996, Israel launched attacks on the South, forcing the Lebanese authorities to take action against Hezbollah. After these attacks, Hezbollah held a number of meetings with the Maronite Christian Patriarch and the Maronite Brothers. In 2001, the Committee on Islamic–Christian Dialogue was set up to discuss further cooperation. Hezbollah youth and students also met with their Christian counterparts. These activities won electoral support for Hezbollah among the Christian communities as well as within the Druze and Sunni communities. In the 2000 local elections, Hezbollah won 61 per cent of municipalities in the South, 95 per cent in the Beqaa Valley and 100 per cent in the suburbs of Beirut. In May 2000, when Israel withdrew from South Lebanon, many Christians who were suspicious of Hezbollah's intentions were relieved that hostilities were not renewed. An additional consequence was that Hezbollah achieved its important military and political objective of freeing South Lebanon from Israeli control, although Israel still occupies Shebaa Farms, an area disputed with Syria and Lebanon (Harik 2005: 75–7; Harb 2007: 216; Hamzeh 2004: 132–3).

In February 2005, the Sunni ex-premier Rafiq Hariri was killed by the blast of a road mine in Beirut. This provoked demonstrations and counter-demonstrations in the city's Martyrs Square. The March 14 Alliance of the Cedar Revolution, a coalition of anti-Syrian political parties led by Saad Hariri and supporters (mainly Christians, Druze and Sunnis), denounced Syria's domination of Lebanon, echoing the UNSC Resolution 1559 which demanded Syria's withdrawal from Lebanon and the disarming of Hezbollah. The March 8 Alliance, a coalition of AMAL, Hezbollah, Michel Aoun's Free Patriotic Movement,[6] the Syrian Social Nationalist Party and the Lebanese Communist Party, organised pro-Syria demonstrations. Syria withdrew its troops from Lebanon on 17 March, but Hezbollah refused to disarm on the grounds that it would be able to defend Lebanese soil in the face of possible Israeli violation of Lebanese territory (Rahnema 2005a: 1xxiii; Shaery-Eisenlohr 2008: 200–201).

When General Aoun returned from exile in May 2005, he found that Saad Hariri, the leader of the Sunni communities, and Walid Jumblatt, the leader of the Druze communities, had formed an alliance. As the leader of the Maronites, Aoun needed a new electoral alliance, as the majority of the Christian middle classes and the poor were tired of sectarian division. Thus he allied his movement with Hezbollah. Each group has its own militia and army. The alliance with Hezbollah was particularly important for Aoun due to Hezbollah's status as a large armed organisation, its ability to bring together different communities, and its role as an effective resistance movement against Israel. In this context, Hezbollah was more acceptable to the grassroots of the Christian communities than any other organisation. Historically, there is also a rural–urban divide: the Shi'a and Christian Maronites are mainly rural communities and the Sunni communities are urban. The Maronite population is shrinking while the Shi'a communities are growing; hence the Maronites needed a strong local ally. This does not translate into an end to the sectarianism between Aoun and Hezbollah supporters. It means that for these diverse communities, resistance to Israel and class issues are also important and Hezbollah fulfils both demands. As an effective resistance movement it fights against Israel, and by providing resources it satisfies the material needs of diverse communities. For many Lebanese people, Hezbollah's concentration on oppression, deprivation and exploitation appears to be based on class analysis rather than religious analysis, an approach which is popular with Muslim and Christian communities (Saad-Ghorayeb 2002: 2–3, 18–19).

After the June 2005 election, Fouad Siniora, a close ally of the Hariri family, was appointed Lebanese prime minister. His policy of forming an armed militia consisting of private security companies did not please Hezbollah, and his neoliberal economic reform led to high inflation and falling real wages, adding to the unpopularity of his government among the majority of the population. At the same time, Hezbollah's unity with AMAL and with Aoun's supporters, who won forty-three seats, gave them a strong voice in parliament. Nabih Berri, the AMAL leader, continued in his role as the speaker of parliament, and Hezbollah joined the cabinet with two ministers in July 2005 (Harb 2007: 214–39).

Since then, Hezbollah has placed an emphasis on Lebanese nationalism, which it defines as a mixture of Lebanese (Christian and Muslim), Islamic (Sunni, Shi'a, Druze) and Arab (all Lebanese). In Lebanon, this mingling of the ideologies of Arabism and Lebanism creates a specific form of nationalism that includes the historical communal identities as well as the socio-political specifities of Lebanon (Shaery-Eisenlohr 2008: 20, 199–204). The existence of different sectarian groups and constant foreign interventions have meant that individuals identify with their community leaders and rely on these to get married, to secure a job, to go to school and to have access to hospital. In this context, the state does not take care of its citizens in a real sense. As Mona Harb explained:

> In Lebanon, the concept of nationalism is a contested issue. There
> has never been a consensus on how to narrate history. Each
> group emphasises its own way of looking at nationalism; from
> Pheonicianism, Maronites to Arab nationalism, each tries to claim
> its narratives as the most legitimate. No one has been willing to
> accept the diversity of our history and to celebrate the fact that we

have such a rich past. Different groups produce their own history rather than connecting them. This has created enclave identities. Many people welcome the alliance between Hezbollah and a part of the Christian community, as they see this alliance as a positive step towards connecting diverse communities and an opportunity to escape the present enclave identities and the polarised situation, which is the product of a long period of history.

The provision of resources by Hezbollah

The Lebanese civil war (1975–90) and Israeli invasions devastated the country and left hundreds of thousands dead, physically and psychologically injured, or displaced. The corrupt, sectarian governments during this time failed to deal with economic stagnation, the refugee crisis, and the widening gap between rich and poor. Former prime minister Rafiq Hariri, a Sunni billionaire entrepreneur, promoted a vision of Lebanon as an urban, secular, upper- and middle-class society (Shaery-Eisenlohr 2008: 22, 185; Deeb 2006b: 118). He played an important role in the rebuilding of Beirut's downtown – mainly through expropriating property from its original owners – which was transformed from a traditional centre into a Western-style business centre with expensive apartments, which have remained empty since no one could afford them. They meant (and still mean) nothing to the majority of the people, who instead need housing, water, health and education for their children. The Beqaa Valley, and the South in particular, historically peripheral areas of the country, have been deprived of public services, clean water, adequate medical care, housing and employment for some time. Hezbollah was the first to provide the social services to those who fought the Israelis in the South and their families. It constructed effective social welfare institutions to bring the Shi'a communities out of marginalisation. Gradually its vast social network supported other deprived communities. The funding for these services came not from government resources but from donations, religious taxes and fundraising (Deeb 2006a: 86–8). Iran's financial assistance was also significant. In the late 1980s, water and electricity services were completely cut off in these areas, while water was flowing in the centre of Beirut. Iran helped to dig wells and deliver water. Since the early 1990s, Hezbollah has taken responsibility for providing health and sanitation for the half a million people who were displaced and suffering from the accumulation of refuse. This service continued for five years until the Lebanese Sanitation Department began to get back on its feet. Hezbollah began to fulfil the function of the state as it was able to mobilise resources that the state was not supplying. It provided schools, clean water and electricity for different communities, and its agricultural development in the Beqaa Valley and the South has been impressive. The hospitals and the health services also provided employment for a large number of health workers (Harik 2005: 84–94, 2006: 270–80).

In some areas, the poorer sections of Christian, Sunni and Druze communities also benefited from Hezbollah's provision of resources. The state and the leaders of their own communities had failed to provide for them and protect them from Israel's constant attacks. For these reasons, such communities, especially those that are Christian, now associate themselves with Hezbollah and vote for it. They do not view it as a Shi'a organisation; they identify with it because it speaks and acts on their behalf. For them, Hezbollah has a sense of commitment that people have not seen in any other group. However, it is not just the poor who identify with Hezbollah, as the anthropologist and writer Judith Harik explained to me:

> in 2003 I did a survey and I found that even sections of the upper classes of diverse communities vote for Hezbollah, because they are the only organisation which stands up against Israel and provide resources for them.

Throughout the years of violence and conflict, the movement of people who fled the Israeli invasions and bombardments altered the sectarian make-up of the South. Formerly the Christian Maronites were in the majority and the Shi'as the minority, but by the late 1990s the majority were Shi'as (Deeb 2006a: 48). Social and political inequalities, sectarian religious conflicts, and ambiguity regarding how the state should be run; how different minorities should function;

what should determine access to the state and resources; how various functions should be aggregated – these factors created a diversity of players in the politics of Lebanon. When the civil war began in 1975, the main players were the Christians and Palestinians. Today the major players are the Shi'as, Christians and Sunnis, and Palestinians have been sidelined. The majority of Shi'as were the poorest of the poor and were mainly illiterate, but now they are educated and are participating in the affairs of their communities and the political life of the country. Jean Said Makdisi, a Palestinian writer, says:

> the poor areas have been gentrified. People in these areas are not rich but in comparison with the 1970s and 1980s they are much better off. Hezbollah is responsible for this change by building roads, schools and hospitals. For the first time in the history of Lebanon, Shi'as are doing well in terms of education, housing, health and employment. They have become visible. This is similar to the days when the PLO was active in Lebanon and many Palestinians were educated; they were doctors, lawyers, engineers and were part of the intelligentsia.

Iran's relationship with Hezbollah

From the 1950s until the 1979 revolution in Iran, the Pahlavi Shah and the government supported a Christian-dominated Lebanon that marginalised Muslims, in particular the Shi'as. In the 1970s, a number of activists opposed to the Shah, notably the Liberation Movement of Iran, lived in Lebanon (Shaery-Eisenlohr 2008: 91–101). This relationship was crucial for Hezbollah's formation. In 1982, a new relationship was formed between Syria under Hafez al-Assad and Ayatollah Khomeini in Iran; Syria was the only Arab country which supported Iran in the Iran–Iraq war. The aim of such an alliance was eventually to defeat American hegemony in the Middle East. Iran dispatched 1,500 Revolutionary Guards to the Beqaa Valley with Syria's support. Syria granted them direct access to its borders. The Iranian Revolutionary Guards offered training, organisation and funding to Hezbollah, and Hafez al-Assad used his control over the

Beqaa Valley to handle political arrangements. Throughout the 1990s this Syria–Iran relationship strengthened. In 2002 when the concept of the 'axis of evil' was adopted by George W. Bush and the USA continued its hostility towards Syria and Iran, Tehran and Damascus cemented their economic, political and cultural relations. Iran built petroleum and gas refineries in Syria. They established a joint car industry (80 per cent Iranian and 20 per cent Syrian), and began to cooperate with each other on Lebanon.

Contrary to the erroneous perception of Hezbollah as an extension of Iran, it is in fact a hybrid organisation, inspired by the Iranian Revolution but independent of Iran. Hezbollah was initially funded by Iran, but since the 1990s this funding has declined. Since 2004, Iran's financial support to Hezbollah has varied between \$60 and \$100 million per year (Rahnema 2005a: lxxii). Hezbollah receives much larger amounts of funding from the Shi'as in Lebanon, Kuwait and Saudi Arabia, and from millions of other Lebanese people who live outside of Lebanon. The example of Salah Ezzeddin, a Shi'a entrepreneur who has been funding Hezbollah, is striking. In 2009 he was declared bankrupt as the result of investing in the global neoliberal money market. Hezbollah disassociated itself from him and downplayed his financial contribution.[7] There are many wealthy businessmen and -women in the region who, like Salah Ezzeddin, financially support Hezbollah.

Religious obligation and pride have led Shi'as to contribute funds to Hezbollah in the form of khums and zakat and through fundraising events for charity organisations affiliated to Hezbollah. They employ hundreds of volunteers, including large numbers of women, as part of their jihad (struggle) against poverty through the distribution of resources. Some women participate in the community work only during the Ramadan period, but many others work as employees in these organisations as well as contributing to their community's welfare. These and other institutions form a holistic network that provides services to a wide group of users needing social and economic services, as well as providing support for the armed resistance (Harb and Leenders 2005: 173–97; Deeb 2006a: 88–92, 204–19).

Thus women supporters of Hezbollah play an important role in accumulating funds for the organisation. For decades, women's rights activists in Lebanon have concentrated their struggle on opposing sectarianism as the source of patriarchy and gender inequality. For them, family law as a sectarian issue has been manipulated by men of diverse religious communities. They have also been engaged in neighbourhood committees to maintain law and order, as decades of war and conflict have destroyed some of the social fabric of their society (Joseph 1978: 541–58, 2000: 107–36). In the pre-1970 context, Lebanese Shi'a women were the least politically organised in the country. However, Shi'a women's increased veiling has been accompanied by an increase in their public participation. Fatima (daughter of Prophet Muhammad) and Zaynab, who by participating in the war against Omayyad ensured the continuity of Shi'ism, are models for these women's participation in the community's religio-political and social life. Zaynab's model in particular symbolises compassion, dedication and courage for these women, who volunteer their time and energy actively participating in their communities' welfare, where fundraising plays an important role (Deeb 2006a: 216–19). However, despite their important contribution, women are not in positions of leadership or decision-making at higher political levels within Hezbollah.

Beside khums and zakat and women's contribution to Hezbollah's accumulation of funds, two institutions have been significantly instrumental in Hezbollah's financial independence since 1984. These are al-Qard al-Hassan (Good Gift, or Good Loan) and Alward (The Promise). Al-Qard al-Hassan is a micro-credit banking scheme that gives loans to people who need them. They have a loan fund of millions of dollars funded by Shi'as in Lebanon and the region.[8] As Judith Harik explained to me:

> The loan is given to anyone who is eligible. To be eligible you have to convince them that you will use it to improve your life. The banking system in Lebanon has been historically attached to the communities' identities, dominated by the Sunnis, the Druze and the Maronites. The Shi'as never had the opportunity that

other communities had. Since the formation of al-Qard al-Hassan, the Shi'as have put their money into this institution. Of course other communities are also welcome to put their money in too. Wealth is also deposited in al-Qard al-Hassan in the form of gold – women put their bracelets and necklaces into the bank. During the bombings of the South, the Shi'as managed to move their money and precious metals out of the area and to safety.

As a large estate agent, Alward has also contributed significantly to Hezbollah's financial independence and the relative prosperity of its supporters. After the destruction of South Lebanon by Israel, Hezbollah obtained funding from the state and its other donors to reconstruct 230 buildings, consisting of 5,400 apartments, 3,000 shops and 2,500 shelters. Judith Harik explains that

> Hezbollah made an offer to the landowners and property owners to reconstruct the properties free of charge by the Jihad al-Bina Construction Agency. People queued to sign up for the scheme because it meant that their old homes which were destroyed by the Israelis would be renovated and they were able to live in newly built apartments.

These two projects have allowed Hezbollah to rely on its own resources and capabilities. Also, a large number of Shi'as who did not have access to money, banking and property now do, on account of these two institutions. Hezbollah's commitment to pan-Islamism, Arabisation and Lebanisation has also overturned the perception that it is an Iranian surrogate organisation. It has been argued that it does believe in *Velayat-e faqih*, but that it works within the Lebanese constitution; its commitment to *Velayat-e faqih* and its affiliation to Iran are not in conflict with its national identity. Nasrallah has argued that, 'just as the affiliation to Christianity, Communism or any other belief system does not conflict with one's Lebanese identity, Hezbollah's affiliation to Iran and *Velayat-e faqih* does not undermine its Lebanese identity or patriotism' (Saad-Ghorayeb 2002: 82–3; Deeb 2006b: 117).

Many Lebanese Shi'as followed Ayatollah Khomeini until his death in 1989, while others followed Ayatollah al-Khoi until his death in 1992.[9] In more recent years, the majority of Lebanese Shi'a have followed Fadlallah or al-Sistani. Fadlallah had been one of al-Khoi's deputies in Lebanon since 1976. He is the most prominent *mujtahid* in Lebanon today. He is internationally renowned and has followers throughout the Shi'a world. Fadlallah is also popular with women and non-Muslims for arguing that it is possible to interpret religious issues, especially those relating to gender or science, according to time and place. Although Hezbollah officially follows Ayatollah Khamenei as the party's *marja* (leader), individual members are free to choose whom they follow. Some follow Khamenei (Nasrallah is one of Khamenei's deputies). However, many Hezbollah members follow Fadlallah or al-Sistani in religious matters; both have challenged the concept of *Velayat-e faqih* and have argued that a single and united spiritual and political authority, the essence of *Velayat-e faqih*, is impossible until the return of the Hidden Twelfth Imam. In fact, both Fadlallah and Hezbollah have denied any organisational association with each other, and Fadlallah's popularity lies in his institutional independence from the organisation (Deeb 2006a: 71, 93–4; Saad-Ghorayeb 2002: 2–4).

Many Lebanese people, and indeed many others in the region, are concerned about Hezbollah's intention to establish an Islamic state, similar to Iran, in Lebanon if and when it comes to power. In response, Hezbollah has argued that it believes in an Islamic identity beyond national affiliation, and, in this context, the establishment of the Islamic state would have to be postponed until an absolute majority of the people in Lebanon were in favour. Fadlallah had spent much time and energy over the years working to promote Christian–Muslim understanding and cooperation as a means of peacefully enlarging Islamic space in Lebanon rather than capturing it. He believes that Islamisation cannot be imposed on Lebanon's large Christian community and would also be rejected by the secular communities. Indeed, Lebanon's diverse and dynamic communities would not be forced into an Islamisation of state and society (Harik 2005: 56–9; Saad-Ghorayeb 2002: 34–8).

In the context of the religio-political relationship between Iran and Hezbollah, the Sunni–Shi'a divide is an issue that affects people's perception of both. Many see Iran as a conservative Islamic country, a fact that may impact on the role of Hezbollah in Lebanon. People in the Middle East know little about the reality of Iran. The Arab world speaks one language, Arabic, while the Iranians speak Farsi, so there is very little communication between them. But the position of Israel and the USA in the region has brought these communities closer to each other despite the limited communication. Intellectuals in the region can communicate with each other through the English language. Ordinary people must communicate through their mutual experience and perception of the role of Israel and the USA. According to UNRWA, 400,000 Palestinians live in Lebanon. Since 1948, hundreds of thousands of Palestinians have had to leave their homeland to take refuge in Lebanon, where they have settled in poor parts of the South among the Shi'a. They have faced prejudice from the Shi'a communities; however, the two communities have both suffered as a consequence of being adversaries of Israel and of total neglect from the Lebanese state. Hence their common fate has brought these communities closer together despite the Sunni and Shi'a divide (Khalili 2006: 57–67). Many Palestinian refugees in Lebanon support Iran's position as a force against the American policy of conflict and war, and their 'greater Middle East project'. However, many people are worried about the role of Iran in Lebanon. Sari Hanafi, an academic, explained:

> Many support Iran, but they realise the complexity of Iran's role in the region and they are critical of Iran's role in Iraq. There is also a fear among some Sunni Palestinians that Iran and Shi'ism can take over the region. There is, therefore, a paradox; they like where Iran stands in relation to Palestinians but they don't want Iran to cross the red line in terms of undermining Sunni religion and culture. Others are worried about the issue of hijab and conservative gender issues.

In the last few years, and especially since Hariri's assassination, the Lebanese media have fuelled anti-Iran, anti-Shi'a and anti-Hezbollah sentiments. Nevertheless, as Mahmoud, a Palestinian activist in Beirut, argued, many Palestinians in Lebanon identify with Iran politically and not in religious terms.

For them, Iran is the only country that is standing against Israel and the crime committed against Palestinians. When they see that their bridges, roads and parks are rebuilt and re-created with Iran's help after Israeli bombings they feel good about it. They feel that the Palestinian nationalist movement and Arab nationalist movement have relatively retreated. In the so-called peace process, Palestinian refugees were forgotten, left behind; the intention of the so-called peace process is to secure the rights of Israel and not the Palestinians. Iran is the only country that is concerned about the cause of Palestinians as oppressed people. People have different views about whether Iran has its own agenda or if its position is genuinely pro-Palestinian. Iran has its own agenda. Hezbollah also has its own agenda. Everyone is playing chess; the Middle East is a battlefield. Iran is strengthening its position in the region by supporting the Palestinians. America is strengthening its position in the region by supporting Israel. We have no choice, we have to take sides.

Israel's wars on Lebanon strengthen Iran's position

Despite the fact that the Shi'a–Sunni divide is historically and culturally a reality, even if it has been exaggerated by the media, the 2006 war brought these communities even closer to each other and with Iran. In July 2006, Hezbollah fighters kidnapped two Israeli soldiers to exchange for Hezbollah prisoners. In response, Israel initiated a full-scale war on Lebanon by attacking the International Airport and Beirut–Damascus Highway, and then continued the destruction of South Lebanon for thirty-four days, producing a shocking level of human suffering. The Bush administration and its European allies, after their catastrophic policies in Afghanistan and Iraq, hoped that an Israeli victory would lead to a 'New Middle East'. For this reason, the USA and Europe repeatedly rejected calls for a ceasefire so that Israel had enough time to punish Hezbollah and, indirectly, Syria and Iran. Not surprisingly, the majority of the people in the region and in Lebanon believe that the USA was responsible for Israel's policy of collective punishment and its war crimes against the Lebanese people. The UN Security Council confirmed the illegality of the war; however, by delaying a ceasefire for thirty-two days it sacrificed the Lebanese people to the interests of the USA and Israel. Hezbollah's resistance and Israel's violence resulted in an increase in the popularity of Hezbollah in the region, transcending the Shi'a and Sunni divide (Makdisi 2006: 9–26). Muhammad, another Palestinian activist whom I met in Beirut, argues:

> During the 2006 war, many Palestinians, the majority Sunni, gave support and help to the Shi'as who were under attack. They opened their homes to the Shi'as. I have a neighbour who is very poor. They had three mattresses and gave one of them to the Shi'as. Before 2006 many Shi'as never went inside the refugee camps. But now there is friendship between the two communities. The Christian communities did not want Palestinians in Lebanon; now they have become aware of Palestinian problems and why they cannot go to their own country. They now realise that they have to support the Palestinians so that they can fight for their rights. In a strange way the 2006 war brought different communities together; they feel that together they are in the fire but they see a way out of the fire if they stick together.

During the 2006 war, the old Arabic saying *Ana ou akhi ala ibn ami, ana ou ibn ami ala il ghareeb* ('Me and my brother against my cousin, but me and my cousin against the outsider') became popular. That is to say, 'despite the Sunni–Shi'a–Christian divide we are all against Israel'. Of course, there is also strong opposition to Hezbollah across the religions, from Sunni, Christian and Shi'a communities. But despite this hostility towards Hezbollah, which is class-based and sectarian, Hezbollah's popularity as the only force to stand up to Israel and to provide resources demonstrates that Lebanese society is diverse and divided but potentially able to unite against the common enemy. This supports Makdisi's theory that the culture of sectarianism, with its roots in European colonialism, is constructed and can therefore be demolished and replaced by an independent state and society (Makdisi 2000: 166–74).

In this war, once again, Israel targeted civilians and infrastructure (roads, airports, ports, bridges, homes, factories, farms, water, electricity, gas and sewage treatment). The damage was estimated in the region of $3.8 billion. The number of displaced people is reported to be around a million, about a quarter of the entire Lebanese population (Quilty 2006: 81; Fattouh and Kolb 2006: 97–101; Deeb 2006b: 115; Harb 2007: 227). Fatimah, whom I interviewed in Beirut, remembers the day they were attacked by Israel:

> The day that the attacks began, we had a wedding on the way. We just took our children and left our homes; we ran towards the east; we were looking behind us and we could see how the bombs were falling on our homes. We ran towards the sea where the Christians live. They helped us; they gave us food and shelter. After a few days when we went back to our neighbourhood we found nothing left of our homes. They would not let us near our house because a rocket had fallen into the middle of it. We were homeless for six months. They rebuilt our house but they could not remove the rocket, because it would likely blow up and ruin a large area of south Beirut. They have built concrete around it so that if it does blow up it won't do much damage. We have now gone back to our home but there is a rocket in the middle of it. Hopefully it won't blow up.

Israel's aim was to destroy Hezbollah, but the action led to the exact opposite of what the USA and Israel had expected: Hezbollah emerged stronger (Achcar and Warschawski 2007: 53–9; Harman 2006: 8–42). The international relief organisations and the state proved ineffective; therefore Iran and Syria emerged as the only supporters of the victims of this war. As soon as the war ended, Hezbollah began reconstruction through the Jihad al-Bina Construction Agency and with the work of hundreds of volunteer architects and engineers. Iran helped in the construction of highways and provided other facilities in poor areas. However, much of the financial backing came, and still comes, from Hezbollah supporters in the region, including many expatriate middle-class Lebanese people (Quilty 2006: 89–95; Fattouh and Kolb 2006: 107–10; Harb 2007: 230–32; Deeb: 2006b: 121)

As the academic Laleh Khalili described to me, Hezbollah's different roles, in parallel with each other, are very effective:

> On the one hand it is a military organisation. It organizes itself as the defence mechanism against Israel. This is an important part of

its identity as a resistance movement. On the other hand, as a conventional force it mobilises forces in the communities. In the first few days of the 2006 war it was the ordinary people in the villages who fought the Israelis rather than the guerrilla forces. They are also extremely disciplined and technocratic.

Immediately after the war, with the help of Iran, Hezbollah rebuilt the villages and bridges that had been destroyed by the Israelis. Mona Harb explaines:

Hezbollah has borrowed ways to manage the city from Iran. Previously, city planning and building was in the European model, as mayors went to Europe and borrowed from them, but now the cities in Lebanon are copying Iran. The culture of city building based on the Iranian model is popular in Lebanon. There are signs in the South thanking Iran for its help.

Lebanese support for Hezbollah and Iran is political rather than religious. People look at how they have suffered for years as the result of Israel's attacks supported by the West, while Arab regimes either supported the West or remained silent, and only Hezbollah and Iran are on their side. In this context, Hezbollah has risen as a powerful political and military player with ties to Iran. In the eyes of millions of people across the Middle East, the governments in Jordan, Saudi Arabia and Egypt that denounced Hezbollah betrayed the Lebanese (Nasr 2007: 256).

Between December 2006 and May 2008, the supporters of Hezbollah, AMAL and Aoun turned Beirut's Martyrs' Square into a tent city and demanded that the government resign. The presidential election of 2007 did not take place. The Shi'a members of the government resigned and Berri, the Speaker, did not convene parliament. As a result, the government was unable to pass any decrees (Shaery-Eisenlohr 2008: 210). The political crisis was exacerbated by an economic crisis. In January 2007, the opposition called for a general strike, demanding higher wages, lower prices and improvements to water and electricity supplies, as over a third of the population live below the official poverty line (Chit 2008). On 1 May 2008 there were demonstrations throughout Lebanon organised by the trade unions. Trade unions in Lebanon were strong in the 1970s but were weakened in the 1980s as a consequence of neoliberal government policies. The unions are independent of religious groups. Although Hezbollah has not indicated any opposition to neoliberal policies, it enjoys support among the poorer sections of the population who are active in the unions (Achcar and Warschawski 2007: 43–4).

On 6 May, the Lebanese government announced that Hezbollah's private communications networks were illegal and challenged the sovereignty of the state. This communications network system coordinates military resistance to a possible Israeli invasion. The government threatened to bring the issue before the Arab League and the United Nations. The authorities also called for the resignation of Wafiq Shuqair, a Shi'a general and head of security at Beirut Airport. Walid Jumblatt, the pro-government leader of the Druze communities, expressed anti-Iranian and anti-Hezbollah sentiments in the media. In response Hezbollah and AMAL and their militias, together with the militias attached to the Free Patriotic Movement and the Syrian Social Nationalist Party, took control of predominantly Sunni West Beirut. They crippled the pro-government media and blockaded the airport. A confrontation followed between these militias and those belonging to Saad Hariri's Future Movement (a Sunni Party) and Prime Minister Siniora.

At a press conference that day, Nasrallah blamed the USA and Israel for creating another civil war in Lebanon, while portraying the tension as a Shi'a and Sunni divide. He emphasised that Hezbollah was trying to avoid sectarian divides, but they would not give up their weapons. They would not use their weapons against the people of Lebanon, but would use them to defend themselves. Nasrallah observed:

> The global media try to demonise Hezbollah as being attached to Iran. But they never mention Israeli aggression. For two years, hundreds of millions of dollars have been spent on discrediting Hezbollah but our reputation has not been damaged. We have

always said that there is a political problem in Lebanon and it
should be resolved politically, through dialogue and referendum.

He further argued that in the 2006 war, Israel had tried to destroy
Hezbollah's communications network and disarm the organisation;
it did not succeed, but now the government was trying to finish the
job. He stressed that 'We will not allow the government to disarm
or to dismantle our communications network. We reject the Security
Council Resolution to disarm; this is the same Security Council which
has failed to stop Israel's aggression over the years.' His speech was
popular throughout the Arab World as the majority of the people in
the region could identify with his arguments. He knew the extent
of Hezbollah's popularity in the region; in his speech he emphasised
Israel's aggression, and sought the support of the Arab world's Sunni
majority in the fight against Israel by arguing that 'our enemy is Israel
whether we are Sunni or Shi'a'.[10]

Fighting continued for a few days in different regions; 80 people
were killed and 250 injured.[11] The army did not intervene directly
as a third of its ranks are Shi'a, and a significant number of officers
have links to Aoun's supporters. In reality, the lower ranking majority of the army who come from poor Shi'a and Sunni families are
pro-Hezbollah. On 17 May, the Emir of Qatar and the Arab League
mediated between the government and the opposition in Doha,
ending eighteen months of impasse. The government had to make
a number of concessions, including electoral law reforms to reflect
more accurately the country's sectarian balance. Of course, many
argue that electoral reform alone cannot present any real solution
to the sectarian system that periodically throws the country into
political crisis. The parties involved agreed on a dialogue to boost
state authority and outlined the relationship between the state and
Hezbollah. Iran and Syria welcomed the agreement. Saudi Arabia and
the USA called the agreement a 'necessary and positive step'.[12] On 25
May 2008, Michel Suleiman, the politically independent commander
of the Lebanese armed forces, became president, and Fouad Siniora
and Nabih Berri remained in their positions as prime minister and

parliamentary speaker, respectively. In this conflict, as in previous periods, the Lebanese government, supported by the USA and its allies in the region, miscalculated the popularity of Hezbollah and its new alliance with AMAL and those sections of the Christian communities led by Aoun. In reality, the conflict led to a major defeat for Washington and Israel. Although the West, Saudi Arabia and Egypt support the Lebanese government over the opposition led by Hezbollah, especially due to Hariri's close ties with the Saudis, President Barack Obama sent his Middle East envoy George Mitchell to the region on an Arab–Israeli peace mission. Also, in March 2009 Britain made a distinction between Hezbollah's military and political activities and announced its willingness to discuss politics with the organisation. As Rima Allaf, a Middle East specialist at Chatham House, the Royal Institute of International Affairs in London, observed, the USA and the UK cannot ignore Hezbollah, a party which represents a significant part of the population of Lebanon.[13]

In June 2009, the ruling March 14 coalition won the election with 71 seats in the 128-member parliament, while the March 8 alliance won 57 seats. Despite losing, the March 8 alliance received 55 per cent of the vote, and Aoun's party defended its alliance with Hezbollah as helping to stabilise Lebanon, arguing that the main threat to Lebanon is from Israel. Laleh Khalili argues that if there was a one person, one vote system in Lebanon, the coalition would have won the election:

> They won 55 per cent of the popular vote. But the Lebanese electoral system is structured on the basis of district vote allocation, similar to an electoral college system. This means that although they had 55 per cent of the popular vote, they did not get enough votes through the districts system to achieve a majority in parliament. Nevertheless, they will be more effective as an opposition force. If they had won they would have become responsible for the corruption and sectarianism of the Lebanese system, in the same way that Hamas has become responsible for the corruption of the Palestinian government.

While the seventy-one MPs from Hariri's coalition could have appointed him prime minister, he reached out to Hezbollah and other rivals in the March 8 Alliance to form a new national unity government. His ally, Walid Jumblatt, also changed his position and declared that Hezbollah should be included in the new government.[14] In October 2009, Ayatollah Fadlallah argued that 'Lebanon has arrived at the point where it is ready to receive any news from the US about peace in the Arab region'.[15] At the same time, Nasrallah called for rapprochement between Iran and Saudi Arabia to bridge the Sunni and Shi'a divide in order 'to put out the sectarian fire'.[16]

In the context of Iran and Hezbollah, the Iranian political establishment offers different levels of support for Hezbollah. Since the 1979 revolution, Hezbollah has enjoyed a close relationship with the security forces in Iran, which has continued throughout Rafsanjani's and Khatami's reformist governments and Ahmadinejad's conservative regime. Nasrallah, as a clever politician, realises that Hezbollah needs the support of Iran regardless of whether conservatives or reformers are in power. In June 2009, when it was announced that Ahmadinejad had been re-elected, he congratulated him, but as soon as the result was contested he stepped back and said that regardless of who wins the election Hezbollah will have a close relationship with Iran.[17]

For the West, in particular for the USA's strategic interests, a strong coalition with the conservative Arab states is crucial. However, improving relations with Iran, Hezbollah and Hamas is also becoming increasingly important. The nature of political Islam – in Iran, Hezbollah in Lebanon, Hamas in Palestine and the Muslim Brotherhood in Egypt – has changed. As I argue throughout this book, there are clear indications that Iran and Islamist modernists in the region are willing to shape their policies according to global politics. It is a change such as this in US foreign policy which could impact the Middle East for better or for worse.

FIVE

The relationship between
Iran and Iraq

Before and after the creation of the Arab Islamic empire, Iraq went through a succession of conquests. Medieval towns disappeared and new towns appeared, old tribes were subdued and new ones flourished. Aramaeans lived in Syria and parts of Iraq (Mesopotamia) from the eleventh to the eighth century BCE and the Arabs migrated to Iraq in late antiquity (500 BCE). The population of Iraq at the time of the Arab conquest was ethnically diverse. With the rise of the last pre-Islamic Iranian Sassanid Empire (224–651 CE), a large Iranian immigration to Iraq comprised the elite as well as a small section of the peasantry. By 644 CE, the formation of the Arab Empire was under way, as the whole of Arabia, part of the Sassanid Empire, and the Syrian and Egyptian provinces of the Byzantine Empire had been conquered. The Arab conquest led to the Arabisation and Islamisation of the population of Iraq, and the major assimilation involved Arabs and Iranians (Hourani 1991: 22–3; Ahmed 1992: 80–83; Batatu 2004: 41).

As discussed in Chapter 3, the Shi'a religion and religious establishment have been identified with Iran since the Safavid era (1501–1722). Between 1623 and 1638 the Safavids seized Najaf and Karbala (where the shrines of Shi'a Imam Ali and Imam Hussein are located) from the Ottomans. The Shi'a character of the cities to the south of Baghdad persisted throughout the dominance of the

Ottoman Turks (1534–1622; 1638–1917) and the Georgian Mamluks (1749–1831), but Ottoman policy favoured Arab Sunnis for state office. The conversion of Iran to Shi'ism led to the rise of a powerful Shi'a clergy in Iran and Iraq. The influential Shi'a clergy who had moved from Iran to Iraq were active in politics and religious life under the Ottomans, and since then this historical relationship has continued. Many prominent Shi'a families were, and still are, of Arabian, Iranian and Syrian origin (Batatu 2004: 24, 156, 233; Cockburn 2008: 30–32). Major figures of Iranian origin in the contemporary period include: Ayatollah Sayeed Mohsen al-Hakim, who was the spiritual leader of the Shi'as globally from 1955 to 1970; Ayatollah Mohammad Baqir al-Sadr,[1] who was executed by Saddam Hussein in 1980; Abol-Qasim al-Khoi, a leading Shi'a ayatollah who died in 1992; and today's Ayatollah Ali al-Sistani (Mallat 2005: 258; Nasr 2007: 67)

The Iraqi city of Najaf is one of the holiest sites in Shi'a Islam, and the city of Qom, the site of the shrine to Fatimeh Massoumeh,[2] is one of Iran's holiest places. These holy cities are centres of Shi'a learning, and the Shi'a clergy reside in them as leaders of the Shi'a communities. Every year, millions of Shi'as from the region and beyond visit these two centres. At different historical periods there has been rivalry between Najaf and Qom over the leadership of the Shi'a communities globally. The Marja'iat (religious leadership) moved between Qom and Najaf. In the 1960s, Ayatollah Borojerdi was the Shi'as marja' (religious leader) and resided in Qom. After his death, the Marja'iat moved to Najaf, which was to the political advantage of the Shah of Iran as he could have a free hand without the interference of the clergy. This gave rise to the importance of Najaf. Later, Saddam Hussein banned the Marjai'at from Najaf, thereby strengthening the position of Qom as many Iraqi Shi'a clerics moved to Iran. After the fall of Saddam, Najaf once again became the place of Marjai'at[3] and has assumed a more prominent position as Shi'as in the region and beyond look there for leadership once again. As was discussed in Chapter 2, Qom and Najaf have become closer since 2003, and are currently centres of debate about whether governance should be left to governments or be the business of theocracy (Nasr 2007: 182–3).

Evidently, the persistence of the Shi'a character of some parts of Iraq is linked partly to the Shi'a sanctuaries of Najaf and Karbala, and also to the historical and commercial interrelationship with Iran. In the nineteenth century, many merchants in Baghdad were Iranian, many Iranian Jews. Historically, many Shi'as who lived in South Central Iraq maintained economic and cultural links with Iran, and many Sunni Arabs of Central and North Central areas maintained economic, political and cultural links with the Arab world (Davis 2005: 20). The ethnic composition of the Shi'as is mainly Arab, except for Iranian Shi'as who have lived in Basra, Najaf and Karbala. However, it is important to note that, despite strong Shi'a characteristics, these areas include Sunni minorities.

Although the domain of Sunnism has been the Euphrates to the north of Baghdad and the Tigris between Baghdad and Mosul, a significant Shi'a minority has lived in these areas too. Some Turkmen settlements are Shi'a and some Sunni. The Kurds in the north and north-east of Iraq are Sunnis and are distinguished from Arab Sunnis; there is also a minority of Shi'a Kurds. Sufism has also been influential among Kurds, Arab Shi'as and Sunnis. The non-Muslim communities of Jews, Christians, Yazidis and Sabeans have also lived in different urban and rural areas. Historically these communities have intermingled in some towns more than others, demonstrating that diverse community identities were not based on adherence to religion alone. However, until the fall of Saddam the state machinery was predominantly under the control of the Sunni Arab minority (Batatu 2004: 37–40; Tripp 2008: 30–31; Chubin and Tripp 1988: 13–15).

The Shi'as have long comprised the majority of the population of Iraq but actually constitute diverse communities. In different historical periods some embraced Arab nationalism, others embraced Iraqi nationalism, some became members of the Ba'ath Party and others joined the Communist Party. Some turned to Shi'ism and its communal leaders, who often are of Iranian origin, in order to struggle against their socio-economic and political exclusion within Iraqi society (Chubin and Tripp 1988: 98–99; Tripp 2008: 3). The

British invasion and occupation of Iraq from 1914 to 1918 led to unity between the Sunnis and Shi'as, who formed a resistance against the British, and later the city of Najaf and its Shi'a *ulema* and community were central to resisting the British and King Faisal in 1924 (Batatu 2004: 23; Mallat 2005: 259; Tripp 2008: 42–4).

From the 1920s on, industrialisation and urbanisation affected class structure and cultural norms. Different ethnic groups interacted with one another in urban areas and, for many, ethnic differentiation was part of the colonial policy of divide and rule. Under the monarchy in the 1920s, the Sunni–Shi'a divide was based on class differentiation rather than religion, as the economically and socially dominant families were mainly Sunni (Batatu 2004: 45–50; Davis 2005: 20). The Shi'a communities' perception of marginality was diverse, ranging from class exploitation to rural–urban and religious–secular divides. The majority of Shi'a grievances centred on the imbalance of the Iraqi state, the relative political under-representation of the Shi'as, and their economic exclusion and political suppression (Tripp 2008: 81–4, 237). Nevertheless, the Sunni and Shi'a communities were united against British control of Iraq (Alexander and Assaf 2005).

In the 1940s and 1950s, there was a relative change in the socio-economic situation of the Shi'as as they began to accumulate wealth and occupy high positions within state institutions. Intermarriages between Sunnis and Shi'as became more common. Nevertheless, the poor were predominantly Shi'a, and for the majority of the Shi'as Arab nationalism was an elitist ideology that re-enforced Arab Sunni domination (Batatu 2004: 45–50; Tripp 2008: 134–9). The land reform of the late 1950s drove millions of Shi'a peasants out of farms and villages towards south Baghdad (today's Sadr City[4]) and the edges of east and north Baghdad, but from the 1940s to 1960s the Shi'as had a dominant place within the Communist Party and played an important role against the Ba'athist coup (Batatu 2004: 649–50; 699–705; Nasr 2007: 85, 116, 187).

Abd al-Karim Qasim, whose father was an Arab Sunni and mother a Shi'a Kurd, had an integrative vision for Iraq. During his premier-ship (1958–63), some within the Shi'a communities enjoyed a relative degree of political power. The emergence of the Hizb al-Dawa al-Islamiyyah, or al-Dawa (the Party of Islamic Call) contributed to a number of Shi'a politicians participating in politics. It was also during this period that Mohammad Baqir al-Sadr's writings on philosophy and economics suggested that the Shi'a view of social justice was compatible with Western concepts of Marxism and liberalism, a view popular with the majority of Shi'as (Chubin and Tripp 1988: 154; Rahnema 2005a: Ivii; Nasr 2007: 86). The Kurdish and the Communist parties also revived during this period, although Qasim ensured that no organisation and no community challenged the army and his authority. In this period, women had access to education and achieved a degree of gender equality. The Personal Status Code of 1959 limited polygamy and granted women inheritance rights, whilst Naziha al-Dulaimi was appointed as a cabinet minister (Zangana 2007: 42–51; Al-Ali 2007: 108). After the coup, the rise of Arab nationalism and Ba'athism once again marginalised the Shi'a communities. Nevertheless, a significant minority continued to embrace Arab nationalism and many joined the Ba'ath Party. In the early 1960s, this party had the characteristic of a genuine partnership between the Sunni and Shi'a pan-Arab youth. However, by the late 1960s it was marginalised (Batatu 2004: 1078–9; Nasr 2007: 186; Tripp 2008: 144–53).

As discussed in Chapter 1, in 1963 a number of Shi'a clergy in Iran objected to the Shah's reforms, which undermined their authority. Following a series of discontented outbursts, Ayatollah Khomeini was deported to Iraq, where he resided in Najaf alongside other Shi'a clergy. From exile he criticised the clergy for their passive stance in the face of Zionism, imperialism and colonialism, and called for the overthrow of the Shah, thereby playing an important role in the 1979 Iranian Revolution (Moin 2005: 87–90). In 1967, a group of Shi'a activists in Iraq, inspired by Ayatollah Mohammad Baqir al-Sadr and Ayatollah Khomeini, began to struggle against the Ba'athist government through the al-Dawa party. This group became popular in the 1970s and 1980s, but when Saddam came to power in 1979 he banned the party they had formed and expelled thousands of Shi'as from

Najaf and Karbala. Some of them went to Lebanon, Jordan, Syria and the Persian Gulf, but the majority settled in Iran (Hiro 1990: 23–4; Nasr 2007: 117, 224; Cockburn 2008: 43–5). In April 1980, Saddam executed Ayatollah Mohammad Baqir al-Sadr and his sister, Bint al-Huda, who was an influential female Islamic scholar. He banned Ashoura commemoration and expelled and arrested thousands more Arabs of Iranian origin. Those who were exiled were sent to Iran and their property was confiscated (Rahnema 2005a: lvii; Nasr 2007: 110, 187; Tripp 2008: 221; Chubin and Tripp 1988: 25–7).

The war with Iran, the invasion of Kuwait, sanctions and the fall of Saddam Hussein

The Iran–Iraq war began in September 1980. Saddam's decision to attack Iran was prompted by the idea that a war with Iran would be short and victorious, would restore Iraqi sovereignty over the whole of the Shatt al-Arab (Arab River) where there had been a dispute between the two countries since 1975, and would demonstrate the power of Iraq as a force in the region to defeat the Iranian Revolution. But this war (1980–88) did not weaken the revolution in Iran. An estimated one and a half million Iranians and Iraqis died, and an estimated \$1.2 billion worth of damage was inflicted on the two countries. Saudi Arabia, Kuwait, Jordan and Egypt supported Iraq politically and financially. For them, this was an Arab–Iranian and Shi'a–Sunni war, and Iran and the Shi'as had to be defeated (Adib-Moghadam 2008: 83–122). Saddam's large army of conscripts were mainly Shi'a and the army elite were predominantly Sunni, but a number of Shi'as who subscribed to Ba'athist rule were promoted to high political and military positions. Saddam's powerful propaganda campaign emphasised Arab-Islamic identity and its supremacy over non-Arab Iranians. The aim was to set the Iraqi Shi'as against the Iranians. However, as is argued by Sami Ramadani (2007), the state was not built on sectarian foundations, even though its policies had a sectarian impact (Ramadani and Zangana 2006, 2007). For example, Saddam's information minister, Muhammad Saeed al-Sahhaf, was among those Shi'as who rose to a prominent position, and it was he who characterised the Iraqi Shi'as as Iranian lackeys and purged the Shi'a members of the Ba'ath Party (Hiro 1990: 1–2; Nasr 2007: 93; 140; 156; Tripp 2008: 224–6; 238; Davis 2005: 3–4).

Throughout the war years, Saddam attempted, on the one hand, to reverse the policy of Shi'a marginalisation symbolically and materially by including them in the national assembly and increasing funding to sustain the Shi'a cities of Najaf and Karbala; whilst, on the other, he ruthlessly attacked the Shi'a communities and forced many more into exile. The Iraqi government provided financial incentives for Iraqi men to divorce their Iranian wives; brought the Shi'a clergy, shrines and mosques under government control; and made the Shi'a *ulema* salaried employees of the state (as discussed in previous chapters, traditionally the Shi'a clergy and the mosques are funded by religious taxes).

In 1982, Mohammad Baqir al-Hakim and his brother Abdul Aziz al-Hakim (sons of Ayatollah Sayeed Mohsen al-Hakim) were forced to live in exile in Iran. In Tehran and Qom they organised the Supreme Council for the Islamic Revolution in Iraq (SCIRI) and subscribed to Ayatollah Khomeini's doctrine of *Velayat-e faqih*. During the Iran–Iraq war, Iran's Revolutionary Guards recruited and trained a number of Iraqi prisoners of war to fight in the Badr Brigade, the military wing of their organisation, against Saddam's army, primarily in Kurdistan. For this reason, Saddam targeted Shi'as involved in political activism involving Iran, and many members of SCIRI, especially al-Hakim's family, were imprisoned or executed. Saddam also ruthlessly attacked the Kurds and destroyed Kurdish areas because the Kurdish Democratic Party and the Patriotic Union of Kurdistan had sided with Iran in 1985–86[5] (Chubin and Tripp 1988: 99–108; Tripp 2008: 225, 236–7; Zangana 2007: 53; Al-Ali 2007: 265).

Despite Saddam's atrocities and propaganda, the Iraqi Shi'a communities did not identify with the Iranians because they valued their tribal, clan, class, urban, rural and political identities as much as their Shi'a identity. Many Shi'as, Sunnis and Kurds felt that foreign intervention would be a national dishonour (Chubin and Tripp 1988:

84–5; Hiro 1990: 88–9; Al-Ali 2007: 156; Tripp 2008: 238). The view of an Iraqi Shi'a soldier quoted by Patrick Cockburn is a powerful reminder of the hybridity of identity construction and reconstruction: 'at the beginning of the war many Shi'as felt that Saddam should fight the Israelis rather than kill Shi'a Muslims. But later on when we had seen our friends killed or wounded in the fighting we shot to kill at the Iranians' (Cockburn 2008: 57).

Despite exclusion and discrimination, the Iraqi Shi'as remained generally loyal to their country. In fact, the Shi'as never demanded an independent Shi'a state, although they struggled for an end to discrimination. However, Saddam's brutality continued. In 1991 he attacked the Shi'a majority towns and tens of thousands were killed in Najaf, Karbala and Hilla. Their mass grave was only uncovered after the fall of Saddam (Nasr 2007: 188–9; Cockburn 2008: 61). Following the Shi'a uprising that year, Saddam placed Ayatollah al-Khoi under house arrest and imprisoned or killed a number of his family members and associates, despite the fact that he had called for an end to the uprising. The supporters of SCIRI and al-Dawa participated in the largely spontaneous uprising and were met with brutal repression by Saddam's army; tens of thousands died and thousands sought refuge in Iran. In many cases, women were tortured and killed for being related to 'the wanted men'. In 1994 Ayatollah al-Sistani was placed under house arrest, and in 1999 Ayatollah Sadiq al-Sadr was assassinated and his family members and close associates imprisoned (Fisk 2005: 1258–9; Nasr 2007: 200; Tripp 2008: 238, 246).

Saddam invaded Kuwait in 1990, which led to UN Security Council sanctions being imposed on Iraq. His attack on the Shi'a and Kurdish communities in 1991 led to further UN resolutions and the creation of a 'safe haven', which effectively created an autonomous Kurdish entity in northern Iraq. Economic sanctions provoked a humanitarian crisis, the consequences of which were devastating for the population of the country. By 1996, an estimated half a million children had died, greater than the child death toll in Hiroshima, but according to Clinton's Secretary of State Madeleine Albright 'the price was worth it'. The education budget fell from $500 million before the 1991 Gulf War to less than 10 per cent of that figure in 1998. Illiteracy increased from 8 per cent to 45 per cent between 1985 and 1999, and the deteriorating education system affected secondary-school and higher-education standards (Fisk 2005: 865–73; Tripp 2008: 250–54; Zangana 2007: 74–5). Throughout the sanctions period, Iraqi people were subjected to bombing campaigns, which also led to the destruction of oil refineries and installations, releasing thousands of tonnes of toxic matter. The child mortality rate, a deteriorating health-care system, malnutrition and widespread poverty ruined the lives of millions of Iraqis. Female employment, which had been the highest in the region, fell from 23 per cent prior to 1991 to 10 per cent in 1997. Poverty, the collapse of the social welfare system, and the practical consequences of an increasingly conservative gender ideology particularly affected women's position within society (Al-Ali 2007: 185–7, 192–5, 210, 213; WLUML 2006).

The Oil for Food Programme, agreed between the UN and the Iraqi government in 1995, was designed to reduce the suffering of the country's people. However, Hans von Sponeck (2006), the UN's most senior and respected official at the time, resigned in response to US policies against Iraq. He argued that the Security Council and the US and UK governments ignored obstacles to the Programme and the suffering of the Iraqi people, despite overwhelming evidence that they were paying a heavy price for crimes committed not by them but by Saddam Hussein. The experience of Haifa Zangana, an Iraqi writer and activist, provides a sad reminder of those terrible circumstances. She writes:

> On December 6, 1995, I sent an A4 padded envelope to my nieces and nephews in Mosul. It contained one pencil case, three erasers, three sharpeners, six fountain pens, two markers, one glue stick, and two ballpoint pens. It was marked 'gifts for children'. The envelope was returned, stamped: 'Due to international sanctions against Iraq, we are not able to forward your packet'. I was told to contact the British Department of Trade and Industry for further information. (2007: 75)

From late 1998, 'regime change' became official US policy. After the 11 September 2001 attack on New York and Washington, the USA, the UK, Australia, Spain and Italy planned the invasion of Iraq. In March 2003, they bombarded Baghdad and carried out massive air strikes across the country. The removal of sanctions and the termination of the Oil for Food Programme took place when, in May 2003, UN Security Council Resolution 1483 removed many of the legal ambiguities in the path of the Iraq invasion; the UK and the USA became the occupying forces and the UN recognised the creation of the Interim Governing Council (Tripp 2008: 283).

Changes in the Shi'a–Sunni balance of state power

The fall of Saddam and the Ba'athist regime in 2003 would signal a change in the Shi'a–Sunni balance of power. The emergence of the Shi'a leadership as a political force, however, must be seen as the consequence of three important factors. First, as in Iran, Lebanon, Egypt and Palestine, was the inability of nationalist, liberal and leftist secular forces to offer an alternative. Second was the systematic persecution of these political organisations by the state in countries allied to the West. Third was the political and economic exclusion of the Shi'a communities, especially since the overthrow of Abd al Karim Qasim in 1963 when Iraq's Ba'ath Party took power.

In March 2003, when US troops marched on Baghdad, Ayatollah al-Sistani asked the Shi'a community not to resist. When the troops entered the holy Shi'a city of Karbala there was no resistance. Al-Sistani chose conditional cooperation with the USA, as he saw the fall of Saddam as the beginning of a major political shift in favour of the Shi'as. He regards Islam as a fundamental part of the Iraqi constitution and national identity. For him, Islam is a source of legitimate authority which should not be excluded from Iraq's legal body. But his model of government is different from those of the dictatorial regimes in the region and from that in Iran. He promotes a democratic Islamic politics and governance rather than authoritarian rule. In this context, he rejects Khomeini's concept of *Velayat-e faqih*.[6]

In his opinion, the responsibility of the *marja'* is to defend Islamic and Muslim communities rather than exercise absolute power over all state affairs. He has advocated accountable government based on majority rule which protects and represents the Shi'a identity. Equally important to his approach has been bridge-building between different communities, a position that has won him majority support in the region. He is recognised by the Shi'a communities in Lebanon, Syria and Iran. As was discussed in Chapter 2, in Iran in recent years a number of clerics, notably Ayatollah Shariatmadari and Ayatollah Montazeri, have supported al-Sistani's position, and, as discussed in Chapter 4, Ayatollah Fadlallah, the spiritual leader of Hezbollah, has also challenged the concept of *Velayat-e faqih*. The religious taxes (*waqf*, *khums* and *zakat*), which amount to millions of dollars donated by millions of people in the region, represent a vote of confidence in him (Nasr 2007: 125–6; 170–73, 182–3, 190, 200; Cockburn 2008: 206; Tripp 2008: 180; Rahimi 2007: 4–5, 10–13).

Although al-Sistani conditionally supported the occupation and the fall of Saddam in 2003, he issued a fatwa, a religious ruling, rejecting the American idea that the new constitution be drafted by those appointed by the USA. Instead, he argued that the constitution should be drafted by those elected by the people of Iraq. He insisted on a one person, one vote system. This was popular with the majority of Iraqis; for five days large numbers of people demonstrated their support for him, and consequently the Americans had to accept this position. He argued with the Iranians and Hezbollah, and convinced them that he should deal with the Americans through practical engagement to ensure the accommodation of Shi'a interests in Iraq without marginalising other communities. For many Iraqis, Shi'a–Sunni–Arab–Kurd diversity has existed historically, especially under Saddam. However, the institutionalisation of sectarianism, including within the state, is a new phenomenon that began with the occupation of Iraq in 2003 (Ramadani and Zangana 2006; Ramadani 2007).[7] Since then, in the face of sectarian conflict, al-Sistani has consistently called upon the Shi'a militia and clergy to avoid civil war and has declared it a 'grave sin' to seek revenge on Sunnis for attacks on Shi'a communities. In this context his nationalist message has been popular with the majority of people in Iraq across the religious and national divides. He also argued that the transitional government should be elected, and demanded that the election take place under UN supervision (Nasr 2007: 175–8; Tripp 2008: 283–5; Rahimi 2007: 8–9).[8]

In January 2005, al-Sistani encouraged different Shi'a communities to join the United Iraqi Alliance (UIA) and participate in the election, and in the process of drafting the constitution, as candidates and voters. Millions of Shi'as and Kurds (a 58 per cent turnout) participated. However, the Sunni Arab population boycotted this election; they felt marginalised and considered the UIA to be a sectarian organisation contributing to conflict. For many within the Shi'a communities the election was a victory as the alliance won 48 per cent of the vote and 140 (nearly half) of the seats in parliament. SCIRI and the al-Dawa Party won the majority of the votes and SCIRI won the majority of the municipal seats. Women won 70 (25 per cent) of the assembly's 275 seats. This election gave the Shi'a communities legitimacy. The challenge to this legitimacy, however, was the low Arab Sunni turnout of 2 per cent. Muqtada al-Sadr's supporters, who participated in the election outside of the alliance, did not do as well as SCIRI and al-Dawa. As a result, they joined the UIA in the December 2005 legislative election (the assembly under the new constitution) and this coalition won an electoral victory for the Shi'as as a whole. They won 46 per cent of the seats in parliament, and Muqtada al-Sadr's followers won the largest proportion of the popular vote. Sunni communities also participated in this election. The turnout was 79.6 per cent, giving it a relatively high level of legitimacy (Nasr 2007: 189–200; Tripp 2008: 238, 295–6; Cockburn 2008: 206; Rahimi 2007: 13).

In April 2005, Jalal Talabani, a leading Kurdish politician who had lived in Iran for many years, became the Iraqi president. Ibrahim al-Jafari, a Shi'a from the al-Dawa Party, became prime minister. He was succeeded in 2006 by Nouri al-Maliki, also a Shi'a and the secretary general of the al-Dawa Party. Mahmoud al-Mashhadani, a Sunni Arab, became speaker of the parliament, succeeded by Ayad al-Samarai, also a

Sunni Arab, in 2009. The predominantly Shi'a presence in positions of state power clearly demonstrates a shift in the balance of power from Sunni to Shi'a political leadership. Many Iraqi Shi'as who had lived in exile for many years, mainly in Iran, and could speak Farsi, returned to Iraq and joined the country's political life. Some are involved in the government, municipalities, mosques and seminaries, and are found in towns from Basra to Baghdad. Some represent Iran's influence in Iraq and strengthen the ties between the two countries. Others feel an attachment to Iran in terms of Shi'ism and blame Saddam for the Iran–Iraq war that resulted in the deaths of one and a half million Shi'as in the two countries (Nasr 2007: 198–9, 224).

Despite religio-political attachment to Iran, the majority of the Shi'as who lived in Iran for many years carried their Iraqi identity with them in exile. Attaollah Mohajerani, an Iranian politician, explains:

> The Iraqi Shi'as who lived in Iran for all those years created a little Najaf in Qom. During the Ashoura commemorations they had their own mourning groups distinct from the Iranian groups; they were called the Najaf Group and the Karbala Group. Their Iraqi Shi'a identity was politically and socially strengthened in Qom. After the fall of Saddam, they went back to Iraq and became engaged in Iraq's politics.

The US occupation of Iraq strengthens Iran's position

The historical link between Iran and the Shi'a communities in Iraq is a matter of record. However, the shift in the balance of state power in favour of Shi'a leadership is evidently linked to the role of the USA in Iraq and not to Iran. SCIRI and al-Dawa have had links with Iran since the 1980s under the Islamic Republic. Both parties have their own militias, such as the Badr Brigade of SCIRI and the resistance group. Since 2003 there has also been Muqtada al-Sadr's Mahdi Army, which has ties to Iran. However, Iran's religio-political influence in Iraq is more complex than its portrayal in the West. These organisations are not simply a manipulated extension of Iran. They are diverse and independent of Iran, and have been competing with each other for power according to their very different visions of state-building in Iraq (Tripp 2008: 296–307, 310).

In fact, Iran's complex relationship with Iraq is more a political than a religious relationship. As discussed earlier, al-Dawa was originally established in the 1960s. Later, Ayatollah Baqir al-Sadr's and Ayatollah Khomeini's supporters concentrated their activities against the Ba'athist regime. This was the biggest Islamist party, which sometimes was clergy-based and sometimes not. In the 1970s, many al-Dawa members and supporters were also members of the Iraqi Communist Party. The organisation had predominantly been against the occupation, but the Americans convinced the leadership to join the Transitional Governing Council.[9] Ibrahim al-Jafari, who under the occupation became the first elected prime minister, lived for many years in exile in Iran and Europe. Nouri al-Maliki, who succeeded him in 2006, also lived in exile in Iran and Syria (Tripp 2008: 280; Cockburn 2008: 166–211).

As discussed earlier, SCIRI was established in Iran in 1982. Its leaders began cooperating with the USA in the 1990s when they were still based in Iran. This was at a time when the relationship between Iran and the USA was at its lowest point; the Bush administration had branded Iran a member of the 'axis of evil', and claimed that all Iraqi Shi'a organisations were manipulated by Iran in opposition to the USA, when in fact the leaders of al-Dawa and SCIRI both have close links with Iran but supported the occupation of Iraq. In 2003, Baqir al-Hakim and eighty-five other people were killed by Sunni extremists in a bomb blast in Najaf. His brother, Abdul-Aziz al-Hakim, who had lived in exile in Iran for many years, became SCIRI's leader. Al-Hakim is a strong supporter of Iran but also supported the occupation and has a close relationship with the USA. Iran has supported both organisations but has consistently been opposed to the occupation of Iraq (Nasr 2007: 117, 192–3; Tripp 2008: 285).

The position of Grand Ayatollah al-Sistani is also important. He was born in Iran, has Iranian citizenship and speaks Arabic with an Iranian accent, but has emerged as a popular leader of the Shi'as in Iraq. As discussed earlier, in rejecting the concept of *Velayat-e faqih* he opposes the political regime in Iran, and in this context he has the support of not just the Shi'as but also other communities in Iraq. Equally important is the fact that he has consistently denounced conflicts between Sunnis and Shi'as.

Thus, Iran has approved the pro-occupation parties (SCIRI and al-Dawa), but has also supported the anti-occupation Sadrist movement and its Mahdi Army (Jaish al-Mahdi). The link between Muqtada al-Sadr and Iran dates to just after the fall of Saddam. He visited Ayatollah Khamenei and the Revolutionary Guards in Iran and named his militia the Mahdi Army, implying that his organisation is a follower of the Twelfth Shi'a Imam Mahdi, who went into occultation in 874 CE. Unlike SCIRI and al-Dawa, which in 2003 joined the Iraqi Governing Council (IGC) set up by the USA, Muqtada al-Sadr refused to join the Council, denouncing it as an illegitimate organisation appointed by an illegitimate occupation (Nasr 2007: 130, 190–94; Cockburn 2008: 167–8; Tripp 2008: 280). His anti-occupation position is not due to Iran's influence; it is because his policy of mixing Islam and nationalism whilst challenging the US occupation is popular with a majority in Iraq – his followers are mainly in the slums of Baghdad and Basra. (He also has support in Kirkuk and among Turkmen Shi'a communities in the north.) As was discussed above, his father, Ayatollah Mohammad Sadiq al-Sadr, believed in unity between the Shi'a and Sunni communities and was popular with the poor; he effectively provided resources to the Shi'a urban poor, especially the 2 million in Sadr City, Baghdad. When Mohammad was killed in 1999 by Saddam, Muqtada continued his father's charity work and advocated unity between the Shi'a and the Sunni communities. His popularity grew in 2004 when his Mahdi Army fought against the US forces. He challenged al-Sistani, the SCIRI and the Badr Brigade, and moved the Mahdi Army into Najaf, occupied the shrine of Imam Ali and confronted US troops. Fearing an American assault on the holy shrine, al-Sistani and Hezbollah intervened and negotiated the withdrawal of the Mahdi Army from the holy city (Nasr 2007: 190–94; Tripp 2008: 280; Cockburn 2008: 202).

In 2006, Muqtada al-Sadr and his movement supported al-Maliki's presidency. But under pressure from Washington, al-Maliki clamped down on the Sadrists. By 2007, the Sadrists withdrew from the UIA alliance as thousands of their members and supporters were arrested, and the USA regarded the Sadr movement, supported by Iran, as the biggest obstacle to the occupation. Muqtada al-Sadr's popularity continued, and in 2008 thousands of people joined the protest marches and sit-ins in Baghdad to support his cause. In 2008, occupation-backed security forces waged savage attacks against the Mahdi Army. The Bush administration, al-Maliki's (al-Dawa) government and the SCIRI, which changed its name to the Islamic Supreme Council of Iraq (ISCI) in 2007,[10] decided to break Sadr's movement. Muqtada left Iraq and relocated to Qom in Iran to continue his theological studies. In the March 2010 presidential election Ayad Allawi, who was prime minister for nine months in 2004–5, leading a transitional government, claimed victory over Prime Minister al-Maliki. His Iraqi National Movement won 91 seats in the 325-seat parliament, 2 more than al-Maliki's coalition. The Iraqi National Alliance, a Shi'a bloc which includes Muqtada al-Sadr, won 70 seats. The Sadrist movement, once again, indicated that its support base is solid and that whoever comes to power has to deal with the reality that Muqtada al-Sadr is a potent force.[11]

These historical events demonstrate that Iran has undoubtedly acted in self-interest and supported the Shi'a organisations according to its own agenda. But the US policy of uniting the government and the ISCI against Muqtada al-Sadr has promoted a Shi'a civil war in Iraq. As Jonathan Steele indicated,[12] this is similar to US policy in Palestine, where the USA is financing and arming Mahmoud Abbas's Fatah movement against Hamas instead of working for Palestinian unity. The USA accuses Iran of supporting the al-Sadr movement, but Iran also supports al-Dawa and ISCI. The difference is that these two organisations support the occupation, whilst al-Sadr opposes it[13] (Cockburn 2008: 231–43).

The issue of federalism, as another form of sectarianism, is also contentious among these organisations. In 2005, al-Hakim and SCIRI argued for a federal state with a confederation of southern Shi'a provinces formed to have access to a percentage of the southern oil fields' production. Al-Sistani, al-Dawa, al-Sadr and secular nationalists rejected this proposal and denounced any form of federalism. Iran has also been against federalism in Iraq as it would be destabilising and threatening to Iran, especially if it created an independent Kurdistan with substantial oil reserves. In the 2009 election, against the pressure of the 86 per cent of the population who opposed the division of Iraq, the federalists were clearly the losers.

Evidently, Iran's religio-political influence in Iraq is personified by al-Sistani and all Shi'a organisations, including the al-Sadr movement, some of which are pro-occupation and some anti-occupation. Iran's motives are more closely related to self-defence than to Shi'a and regional domination. The reality is that the fall of the Taliban in Afghanistan and that of Saddam in Iraq were to Iran's advantage, especially in Iraq where a Shi'a-dominated political system came to power. Nevertheless, Iran faces the ever-present threat of military intervention by the USA and Israel or even another attack from Iraq. As is argued by Milani (2009: 349–66), if Iran's legitimate security is threatened, it will react and the region as a whole could suffer. Indeed, US Special Forces have been conducting cross-border operations from northern and southern Iraq. By 2008, the scale and scope of CIA and Joint Special Operations Command (JSOC) missions against Iran had expanded with the authorisation of the Iraqi government. Iran, fully aware of this situation, continued to support the Iraqi government and all the Shi'a parties. To achieve security against the possible threat from the USA and its allies, Iran has been building complex and often unstable and uneasy alliances with Shi'a movements across the political spectrum in Iraq. When in 2008 al-Maliki declared that 'Iraq was not willing to be a staging ground for covert operations against Iran' this clearly demonstrated that Iran had succeeded in convincing the Iraqi government not to allow the USA to use Iraq as a base to attack the country (Tripp 2008: 310–11; Cockburn 2008: 166–211).[14]

Criticisms of the role of Iran

Many Iraqis in Iraq and in the diaspora, including Shi'a communities in Tehran, Damascus and London, agree that the sheer disaster that exists in Iraq is the result of the US occupation, but they are highly critical of, or even hostile to, Iran's position. In their eyes, all three governments are equally responsible for the continuation of corruption, violence and economic deterioration. As Zaynab, an Iraqi academic, observed:

> After the fall of Saddam, people were hoping for reconstruction and democracy. But now Iraq has become an open *sofra* [dinner party] that everyone is entering into for their own interests and not for the interest of the Iraqi people. Iraq has become the battle ground between Iran and America. They compete with each other over funding different groups and the fund is spent on arms to kill each other. Even Shi'as are killing Shi'as and the Sunnis are killing Sunnis these days, in the same way that the Sunnis are killing Shi'as and the Shi'as are killing Sunnis.

In response, Iranian politician Attaollah Mohajerani argued that:

> Iran supports the Iraqi government as the representative of all Iraqis and not just the Shi'as. If the Iraqi government is not working for the interest of the Iraqi people, even the Shi'as, this is because Iraq is under foreign occupation. Iran never recognised the occupation of Iraq and has systematically called for the withdrawal of foreign forces. The Iraqi government has accepted the occupation. The USA has failed in Iraq and Afghanistan; they have created chaos and catastrophe. However, Iran cannot do the job of the Iraqi government for the Iraqis, but at the same time Iran has to support the Iraqi government.

Sami Ramadani argues that we cannot equate Iran and the USA as Iran is reacting to the US presence in Iraq, and we cannot forget that the West supported Saddam against Iran in the Iran–Iraq war in order to crush the revolution. He explained to me:

> If we take this background into account, we understand why Iran is reacting to the USA in Iraq. Iran is the party that is under threat and Iraq is potentially the biggest base for attack against Iran. There are over 5,000 Mujahideen Khalq Organisation (MKO) members, armed and trained by the USA, in Iraq, ready to carry out 'regime change' in Iran. On different occasions they have crossed from

their camp into Iran to mount assassinations and sabotage. Israeli units go to Iran through Kurdistan.[15] They are also arming the Kurdish party [The Party for a Free Life in Kurdistan – PJAK] to attack Iran.

In order to undermine the nationalist anti-occupation resistance, the USA is financing the Sunni militias and fuelling anti-Shi'a and anti-Iranian prejudice. At the regional level the USA has also created an anti-Iranian alliance of Sunni-led Arabs and at the international level portrays Iran as a regional threat in order to police the Gulf region on the pretext of mediating in the deliberately constructed vision of Sunni-versus-Shi'a conflict,[16] This is accompanied by racist anti-Iranian propaganda in the Arab media. Nevertheless, Iran is popular with the majority of people in the Middle East, despite the Shi'a and Sunni divide. However, most Iraqis view Iran very differently from those in Palestine, Lebanon and Egypt. They feel that they have been betrayed by Iran, in the same way that the Palestinians and Lebanese feel that they have been betrayed by the pro-West regimes in the Arab world.

Lebanon's Hezbollah model is not working in Iraq. In Lebanon, as was discussed in Chapter 4, Hezbollah's unity with a significant part of the Sunni and Christian communities has led to a decline in ethnic and religious conflicts; they provide effective social welfare to communities and have been successful in their struggle against Israel. In Iraq, however, a Shi'a-dominated state as a client state of the USA has not been able and willing to resolve conflicts between and within Shi'a and Sunni groups. Armed criminal gangs are engaged in warring political factions and are competing with each other over control of the black-market trade in oil. Many use violence and crime opportunistically against different communities for their own material gain. Oil and drug smuggling and kidnapping have become widespread; basic necessities such as water, electricity, health, education and employment are rapidly deteriorating; and sectarian killings are being waged by both Shi'a and Sunni extremists. In 2005 and 2006, sectarian violence was mainly the work of non-Iraqis, such as the group led by the Jordanian Abu Musab al-Zarqawi and affiliated to al-Qaeda, which led the most violent attacks on different, but predominantly Shi'a, communities. Since then, however, the sectarian conflicts have been intensifying and extending beyond Baghdad. These attacks are from Sunni Islamists, Ba'athists and Shi'a Islamists. Many Iraqis believe that the Shi'a-dominated client state of the USA, supported by Iran, is responsible for the violent conflict, as well as for corruption and economic deterioration (Nasr 2007: 196–8; Tripp 2008: 286–8; Tripp 2009).

There are approximately 2 million actively organised armed men in Iraq, a combination of occupation forces, contracted foreign mercenaries, occupation-backed Iraqi forces, death squads, US-trained army and police, US-controlled secret Iraqi militia, private kidnap groups, and the militias and resistance forces of various parties. The accuracy of the information available on different types of casualties varies greatly. Haifa Zangana[17] argues that more than 1 million Iraqis have been killed since 2003. People are suffering due to US and British depleted-uranium shells. The country's infrastructure has been destroyed and there are hundreds of hazardous sites related to cluster bombs in Baghdad alone (Zangana 2007: 20). By 2005, only 23 per cent of Iraqis had access to clean water, and by 2006 electricity supply had fallen to 4,100 megawatts, both figures much below pre-invasion levels. Unemployment has increased sharply, and the majority of people are on the edge of destitution (Cockburn 2006: 4–5; ICRC 2008). Similar to the situation in Afghanistan, the Iraqi people are not benefiting either from billion-dollar, US-funded NGOs and democracy-building, or from the market economy encouraged by the USA and international financial organisations. These factors have been used to justify the US military occupation of Iraq, and benefit only the private corporations and companies that are exploiting Iraq's resources (Zangana 2007: 74–5; Tripp 2008: 289–90).

As in Afghanistan, there is very little change in women's and gender issues in Iraq, despite the fact that women hold more than 25 per cent of the seats in parliament (Rostami-Povey 2007b). Iraqi women are also concerned[18] about the rise of religious extremism and the domination of state institutions by conservative Islamist men. They do not want conservative gender practices, such as the compulsory veiling that is practised in Iran, to be imported to Iraq. Nadje, a journalist, argued:

> The Shi'a politicians are encouraging the hijab. I was told by some of them that if I wear the hijab I will be promoted to the state media. But I rejected the offer. Hijab is a personal issue for women; we have to decide whether we need to wear it or not, not to be told by the politicians to wear it in order to be promoted.

Violence against female politicians has intensified. Examples of attacks on women within state institutions include the assassination of Aqila al-Hashimi, a member of the Iraqi Governing Council (IGC), in 2003; the assassination of Amal al-Ma'malchi, an adviser to the ministry of municipalities and public works, in 2004; and an assassination attempt against Salama al-Khafaji, another member of the IGC, in 2004. There are, of course, hundreds of attacks on a daily basis on ordinary women which are not reported (Tripp 2008: 305). Government militias, tribal groups and sectarian militias (both Sunni and Shi'a) are fighting one another. Public goods and public institutions, such as the health, education and other institutions which existed under Saddam Hussein, have been destroyed. This has led in turn to the re-emergence of the old as well as new powerful sectarian networks, which are in conflict with each other not over religious issues but over political power.[19] Under these circumstances, many see Iran as partly responsible. By 2006, 2 million Iraqis had been internally displaced and another 2 million had taken refuge outside of Iraq. According to the Iraqi Red Crescent, two-thirds of the displaced are women and children (Zangana 2007: 17). Ahlam, who has witnessed the refugee crisis in Syria, explained that

> Since the occupation so many people have been forced to leave Iraq. Many were killed in the process, many women were raped, many lived in the border areas. There is a large number of forced migrants in neighbouring countries who live in terrible conditions. Refugees have many problems, especially female-headed households and other vulnerable people who need care, and no one is even aware of their conditions and nobody talks about them.

Even in Kurdish areas where the level of violence is relatively low and a degree of economic stability is present, people are protesting against corruption, political repression and economic inequalities. In Halabja, people burned down a memorial museum and argued that 'the government does not do anything about lack of resources and only come here once a year with their limousines to bask in our sufferings' (Tripp 2008: 305–9, 2009). Um Iman, a refugee observed:

> The politics of Kurdistan is run by Talabani and Barzani. They have all the resources under their own control. Very little has been done for ordinary Kurds. We have no electricity or water and very few economic activities; the old tribal traditions such as honour killing, forced marriages and old men marrying young women are becoming social norms. These, together with economic problems, have created a terrible situation for women. The same problems exist for women everywhere in Iraq; in the Kurdish part we see crimes against women, but in the rest of Iraq the lack of security does not allow crimes to be seen. People are killed on a daily basis, women are killed on a daily basis; young women are sold on a daily basis for prostitution.

The rape of Iraqi women by the invading forces' soldiers and the Iraqi police is widespread through home raids and random arrests. Women are raped in prisons, inside their homes after the arrest of their male relatives, and after being taken to police stations, accused of helping the insurgents (Zangana 2007: 119–20). Torture, Abu-Ghraib style and otherwise, is widely practised in Iraqi prisons. The Iraqi people's anger against and defiance of the US-supported Iraqi government was symbolised by Muntadher al-Zaidi, a young socialist journalist who threw his shoes at George Bush in December 2008, saying: 'This is the farewell kiss, you dog; this is from the widows, the orphans and those who were killed in Iraq.' He became a national and regional hero, and anti-government and occupation demonstrations in Najaf, Falluja, Baghdad, Mosul and Basra supported him following his imprisonment and called for his release.[20]

Certainly, the role of Iran is not comparable to the role of the USA in Iraq. In the minds of many Iraqis, however, there is a joint occupation by the two countries. Aysha also explained to me that

It is like the Cold War, when the two sides collaborated on certain issues and also fought against each other and only ordinary people suffered in between. Iran and the USA use Iraq to settle their differences. It is more than hypocrisy, it is power politics and Iraqis are suffering.

Of course, resistance to the occupation and the government, which has Iran's support, has also been organised by genuine civil organisations. In 2004 the Iraqi National Foundation Congress (INFC) was established. This organisation opposed Saddam's regime, the occupation and any division based on sectarian, religious and ethnic divides. The secretary general of the organisation was Sheikh Jawad al-Khalili, a prominent Shi'a scholar. The other founding members were Muthana al-Dhari, the spokesperson of the Sunni Association of Muslim Scholars, and Wamidh Nadhmi, a secular Arab nationalist. They condemned terrorism and called for an end to the occupation and for the unity of the Iraqi people. However, they do not have a military wing and only operate at the political level. They are taking a big risk in being active and their influence is limited, but they continue their work in Baghdad (Zangana 2007: 129–31).

In 2000, a London-based women's organisation called Act Together was established to raise consciousness about women's issues under the occupation (Al-Ali and Pratt 2009: 121–62). Maysoon Pachachi, a film-maker, opened a film school in 2004 in Baghdad. She had to close it down in 2007 as a result of the escalation of sectarian conflict. But it reopened in 2009. Her school has trained eighty Shi'a, Sunni, Kurd and secular film-makers, who have made eleven documentaries.[21] The efforts of individuals and groups to keep their communities together demonstrate how hopeful Iraqis are for their future. War, conflict, foreign occupation and invasion destroy communities. Women, in particular, play important roles in generating networks and setting norms in their communities. In this way they collectively reject foreign and sectarian forces, especially in Baghdad where walls are built to separate the Shi'a and Sunni communities. Hana, a women's rights activist and the founder of Iraqi Women's Will, established in 2002, remarked:

Theologically, historically and culturally there is a divide between the Shi'as, Kurds and Sunnis, but this issue has been politicised since the occupation. There have been intermarriages and harmony between these communities for many years. It is the occupation which has created a violent conflict between them. Even today, the Sunni and Shi'a communities are not killing each other, are not against each other; there are groups which are created by the occupying forces and the government who fight with each other and kill each other. In my organisation, even today, many Shi'a, Kurdish and Sunni women work side by side trying to help diverse women and communities who need help. They have built concrete walls to separate different communities from each other. These walls have created more tension and conflict. But people celebrate their weddings in two places as a way of breaking the wall which has been imposed on their communities.

The oil and dock workers' unions have also raised their voices. They took control of the ports and major oil fields and opposed the 'Oil Law' which privatised the oil industry and allows international oil companies to control the production and marketing of Iraq's oil.[22] Sami Ramadani explained:

The idea of the Oil Law was conceived before the invasion of Iraq in the USA, where a committee was set up in the state department and included a number of Iraqis as members. They drafted the Oil Law in 2007, and it means the control of the production, marketing, sale and price of the oil by oil corporations, who will extract 70–80 per cent of the profit. The majority of the population opposes this law and the oil workers' union has played an important role in opposing it. As the result the Oil Law has not gone through yet, but the government signed the contract with BP in 2009. There is also disagreement between the government and the Kurdish leadership, who want complete control over the oil production in Kurdistan and the freedom to sign independent oil contracts. The central government opposes the Kurdish leadership as they want to continue with the present agreement of allocating 17 per cent of oil revenues to the Kurdish area for the Kurdish population.

The USA as the superpower has destroyed Iraq as a functioning country and has used it as a base to threaten Iran's sovereignty. Iran, on the other hand, has manoeuvred to find a presence in Iraq in order to combat the possible threat from the USA. This combination has turned Iraq into a mosaic of warring factions where a great number of people are being abused. Different parts of the Iranian political establishment have diverse views about Iraq. But generally there has been a consensus in Iran on the need to see the USA out of Iraq. At the same time different Iranian governments have done everything they can to force the USA to cooperate with them. However, they have realised that as long as Iran continues to support the anti-occupation forces, the USA will not leave Iraq or end the occupation. For this reason, Iran began to pull back from supporting the Sadrist movement and other anti-occupation forces. In response, the USA handed over Camp Ashraf to the Iraqi government in January 2009 as part of its plan to withdraw from Iraq. This was in Iran's interest as the camp was used by the Mujahideen Khalq Organisation against Iran (Tripp 2009).[23]

In 2009, the UK and the USA announced their timetable for withdrawal from Iraq. But the majority of the population feel sceptical that the withdrawal of these forces will be total. UK military forces have remained in some bases, 132,610 foreign military contractors are staying, and US troops have redefined the borders of cities such as Mosul and Baquba and are remaining in those areas until August 2010.[24] Under these circumstances, as long as the USA remains in Iraq, Iran will feel threatened and will continue its role in Iraq. Sami Ramadani argued in an interview with me that

> The strategy of the USA is to have a client state in Iraq, but they cannot achieve this through the ballot box; they can only do it with a strong physical presence in Iraq. They claim that they are building the Iraqi army, the security forces and other state institutions, but they are all heavily staffed by American advisers. This situation is not acceptable to Iraqis and they will continue to resist the presence of foreign forces. For this reason, the USA will not withdraw from Iraq in the foreseeable future, unless they change

their policy on Iraq and the Middle East. That would be to leave Iraqi people to make their own alliances with their neighbouring countries such as Iran, Lebanon and Palestine. I am, therefore, not optimistic in the short run, but in the long term I am confident that we will gain our independence.

SIX

The relationship between
Iran, Palestine and Hamas

As a geopolitical entity, Palestine dates back to 3000 BCE. From 1500 BCE it was the land of the Canaanites. These ancient people were subsequently ruled by the Egyptians, Philistines, Israelites, Phoenicians, Assyrians, Babylonians, Persians, Macedonians, Romans, Arabs, Crusaders, Ayyubids, Mamluks and Ottomans (Hilal 2007: 30). Muslims conquered Palestine in 638 CE, allowing people of other faiths to live in peace there and welcoming pilgrims of all religions. Under Islamic rule, the indigenous Muslims, Christians and Jews of the Middle East lived together peacefully. This is in comparison to the lack of religious tolerance and the Christian fanaticism in medieval Europe at this time. Between 1097 and 1291 Western crusaders fought wars to gain control of Palestine, and, by slaughtering the Muslim population, ruled in Al-Quds (or Jerusalem) for seventy years until Saladin defeated them in 1187 (Hroub 2006: 2–3, 31).

Under Ottoman Islamic rule, Palestine was again very tolerant towards Christians and Jews. These communities were autonomous and had considerable power of self-rule, including collecting and distributing their own taxes. This system was much more advanced than any contemporary system in dealing with religious minority groups. Soon after the collapse of the Ottoman Empire and the imposition of British colonial rule, Palestinians demanded a sovereign state.

However, the Balfour Declaration of 1917, which was the product of British imperial interests and Jewish and Christian Zionism, facilitated the establishment of a Jewish state in Palestine. After the First World War, Zionism consolidated British colonial rule over Palestine. To justify Palestinian displacement, European settlers were portrayed as civilised and the Palestinians as 'non-Jewish communities' or uncivilised Oriental Arabs. The Palestinian anti-colonial uprising of 1936–39 was crushed by the British military and the force of Christian Zionist ideology, and after the Second World War the newly created Jewish State of Israel became a strategic asset for the USA in the region, as a military structure and to protect Western oil supply. This highly militarised state and society has since been in constant war with the Palestinians and the people of the Middle East (Hilal 2007:1; Masalha 2007: 98–102, 236; Rose 2004: 4–21, 154; Chomsky 1999: 9–38; Said 1980: 25–8; Sayigh 2007: 198–200).

Palestinian women have played an important role in resistance and national movements. A brief look at the history of the women's movement shows how in 1921 the Palestinian Women's Union organised demonstrations against the Balfour Declaration. In 1929, 200 delegates attended the first Arab Women's Congress in Palestine. From 1936 to 1939, women resisted the British and the Zionists. Between 1948 and 1964/5, various women's organisations generated new forms of activism (Jad et al. 2000: 137–56).

The Holocaust was repeatedly used to justify the State of Israel in the bid to recast Palestinian land as 'Jewish land'. For Palestinians, the 1948 Nakba (Catastrophe), like the Holocaust, was a crime against humanity, punishable by international law and comparable to the colonial history of ethnic cleansing in the Americas, Africa and Australia. In the war, which began in 1948, the Zionists murdered Palestinians in seventy massacres. The famous Deir Yassin massacre symbolised the level of terror that was used to force Palestinians out of their lands and homes (Said 2000: 205–9; Pappe 2006: 1–9, 55–61, 90–91; Rose 2004: 135, 149–53). The Israelis created the Law of Absentee Property, and under this law confiscated the Muslim *waqf*, the Islamic institution which owned a sizable amount of land in historical Palestine. The Palestinians lost more than 78 per cent of their country, including the western part of Al-Quds or Jerusalem, and were left with East Jerusalem, the West Bank and Gaza. Palestinians became refugees, many of them expelled to the West Bank, Gaza, Lebanon and Syria; they were deprived of their national territory and identity and many were condemned to refugee status in exile (Hilal 2007: 2–3; Masalha 2007: 234; Hroub 2006: x; Pappe 2006: 216–17; Pappe 2004: 142–7).

Against this background, the role of Iran in the Middle East in the 1950s is significant. As was discussed in Chapter 1, the victory of Mossadeq's nationalist government in Iran, supported by the Communists and the Islamists, was popular in the region. The Iranian oil nationalisation inspired a wave of anti-imperialist movements throughout the Middle East. However, the American and British coup in 1953 changed the position of Iran. The Shah of Iran, Israel and Turkey formed an alliance (the Alliance of the Periphery) against the Arab World. In the face of rising nationalism and communism in the region, this alliance was important for Iran as a front-line state in the Cold War. Israel's pact with the Shah of Iran was cemented by the USA. Iran recognised Israel and supplied 80 per cent of the country's oil requirements. Although a number of UN resolutions affirmed the Palestinians' right to compensation or repatriation, Iran continued its economic relationship with Israel. As is discussed in the next chapter, in the aftermath of Suez the Iran–Israel relationship became stronger, particularly in terms of military and intelligence cooperation, including close collaboration between Mossad (the Israeli secret police) and SAVAK (the Iranian secret police), which continued until the fall of the Shah in 1979 (Chubin and Zabih 1974: 160–63; Shlaim 2000: 192–204).

From the 1950s to the 1970s secular Arab nationalism and Marxist ideologies were popular in Palestine, as in most countries in the region. The Palestine Liberation Organisation (PLO) was established in 1964, advocating armed struggle to liberate Palestine, including the accommodation of pre-1948 Jews in a secular democratic state. Yasser Arafat and Fatah, the principal faction within the PLO, struggled hard and won the recognition of most people in Palestine and throughout the majority of the Muslim world. However, the weakness of Arab nationalism and continuous Western support for Israel made it impossible for the PLO to pursue its goal of liberating Palestine.

In 1967, Israel attacked Egypt, Syria and Jordan, seizing Sinai and the Gaza Strip from Egypt, the Golan Heights from Syria, and the West Bank and East Jerusalem, which were under the control of Jordan. After the 1967 war, women resisted the Zionist occupation of the West Bank and Gaza. In 1969–70 Leila Khaled, a member of the Popular Front for the Liberation of Palestine (PFLP) and the Palestine National Council, became a legend for participating in plane hijackings to draw the attention of the world to the atrocities committed against the Palestinians. In the late 1970s and early 1980s, diverse women's committees and women's centres worked to put gender issues on the agendas of the nationalist movements (Sharoni 1995: 56–89; Ababneh forthcoming).

After the Black September of 1970, the PLO was forced to move its headquarters to Beirut. Meanwhile, the USA provided Israel with billions of dollars in aid and sophisticated weapons. Egypt, historically, was the leader of the united Arab front against Israel. After its defeat in the 1973 Arab–Israeli War, Egypt was detached from the Arab opposition to Israel in return for US military and economic aid, and Israel's role was consolidated as the USA's strategic asset in the Middle East (Rose 2004: 157–160; Hroub 2006: xii, 6; Gunning 2007: 28–34; Chomsky 1999: 10; Sayigh 1997: 470–84).

Nevertheless, in the 1970s, the Palestinian secular left and nationalists were in the forefront of the struggle against Zionism. These organisations had diverse political ideologies, ranging from communism to nationalism, and identified with different movements around the world. The Iranian Marxists and Islamist guerrilla organisations looked to the Fatah movement as well as to Algerian, Latin American and Vietnamese movements as models for their struggle against the Shah. Some members of these organisations escaped from Iran to PLO camps in Lebanon. The Palestinian military camps in Lebanon trained fighters from around the world, including Iranian guerrilla groups (Behrouz 2004: 199; Khalili 2007: 49; Abrahamian 1982: 409).

Despite a decade of dominance, the leadership of the PLO failed to deliver, as they were forced to make concessions to Israel under pressure from the Zionists. The 'peace treaty' between Israel and Egypt in 1979 coincided with the 1979 revolution in Iran. The slogan of the Iranian Revolution, 'Iran today, Palestine tomorrow', and the resistance against the Israeli attacks on Lebanon had considerable significance for the Palestinians. Saleh, a student activist at Birzeit, commented:

> The 1979 revolution in Iran was important for Muslims in the region. Ali Shariati's books became popular in Palestine. Many began to criticise the Islamist movements in the region for not achieving much, while in Iran they managed to defeat the Shah and his client state of the USA and the friend of Israel. Islam became relevant as a political force because of the Iranian Revolution.

Laleh Khalili also argues that many Palestinian intellectuals who believed in the national liberation of Palestine saw a 'family resemblance in the nation-statist, liberationist, and Islamist discourses'. For example, Fathi al-Shiqaqi wrote a book, *Al-Khomeini: Al-Hall al-Islami wa al-Badil* (Khomeini: The Islamic Solution and the Alternative), in which he declares Khomeinist Islamism to be the only possible liberation strategy (Khalili 2007: 33).

After the 1979 revolution, the Israeli ambassador to Iran revealed that over the years the entire Israeli leadership had visited the Shah, including Ben-Gurion, Golda Meir, Yitzhak Rabin, Menachem Begin and Moshe Dayan (Rose 2002: 27). The establishment of the Islamic Republic ended this relationship. Arafat visited Iran and met with Ayatollah Khomeini. Iran also ended the previous policy of recognising the State of Israel, and demanded the liberation of Palestine and Al-Quds (Jerusalem). It broke all diplomatic relations with Israel, and the Israeli embassy in Tehran was turned into the Palestinian embassy. Turkey became the key player for Israel and the USA as a counterweight to Iran and Syria (Shlaim 2000: 558).

The emergence of Hamas

Historically political, Islam in Palestine has long had anti-colonial and Palestinian nationalist dimensions. The failure of the Arab secular left and nationalism as a political force paved the way for Islamic resistance to Zionism and imperialism.

The religio-political origin of Hamas lies with the Muslim Brotherhood movement, founded in Egypt in 1928.[1] The Palestinian Muslim Brotherhood was involved in the anti-colonial struggle of 1936–39. Following this, branches of the organisation were first established in Jerusalem in 1946 and later in Gaza, Jaffa, Haifa, Lydda and Ramleh. During the 1948 war, the members of this organisation fought the Israelis with the support of Brotherhood volunteers from Jordan and Syria. In the West Bank, under the influence of the Jordanian Hashemite regime, they advocated non-violent resistance. In the Gaza Strip, the Palestinian Muslim Brotherhood had close ties to the Egyptian Muslim Brotherhood, and by the mid-1950s they were a strong political force in Gaza. After 1967, when the PLO was engaged in armed struggle against the occupation, the Brotherhood's activities were concentrated on the provision of social welfare in refugee camps and poor urban areas. In this context, the organisation was able to operate openly without fear of an Israeli clampdown. They also re-emerged faster and stronger in Gaza than in the West Bank since their main institutional competitors, the Communist Party and the nationalists, were weaker there.

In 1987, the Harakat al-Muqawama al-Islamiya (Hamas) was founded at the beginning of the first intifada (1987–93) – the uprising against the Israeli occupation. At first, the USA and Israel had official contact with Hamas, hoping that the organisation's growing power would undermine the secular nationalist PLO and their widespread support.[2] In 1989, however, Israel declared Hamas an illegal organisation. The PLO's support for Saddam Hussein in the Iran–Iraq war weakened the Iran–PLO relationship. However, Iran continued its anti-Zionist and pro-Palestinian policy and openly supported Hamas (Sayigh 1997: 476; Hroub 2006: 12–16, 110; Gunning 2007: 30–33,

57–68; Masalha 2007: 215–21; 234; Kadivar 2007: 73–81, 1997: 109, 220).

The first intifada began in December 1987 when a number of Palestinian prisoners escaped and killed an Israeli soldier. The Israelis also killed and injured a number of Palestinian workers who were returning from work in Israel. In response, mass protests took place in the West Bank and Gaza, and young Palestinians began throwing stones at Israelis. The whole population of Gaza and the West Bank soon joined the intifada. In response, Rabin's Israel imposed unprecedented collective punishment – including mass arrests, torture, curfews and house demolitions – which led to tens of thousands of deaths and injuries.

Hamas played an important role in the intifada; it mobilised its members and supporters through the network of mosques and universities. It demanded the abolition of the State of Israel and advocated armed struggle against Israeli occupation. Hamas's insistence that all historical Palestine was an Islamic *waqf* led to civil rights campaigns to recover confiscated Muslim *waqf* property in Israel. These policies and demands were popular with the majority of the Palestinians and were in contrast with the PLO, which signed the Algiers Declaration in 1988, in effect abandoning its original goal of establishing a Palestinian state throughout historical Palestine. Hamas, for its part, rejected the Declaration and its central concept of the two-state solution – the emergence of a Palestinian state on the West Bank and Gaza. This was the beginning of tension between Hamas and Fatah, as the Fatah leadership felt that its authority had been challenged. By 1992, Hamas was a strong resistance movement in the Occupied Territories. This was a period of mass deportations and expulsions of Palestinian academics, doctors, engineers, clergy, teachers, health workers and intellectuals to the southern Lebanese border, where many of them were killed by the Israelis. This led to stronger resistance against Israel and insistence on the right of return, as the large-scale deportation was a reminder of the 1948 and 1967 displacements. Gradually, Hamas developed a closer relationship with Hezbollah and consequently with Iran (Tamimi

2007: 52–75; Masalha 2007: 221–6; Gunning 2007: 47; Mishal and Sela 2000: 97).

As with Hezbollah, the emergence of Hamas as a popular resistance movement was the direct result of Israeli and US policies in the Middle East. In 1993, the PLO signed the Oslo Accords, hosted by President Clinton, and Arafat shook hands with the Israeli prime minister Rabin.[3] This agreement was claimed as another step towards the two-state solution. However, the number of Jewish settlements on the West Bank and Gaza continued to rise and the Israelis continued building roadblocks and the 'apartheid' wall in order to uproot Palestinians and make them invisible (Khalili, 2010). In reality, the Oslo Agreement legitimised Israel's seizure of Palestinian land and water resources, which meant that as the Palestinians were suffering from lack of water, Israelis were filling their swimming pools and their flower beds were blooming (Rose 2004: 161–4; Masalha 2007: 226–7; Chomsky 1999: 550–51; Said 2000: 14–20, 265). Some 90 per cent of the West Bank's water is under the control of the Israelis. Water has been diverted to settlement areas. Palestinian lands and trees have dried up. For their daily use they have to buy water from the settlers or the State of Israel. Omar from Qalqiliya explained:

> They are particularly interested in Qalqiliya because it has great water resources. They are starving us of our water resources. But we are still resisting after all these years. On the other side of the wall they have created a mountain of flowers to pretend that there is no wall between the settlers and us.

The Oslo Agreement also denied the 5 million Palestinian refugees and exiles the right to return to their country. This was facilitated by Clinton ignoring UN Resolution 194 of 11 December 1948, which states the rights of the Palestinian refugees who were driven out of their country.[4] Total dependence on foreign aid, exclusve reliance on private investment, and the US funding of Fatah against Hamas have had a devastating impact on Palestine's economy (UNCTAD 2006). In 1994, the Palestinian Authority (PA) was formed, headed by Arafat, and took over from the Israeli military in the Gaza Strip, in Jericho and, later, in other parts of the West Bank. As Edward Said argued, under the Oslo Agreement the PLO became the policing mechanism for apartheid Israel, which continued its expansionism and its marginalisation of the Palestinians (Said 1995: xxxv; Masalha 2007: 299).

While the PLO's popularity was diminishing, Hamas was rising in popularity for its stance against Israel. Throughout 1995 and 1996, Hamas, supported by Iran, followed the example set by Hezbollah in Lebanon (in the 1980s) by embracing the tactic of suicide bombings, which at the time was seen as the only means available to the Palestinians to deter the increasing Israeli attacks on the defenceless Palestinian population. Hamas was the first Muslim Sunni group to adopt the strategy of suicide bombing. This is significant, as the notion of suicide bombing had been alien to secular Palestinian guerrilla organisations. As Nur Masalha explained to me:

> The notion of martyrdom has been a powerful weapon in the Palestinian struggle against Zionism and the British since the mandatory period, but not suicide bombing. The military wing of Hamas, Kataib Izzidin al-Qassam [The Qassam Bridges], is named after Shaykh Izzidin al-Qassam, who was killed (with his followers) by the British army in 1935 in a well-known battle in the Palestinian countryside. The martyrdom of the Qassamites (Qassam and his followers) helped to spark off the Palestinian rebellion of 1936–39. In the post-1967 period, walls and side streets in Palestinian cities and refugee camps in the West Bank and Gaza were covered with posters of shahids [martyrs], often with actual photos and names of those individuals killed while resisting Israeli occupation. Also, among the Palestinians the names of the most famous martyrs, especially those killed by the British in the uprising of the 1930s, are celebrated in popular Palestinian songs.

From the 1990s, therefore, the tactic of suicide bombings, which was associated with Shi'ism and Lebanon, was adopted by Palestinians. The first suicide bombing carried out by Hamas was in the aftermath of the 1993 massacre of twenty-nine Palestinian worshippers by an Israeli-American settler and army reservist, Dr Baruch Goldstein, at the Ibrahimi mosque in al-Khalil (Hebron). Palestinian women also adopted this form of protest. Wada Idris, aged 26, was the first female suicide bomber in 2001, and Zaynab Ali was the last in 2004 (Hasso 2005; Tamimi 2007: 163). For many Palestinians, Hamas suicide bombings were a response to the massive rise in the number of Palestinians killed by the Israeli army. Hamas's response to the Israelis portraying Palestinian struggle as terrorism was: 'Stop killing Palestinian civilians and we will stop killing Israeli civilians.' Of course, the number of Palestinians killed by Israelis has been much higher than Israelis killed by Palestinians, and the Western media and politicians' condemnation of the Palestinians has been far harsher than their condemnation of the Israelis. In response to Hamas suicide bombings in Jerusalem, Israel imposed collective punishments on the Occupied Territories and, together with the USA, exerted enormous pressure on the Fatah-led PA to suppress Hamas. This led to increasing rivalry between Hamas and Fatah between 1994 and 2000, when the Palestinian police killed Hamas supporters in Gaza.[5] Millions of dollars were spent on policing, while very little was spent on health, education and employment. Many Palestinians blamed the situation on the Oslo Agreement, which was forced on the PA, turning it into a police force for Israel (Said 2000: 32–7; Hroub 2006: 53–4; Masalha 2007: 226–9; Tamimi 2007: 101–2; 159–70).

The deterioration of the Palestinian situation and a lack of support for the Palestinians from the Arab regimes strengthened Iran's relationship with Hamas, as Iran remained the only government that openly supported the Palestinians against Israel. In 1998, Sheikh Ahmed Yassin, the leader of Hamas, made a state visit to Iran under Khatami's premiership. He praised Iran for supporting the Palestinians. Following this visit he went to the United Arab Emirates, Kuwait, Qatar, Syria and Yemen. In these visits he criticised Yasser Arafat's discussions with the UK and the USA as fruitless (Tamimi 2007: 113–17).

The second intifada began in 2000 when Ariel Sharon provocatively visited al-Haram al-Sharif, Islam's third holiest place, in Al-Quds (Jerusalem) to demonstrate that even the Muslim holy places are under the control of the Israelis. The uprising was also in response to the failure of the Oslo Accords and the continued building of settlements in East Jerusalem, the West Bank and Gaza. Moreover, by this time the Palestine economy was disastrously weakened, with 31 per cent unemployment and 47 per cent of the population living below the poverty line. This second intifada turned into an armed confrontation with Israelis and was popular with all Palestinians, including Fatah and PLO supporters. Contrary to popular perception, the Palestinian weapons involved in this intifada did not come from Iran; they came from Egypt, despite the Egyptian government's position, and from the black market and discontented individual security forces.[6] Hamas also developed local manufacturing processes for primitive weapons (Hroub 2006: 47–50; Mishal and Sela 2000: xvi).

At the beginning of the twenty-first century, the Bush administration developed an even closer relationship with Israel.[7] When Bush became president in 2001, the Oslo peace process had broken down and the second intifada was raging. Ariel Sharon was elected Israel's prime minister and used maximum force to crush the intifada. After 9/11 the Bush administration launched its 'war on terror' and the neoconservatives attempted to impose an even more fanatical version of Zionism on US–Israeli policy, as Bush began to talk about a 'viable Palestinian state'. But he and his administration made no attempt to stop Israel building more and more settlements in the West Bank and Gaza, and there was no mention of Al-Quds (Jerusalem) and the right of refugees to return. In early 2003, the Bush administration published its 'Road Map' for an Israeli–Palestinian peace. Arafat and Hamas agreed that the Road Map would not be to Palestinian advantage. But Mahmoud Abbas (Abu Mazin), the prime minister at the time, agreed to it. He succeeded Arafat as chairman of the PLO Executive Committee when Arafat died on 11 November 2004. To many Palestinians, his conciliatory language appears more sympathetic to Israel than to Palestine, including his remarks about renouncing Palestinian refugees' right to return (Rose 2004: 165–71; Tamimi 2007: 202–3). Ayham, a life-long Fatah supporter and a refugee in Damascus, explained to me why he lost confidence in Fatah and the PA:

Originally Fatah was a national liberation movement. It genuinely represented Palestinians. For decades we faced failure after failure. As a result, Fatah lost the confidence of the people, mainly because of the Arab regimes' pressures on them. In recent years, Mahmoud Abbas has been trying to deal with the USA under pressure from Saudi Arabia. But he is systematically compromising, giving more and more concessions and not working in the interests of Palestinians. For me, if you give concessions to the enemy there is no return from continuing that path, until eventually you do what they want you to do. Privileges also corrupted the organisation and its leaders. Unfortunately, the Fatah conference in 2009 concentrated on how to oppose Hamas rather than on how to struggle against Israel's increasing aggression towards Palestinians. There was no discussion about learning from the past and having a vision for the future. The election of Marwan Barghouti[8] was positive, but this will not make much difference as he is in jail and cannot participate in decision-making. For all these reasons, Hamas has become the only alternative.

The USA and Israel have systematically sidelined the national liberation dimension of Hamas and have not just portrayed it as a terrorist organisation but have included it as part of the 'global terror' discourse. In 2003, Hamas called a temporary ceasefire, which lasted until 2005 despite continued Israeli raids into Gaza. In 2004, Israeli helicopters killed Sheikh Ahmed Yassin, the Hamas leader, along with nine other Palestinians. He had been behind the idea of hudna (a truce), which had led to the ceasefire with Israel, while demanding Israeli withdrawal to the 1967 borders, the return of Palestinian lands, the removal of Jewish settlers and the release of Palestinian prisoners. In his view this was the only way to end the suicide bombings. He also opposed the developing civil war between Palestinians as a result of the rivalry between Hamas and Fatah (Hroub 2006: 123–5; Tamimi 2007: 157–9, 210–19; Masalha 2007: 229–30).

Taking this background into consideration, the Palestinians see that no government in the region, with the exception of Iran and recently Turkey, is publicly objecting to Israel's atrocities. In order to be able to appreciate fully the popularity of Hamas and of Iran's support for the organisation, we need to understand the scale of Israel's efforts, supported by the West, to uproot Palestinians. As part of its policy of uprooting Palestinians, Israel is systematically maximising the number of Jews, minimising the number of Palestinians, and refusing to withdraw to the 1967 borders. The apartheid wall is the continuation of ethnic cleansing and leaves Palestinian communities divided and isolated from each other in East Jerusalem, the West Bank, Gaza, and throughout the rest of the country. As part of its agenda, the Zionist state encourages migration to Israel. A large number of poor immigrants from Africa, Russia and Southeast Asia have settled there. Those with a Jewish background have been given Israeli passports and work as cheap labour, security guards, police officers or join the army. The Israelis give employment priority to these immigrants, while in many cases they refuse to employ Palestinians or systematically humiliate them at all levels of employment. Zionists in Israel and the USA are funding a plan to build the Jewish Third Temple on al-Haram al-Sharif, which would destroy the Muslim shrines, and could lead to local and regional conflict (Said 2000: 247–55; Masalha 2007: 123; Hilal 2007: 11–15).

Following the violent incidents that occurred at the Al-Aqsa Mosque in October 2009, no Arab leader objected. Only the Lebanese Shi'a leader Ayatollah Fadlallah argued that 'Israel had entered a new phase of making occupied Jerusalem fully Jewish. Israel's strategy is to deny the mosque its holy status by letting its soldiers step inside it'. He blamed the Arab regimes for the increasing Israeli violations, saying, 'Israel would not have been able to expand its aggressions had the Arab world and the Muslim world made one step toward stopping the Israeli invasion.'[9] In an interview with me in Ramallah, Samia argued that

> Zionism is worse than the apartheid regime of South Africa and fascistic regimes elsewhere. It has the support of the West because of their guilt over the Holocaust. It is nothing to do with the original Jews in the region. The Jews were an integral part of Palestine. The issue of who is Muslim, who is a Jew, who is Christian is a new phenomenon created by the Zionists. They want to create a pure Jewish Zionist state free of all other ethnic and religious groups.

Silwan is just outside the Old City and historically was a Palestinian village, with 15,000 people living in the area. In recent years, 300 settlers have been moved to this area. They are armed, have put the Israeli flag on their buildings, and are constantly threatening the Silwan community. Khaled, who is campaigning to save the Silwan community, explained:

> In 2009, the Israeli government created a pretend and futuristic map of the area to show that there was no Silwan community and the area is part of the 'Jewish temple mountain'. We will fight them, as we have no other solution. This is our home, we will not leave.

Since 2008, the Israelis have repeated 1948 levels of destruction of Palestinian homes and communities. The apartheid wall, the green line, and the building of new settlements are strangling the Palestinian communities on a daily basis. The combination of a lack of economic activity and the absence of schools and hospitals forces people to leave. Fadwa described the situation:

> The wall divides our homes from our lands, our homes from our schools, universities,[10] hospitals and workplaces. Their aim is to paralyse our lives. We cannot go to hospital, to school, to university, to our workplaces unless we travel for hours and go through checkpoints to reach our destination. By ordinary roads and routes it takes only a few minutes. Sometimes they create flying checkpoints to deliberately stop students getting to school and university on time, especially during their examination period. The wall is concrete in some parts; in other parts it is barbed wire, razor wire and electric wire with cameras. People in these cities and villages live like prisoners. Their roads have been closed and they can only go in and out through checkpoints, flying checkpoints and road blocks. Sometimes there are permanent checkpoints. In many cases they have no way to get in and out of the village with their vehicles to purchase food and daily necessities. They have to walk miles to get to shops and then carry goods by hand back to their villages.

Mohammad, a leading activist in the 'Stop the Wall' campaign,[11] told of his family's experience:

They only give permits to older people to move from their homes to their land separated by the wall. But old people cannot work on their land. Since 2003, they have not given me and my brothers and sisters permits to go and work on our land. So our olive trees are dying because my 75-year-old father cannot work. The settlers are armed. They attack Palestinians, burn their houses and force them to leave their homes. The settlements' sewage is directed onto Palestinian lands and villages, killing their agricultural products and ruining the environment. They are also rewriting history by changing the names of villages and cities from Arabic to Hebrew to pretend that these communities never existed.

Yasser Arafat's efforts were the closest the conflict has come to a two-state solution, and Hanan Ashrawi, as the spokesperson for the Palestinian delegation at the Madrid Peace Conference in 1991 and after, has struggled ceaselessly for peace. However, the Israelis treated their and others' efforts and compromises with contempt and have continued the construction of the apartheid wall, the settlements in the West Bank and the strangling of the Palestinians' livelihoods.

In 2009, Barack Obama's new presidency raised speculation regarding pressure on Israel to accept the idea of a meaningful Palestinian state alongside Israel. His Persian New Year (21 March 2009) greetings to the Iranians and his speech in Cairo on 4 June 2009 raised some hopes. However, he has failed to persuade Israel to impose a freeze on settlements. Binyamin Netanyahu has refused to agree to the return of Palestinian refugees and has insisted that Jerusalem would remain under Israeli control.[12] In October 2009, the UN Human Rights Council's vote to condemn the January 2009 Israeli assault on Gaza was rejected by Netanyahu. And in March 2010 Netanyahu refused the USA's demand for a freeze on the construction of Jewish homes in East Jerusalem. These were fresh blows to Obama's efforts for a two-state solution; even the Fatah leadership has expressed its loss of hope, believing that Obama could not withstand the pressures of the Zionist lobby.[13] As Anne Alexander and John Rose have argued, the only way to end Zionism is in the same way that the apartheid system in South Africa was ended, through a one person, one vote system under which all the peoples of Palestine could live democratically in one state (Alexander and Rose 2008). Mahmoud, an activist, declared:

> I am hopeful. The change may not happen in my lifetime, but Palestinians are prepared to sacrifice another hundred years to achieve what is legitimately theirs. We have had the crusaders come and go, the British and the French have come and gone, and the present occupiers have come and they will have to go. There has to be an end to this injustice.

Hamas participation in electoral politics

Hamas inherited the idea of participating in electoral politics from the Muslim Brotherhood and from Hezbollah's example in Lebanon. Since 1992 Hamas supporters have competed with Fatah supporters in professional associations and student-union elections. Hamas supporters are mainly concentrated in urban areas, in both middle-class and poor neighbourhoods, as well as in some rural areas. In 2004 and 2005, Hamas won a third of the seats in municipal elections. Hamas's landslide victory in January 2006 was particularly significant. According to Khaled Hroub, the Palestinian academic and writer, Hamas has the support of 30–40 per cent of the population. The basis of support for Hamas is the frustration felt by the Palestinians at continued Israeli military aggression and the failure of the PA to stop Israel's crimes against Palestine. This election ended Fatah's monopoly in Palestine in a free and fair democratic vote, in which an unprecedented number of people participated. Under the electoral system, while Hamas received 44 per cent of the popular vote, it become the majority party in the Palestinian Legislative Council (the Palestinian parliament with limited sovereign power in the West Bank and Gaza) as it won 74 out of 132 seats. In the June 2007 election in Gaza, Hamas defeated Fatah and took over the Gaza Strip; in the West Bank, President Mahmoud Abbas and Fatah remained in control of the PA, its ministries and its security forces. Many Christians, secular leftists and nationalists, as well as Muslims, voted for Hamas. This support was also a vote of no confidence in Fatah and a demonstration of opposition to the USA. Eileen Kuttab, an academic at Birzeit University, explained:

> There are a number of villages with a majority Christian population. Ramallah was originally a Christian village. Many Christians live in Ramallah, Birzeit, Nazareth and Jerusalem. Some villages in the Ramallah area voted for Hamas, primarily because they needed a change of government. Second, they consider Islam as a part of their culture which does not contradict their national aspirations. Third, they have also been squeezed out by the new settlements and suffer because of the wall and the checkpoints. Much of our land and many of our homes have been taken over by the Zionists. People are tired of Western and US hypocrisy and the leadership of the PA, which is corrupt and repressive. Hamas also provides social services, which are important for all communities.

Hamas has developed a relatively close relationship with two left-wing organisations, the Popular Front for the Liberation of Palestine and the Democratic Front for the Liberation of Palestine. In the 2007 election Hamas supported two independent Christian candidates in Gaza and Bethlehem, and a Christian was appointed to the Hamas cabinet as the minister for tourism. It has also achieved landslide victories in municipal elections, student-union elections and syndicate elections (Gunning 2007: 143–55; Hroub 2000: 216–17, 2006: 80–91).

As discussed earlier, the massive political mobilisation of women during the first and the second intifadas once again demonstrated Palestinian women's agency and identity. More recently, within Hamas, women have also been visible in political mobilisations and their votes have been instrumental in putting Hamas in the lead in universities, and at local and national levels. They are particularly visible within education, health and charity organisations, as well as the media. As in Hezbollah, however, women are not in positions of leadership and decision-making at the higher political levels. In the 2006 parliamentary election, 13 women out of 66 stood on the Hamas platform; 7 of them won seats, but when Hamas formed the government only Myriam Saleh, an academic and founder of several women's organisations in the West Bank, was appointed to the cabinet, as the minister for women. Nevertheless, the female MPs and activists encourage women to participate in political life and stand up for gender equality. According to Huda al-Qrenawi and Jamila al-Shanti, Hamas will in due course scrap many of its gender-discriminatory politics. All Hamas female candidates elected in the 2006 election are educated professionals or community activists. Huda Naeem, elected MP in 2006, calls for an end to forced marriage, 'honour killings', low pay and girls being kept out of school (Hroub 2006: 75–8; Gunning 2007: 168–9; Alexander and Rose 2008: 28).

The democratically elected Palestinian government led by Hamas was opposed by Israel, the USA, Europe and Fatah (Hroub 2006: xxi–xxii). Following its successful election, the USA and Israel put a freeze on all funds entering the Occupied Territories. Israel's economic blockade of Gaza meant that all exports were halted and imports were heavily restricted. The Gaza Strip, home to 1.5 million Palestinians, was left without power for several hours every day.[14] In June 2006, Hamas called for the formation of a government of national unity ready to open peace negotiations. The next day, Israel bombed power stations and civilian houses in retaliation for the capture of one Israeli soldier by Palestinians.

The provision of resources by Hamas

Hamas provides the social welfare, health care, education, and cultural and sporting institutions that are crucial for Palestinians living under Israeli occupation. This has greatly contributed to their popular support. Similar to Hezbollah, Hamas's provision of resources is transparently conducted through charity organisations, mosques, unions, schools and sports clubs. The Israelis have tried, with the help of the PA, to close down Hamas's social work institutions and to freeze their bank accounts. But they have faced street demonstrations by hundreds of thousands of Palestinians, including Fatah supporters,

Christians, secular groups and other communities, who receive the social welfare services provided by Hamas.

Without the provision of resources by Hamas, Palestinians could not survive. Palestinians pay taxes to Israel, but the Zionist state refuses to provide resources for them. As an occupier, according to international law, the State of Israel is responsible for providing resources for the occupied population, but it refuses to do so on the grounds that this is the responsibility of the PA. However, the bulk of PA revenue goes towards strengthening the Palestinian police force, which is often used to silence the resistance movement. The social, educational and medical provision from the UN and an army of NGOs is ineffective, mainly because the USA and Europe allow Israel to dictate what aid can be given and what cannot (Said 1995: 47–50; Masalha 2007: 217: Hroub 2006: vii–xix, 18–19, 66–8, 90–91; Tamimi 2007: 220). In fact, many Palestinians are hostile to aid agencies as they see them as perpetuating the Zionist political agenda. In an interview with me in Jayyus, Hannah commented:

> This school was built by the US Agency for International Development [USAID]. We asked them to build the school away from the wall, because we don't want our children to see the wall on a daily basis. But they insisted on building it here so that, in their view, the children accept it as a reality and do not fight it. People in the village hate USAID, and in response children have drawn massive paintings on the wall of the school facing the Zionists' wall saying that we will continue to resist.

These experiences of Palestinians clearly demonstrate that the popularity of Hamas is due to the brutal occupation of Palestine and the systematic marginalisation of the secular left and nationalists by the West. In this context, similar to Hezbollah, Hamas emerged as an effective resistance movement and has provided social welfare where the state fails to play this important role for its citizens. Of course, Hezbollah and Hamas are quite different organisations in terms of the Sunni and Shi'a divide, and there are other differences based on the different state formation, social structure and politics of the two countries (Hilal 2007: 7).

As with Hezbollah, the funding of Hamas is wrongly perceived by the West as coming from Iran alone. For decades, funding has come from both pro- and anti-US countries in the region (Kuwait, Iran, Saudi Arabia, the Gulf States, Sudan and Algeria). During the Iraqi occupation of Kuwait, the PLO supported Iraq but Hamas criticised the occupation and also blamed US policy in the region. It was in this context that it continued to receive funding from Iran and Kuwait. This was also a period of ascendancy for the Islamic movements. Many Gulf countries and other Muslim-majority societies in the region which were funding the PLO saw Hamas as the alternative to the PLO and transferred their financial support in order to weaken the secular group and strengthen Hamas. Rich Muslim business people are the main source of Hamas's funding, and Hamas also receives money from Islamist organisations and individuals in the USA and Europe. All money transfers to Hamas are carried out by Western and Israeli banks under close monitoring (Ahmad 1994: 93; Hroub 2006: 95–7; Masalha 2007: 223).

In August 2009, Israel allowed a limited number of trucks supplying food to enter Gaza, and the 'tunnel economy' between Egypt and Gaza also became operational. Hamas is in charge of profitable trade and investment, has managed to establish an insurance company and a bank, and is buying up much of Gaza's real estate. Nevertheless, the 'Tunnel Economy' remains highly vulnerable to continued Egyptian and Israeli pressures,[15] and Hamas has faced systematic blockades by the USA, the EU and the PA. Moreover, the organisation faces acute funding shortages, as it inherited from its Fatah-controlled predecessor massive bank debts and a huge bureaucracy with more than 160,000 employees, including a police force committed to repressing the resistance movement. Furthermore, the organisation faces sanctions by the USA, the EU and Israel and for withholding millions of dollars every month as tax revenues it collects from the PA. Nevertheless, Hamas has survived[16] (Hroub 2006: 70–72; Tamimi 2007: 230).

The acute shortages of funds, as well as divisions within the leadership of the Palestinian resistance movement, have impacted on Hamas's ability to provide social services. As a result, many women have taken the initiative to work with grassroots communities, offering health care, education and sports, and empowering projects through confidence-building and the creation of solidarity and cohesion. Eileen Kuttab, an academic and activist and a leading member of Bisan Research and Development Centre, explained to me in Birzeit:

> Bisan is part of the historic Palestine. We work in Jenin, Hebron and other villages and link them with Bisan. We try to raise awareness by talking to them about the resistance movement and boycotting Israeli goods. We follow Paulo Freire's method of educating them to resist.[17] We try to promote the concepts of self-reliance and community-based organisation and through participatory work help people to survive. In this context the model of Hezbollah is important for us because they have managed to unite different communities.

Hoda, an academic and activist at Al-Quds University, is an elected member of a women's association in East Jerusalem, which is under Israeli control. They also try to provide education and health care and to help families with their day-to-day problems. She observed:

> There are many Women's Associations in Palestine run by Fatah, Hamas and other political organisations. But the Israelis put massive obstacles in our way. For this reason, some of these associations work from Abudis with women in East Jerusalem. Outside of Israeli control we are more effective. We do networking with other Women's Associations, no matter what their political affiliation (Fatah, Hamas, Jihad, PFLP and others...); we work together to meet the needs of women.

Israeli wars unite Palestinians against Israel

As was discussed in Chapter 4, Israel's attack on Hamas and Hezbollah in the summer of 2006 was intended to demonstrate that it is prepared to destroy those organisations that challenge its military might in the region. It is also indirectly a message to Iran and Syria about what they may face if they do not toe the US policy line in the region (Hilal 2007:10–11). According to Ehud Olmert (Israel's prime minister, 2006–09), the large-scale military assault on Gaza was carried out to free an abducted soldier. On these grounds, they attacked power plants and left Gaza in darkness. They fired missiles at civilian areas including a playground, a funeral procession and children playing on the beaches.[18]

The 2009 war on Gaza (27 December 2008–18 January 2009) became known as the Gaza massacre. Israel launched a military attack and used phosphorus on civilian areas in retaliation for rocket attacks on southern Israel and alleged arms smuggling into Gaza. They killed 1,400 Palestinians. More than 400,000 Gazans were left without running water and 4,000 homes were destroyed or badly damaged, leaving tens of thousands of people homeless. Eighty government buildings were hit and unarmed civilians carrying white flags were killed. They used Palestinians as human shields, a breach of the Geneva Convention. Israeli forces targeted Hamas bases, police training camps, police headquarters, offices and civilian infrastructure, including mosques, houses, medical facilities and schools, on the grounds that these buildings were used by Hamas fighters and as storage spaces for weapons and rockets.[19] According to the Red Cross, thousands of Gazans whose homes were destroyed in this massacre are still, in 2010, without shelter, despite pledges of almost $4.5 billion in aid, because Israel refuses to allow cement and other building materials into the Gaza Strip. Hospitals continue to struggle to meet the needs of their patients due to Israel's disruption of medical supplies,[20] and 95 per cent of Gaza's water fails to meet World Health Organisation standards. The extremely high nitrate levels in the water supply are placing thousands of newborn babies at risk of poisoning. Aid agencies are banned from having any contact with Hamas. This means that the aid agencies are not able to repair water and sanitation facilities.[21]

During the Gaza war, there were three attacks on Israel from Lebanon by Hezbollah's supporters. The war on Gaza united Palestinians against Israel. Yousef, a teacher and activist and a Fatah supporter in East Jerusalem, observed:

The infighting that we see between different communities in Palestine is between the elites, not among the ordinary people. The ordinary people feel that they have been cheated by both leaderships. For ordinary Palestinians, our enemy is Israel, no matter whether we support Fatah, Hamas, Jihad, PFLP or the communists. In Gaza we fought alongside each other against Israel. There is a saying in Arabic: Me and my brother against my cousin, and me and my cousin against the outsider.

Israel's policies strengthen Iran and Hamas

The Palestinians are the most secular people in the Middle East. Palestinian secular nationalist orientation persists and there is very little in the way of sectarian politics in Palestine. In this context, the support for Hezbollah, Iran and Hamas can only be explained by the success of Hezbollah in South Lebanon; its hugely effective resistance eventually managed to drive the Israeli army out of Lebanon in 2000. Since the Iraq invasion in 2003, the pro-West and Israeli media have emphasised and exaggerated the Sunni and Shi'a divide in order to weaken the social fabric of the region and ensure Israel is its only power. Despite this powerful propaganda, when Hezbollah won the war against Israel in 2006, this victory once again made a big impression on the Palestinians. People forgot about the Shi'a–Sunni divide and supported Hezbollah and Iran. For them, their national identity and dignity are more important than the Sunni and Shi'a divide. Islah Jad, an academic at Birzeit University, commented:

In that war, people witnessed that Hariri, who is a Sunni supported by the West, did not care about Israel's attack on Lebanon. In contrast, Hezbollah united with Christian and Palestinian Sunnis against Israel's attack. In this context, for the majority of the people in the region Hezbollah and Nasrallah have been the Arab leaders since 2006. In most households and shops people have put up Nasrallah's picture on their walls. In demonstrations, people hold up his picture and the Hezbollah flag, chanting 'he is our leader'. This is because Hezbollah and Nasrallah are defiant, dignified and victorious over Israel, the avowed enemy of the Palestinians and the Lebanese. After the war, the PA began to point again to the

Sunni–Shi'a divide, saying that the situation was about Iranian and Shi'a domination over Sunni religion and culture in the region. People began to ask why no Sunni leader in the Arab world had supported the Palestinians against the Zionists. As a consequence, they came to the conclusion that, despite the insistence of the Western, Zionist and most Arab media, the conflict had nothing to do with religion or the Sunni and Shi'a divide. Instead, it was a case of who wanted to be submissive to the Israelis and their Western allies and who did not; who was supporting the Palestinians against the crimes of Israel and who was not.

Many Palestinians are impressed with Hezbollah's pluralism and see them as modern Islamists and a model to emulate. This also means that the majority of Palestinians are not supporters of al-Qaeda, bin Laden and other fanatical Islamists. The Hamas and Hezbollah cooperation represents the new face of political Islam. It is not fanatical and conservative; it is pluralistic and concentrates on the struggle against Zionism and imperialism, which is popular in the region. May is a member of Ibn Albalad, a democratic secular organisation believing in the one-state solution which was the original manifesto of the PLO. When we met, she argued that

> Since 1983, Hezbollah have became popular in Palestine because they have allied with Christians, Druze and Palestinian Sunnis in Lebanon; they have supported the whole of the resistance movement, not just Hamas; and they have advocated unity between all groups in Palestine. In Lebanon, we see cooperation between Hezbollah and other forces, including the leftist and secular groups. In Gaza, we see cooperation between Hamas and different groups, including the grassroots Fatah supporters. According to Fatah and PFLP supporters in Gaza, the Hamas leadership is learning from the majority of their supporters that they cannot impose their rigidities on their supporters and have to be tolerant. At first they imposed the hijab on women, but later stopped this imposition. Now many women without the hijab support Hamas in Gaza and other parts of Palestine.

As discussed in Chapter 4, the inherent contradiction in Hezbollah's religio-political stance and pressure from the grassroots changed the nature of the organisation.[22] Whether Hamas will also change to that extent remains to be seen. The religious drive within Hamas is visible and powerful. Consequently, many Palestinians are concerned about Hamas's intention to Islamise politically secular and socially liberal Palestinian institutions and replace them with a socially conservative agenda. Omar Barghouti, a founding committee member of the Palestinian Campaign for the Academic and Cultural Boycott of Israel (PACBI),[23] explained to me in Ramallah:

The Wahabi strand of the Sunni sharia can be devastating, especially that it is supported by the autocratic and culturally repressive Saudi Arabian monarchy, which has ample financial resources that enable it to bankroll the spread of its medieval view of Islam. The concept of *ijtihad* in Shi'ism has, in my view, contributed significantly to Hezbollah's openness to alliances with Lebanese Christians, Palestinian Sunnis, Arab nationalists, secularists and even Marxists. Hamas leaders, on the other hand, have not displayed any similar tendency in accepting, let alone creating, significant partnerships with political forces or political activists whose ideologies are not in harmony with their own. Hezbollah employs professionals who may be communist, Christian or unveiled women in their vast network of schools and health-care centres; Hamas do not. By most standards, and despite any criticism of their Islamist views at the socio-cultural and intellectual levels, Hezbollah has proved to be the most sophisticated resistance movement in modern Arab world history. Since 2006 Hamas has effectively hindered the development of arts and cultural centres in Gaza. Hip-hop, for instance, was a flourishing form of cultural expression in the overcrowded refugee camps; now the lyrics are subject to gruelling censorship and performances are substantially constrained by the Hamas authorities. Theatre plays are also subject to heavy censorship and bans. Dance in Gaza has become virtually extinct, except for some bland, male-only performances of folklore. In this respect, Hamas thus displays a Wahabi tendency that many thought was abandoned – or comprehensively reformed – in the movement's transformation from its Muslim Brotherhood origins to a leading Palestinian national resistance movement with a more moderate Islamist outlook on life.

In response, Hamas has frequently declared that it will not impose any religious practices on Palestinians. Indeed, Palestinian society is diverse, with secular, religious, Muslim and Christian members, who have lived side by side for centuries. The majority of this diverse population supports Hamas as a resistance movement against Israel and as a provider of social welfare provision, but not its cultural and religious agenda (Hroub 2006: xviii; 73–5; Masalha 2007: 238–9).[24]

Iran's relationship with Hamas

The relationship between Iran and Hamas is multidimensional, political, ideological and cultural. At the political level, it relates to the isolation of the Palestinians in the Arab world. This relationship must also be seen in the context of the failure of the Arab regimes to support Palestinians. In the eyes of many Palestinians, therefore, Iran is the only country supporting them. Like Hezbollah, Hamas has a full diplomatic relationship with Tehran; it has offices and spokespersons in Iran, operating at political and media levels. But the relationship between Hamas and Iran is different from Iran's relationship with Hezbollah. It has not stemmed from a religio-historical relationship based on Shi'a ideology; it is more a political union. Hamas has similar links with Syria, Sudan, Lebanon and Libya and also enjoys the support of states such as Egypt, Saudi Arabia, Qatar and Kuwait, but of a different kind. These pro-West and pro-US states support Hamas in order to counterbalance the Iranian–Syrian influence. Other countries, such as Pakistan, Malaysia, Indonesia and Turkey, have also received delegations from Hamas in support of the Palestinians.

Contrary to the popular perception created by Western media and politicians who associate the organisation with Iran, Hamas, under the influence of the Muslim Brotherhood, is particularly impressed by the moderate Islamist ruling parties in Turkey and Malaysia, more so than it is by Iran. Senior Hamas officials have visited these countries, which have sent diplomats to communicate with Hamas. These official links are important for Hamas, as it tries to change its image as a 'terrorist organisation' and to take over from the PLO in representing the Palestinians. At the same time, its relationship with anti-Israel and anti-US camps, such as Iran, has been instrumental in raising funds and mobilising public opinion in the region and beyond (Tamimi 2007: 77–8; Hroub, 2006: 93–5).

Palestinian views about Iran's support for Hamas are divided. Tania, who identifies herself as a secular (from a Christian background), left-wing nationalist and feminist, argued:

> In my opinion, Iran may have its own agenda in the Middle East, but I prefer its role in comparison with the role of the USA. For me, the real enemy is Zionism and not Iran. In this context, I support Iran and Hamas. We have to unite against the occupation. Of course I am worried about the influence of sharia laws associated with Sunni Hamas or Iranian Shi'ism. But we have to look for alliances in order to win. We suffer enormously from the occupation, and Hamas, Iran and Hezbollah have been able to stand up against Zionism.

But the Fatah leadership accuses Hamas of following Shi'a Iran and its agenda. Ammar, a Palestinian Fatah supporter in East Jerusalem, explained to me:

> Iran became important for Palestine after the 1979 revolution, especially when Arafat visited Iran. But today we feel that Iran's support for Hamas is divisive. The movement in Palestine is not just Hamas; it is Fatah, the communists, Jihad and Hamas. Iran supports Hamas because it has its own agenda of dominating the region with its Shi'a ideology. US support for Fatah and Iranian support for Hamas are negative for the Palestinian movement. The Sunni and Shi'a divide is dangerous in the region and Iran is intensifying the situation. These alliances are not in the interest of the Palestinian people because each side has its own agenda. The unity between Hamas, Fatah and Hezbollah is only positive when it is free from the agendas of different governments in the region. The unity between Shi'a, Sunni, Christians and Jews is positive, but governments in the region use religion to divide people. We have to liberate ourselves with our own efforts. The Iranian Revolution succeeded because the people of Iran did it themselves. The first intifada was successful because the Palestinian people initiated it

themselves. The second intifada was not successful because the leaders, who had their own agenda, influenced it.

Islah Jad, an academic at Birzeit University, does not agree:

> The internal divisions within Palestinian politics are due to the USA and Israel pushing the PA to be passive in the face of the brutal occupation of our land and daily humiliation. In this context, the Palestinians see Iran, Hezbollah, Hamas and Syria as on their side, despite the Shi'a and Sunni divide. Before the 1979 revolution in Iran, the Shah was controlling one side of the region and Israel the other side. Since then, Israel has tried to control and have hegemony over the region. The people of the region cannot accept this, not because of religion, but because the Zionists are committing crimes against Palestinians and are supported by the West. People ask themselves what the Iranian agenda is. If it is opposing Israel, then that is good enough for them to follow that agenda.

It is not just Iran and Hezbollah that are popular. During the war on Gaza, people carried the Venezuelan flag because President Hugo Chávez had supported the Palestinians against Israel. In January 2009, Recep Tayyip Erdogan, the Turkish prime minister, stormed out of a discussion on Gaza at the World Economic Forum in Davos. This was a verbal and political response to Israel's war on Gaza. He received a hero's welcome when he returned to Istanbul, which reflects the growing opposition among the Turkish population to the country's good relations with Israel. The following day he became a hero to the Palestinians. His picture and the Turkish flag were put up in shops and on the streets. Hezbollah also issued a statement praising Erdogan for his speech at the UN General Assembly in New York in September 2009. His statement described Erdogan's speech as 'courageous and committed to international causes, especially the Palestinian cause'. Hezbollah's head of foreign relations, Ammar al-Mousawi, also praised Erdogan's call to the international community to focus on Israel's nuclear weapons rather than Iran's nuclear programme, adding that he also hoped that the Arab countries would follow Turkey's footsteps.[25]

As many Palestinians will explain, religion and politics overlap in the region. People in Palestine and nearby, for the first time since Gamal Abdel Nasser, are hearing a voice that stands up to the crimes committed by Israel and the USA in Palestine. It is in this context that Iran has become an alternative power to the USA for the region. People in Palestine welcome Iran's support in fighting Zionism and the occupation, but they don't want it to dominate the region in terms of Arab nationalism and Shi'ism. For them, Iraq is an Arab country that is being destroyed by the Americans, with Iran complicit in its ruin. But they see Iran's role as less problematic than the shameful position of Arab leaders who are openly pro-US and pro-Israel. The Arab regimes in the region have focused all their energy on portraying Iran as the enemy and not Israel. Some governments have now realised that they could be toppled by the anger of their own populations, which are subjugated terribly by Zionism and imperialism. This is parallel to Hamas's situation: people support Hamas not because it is religious and fanatical, but because it is the only resistance movement.

Osama, a political activist in Haifa, argued:

Iran presents a model which is new to the Arab public. The Arab public is used to associating civilisation and development with the West and Westernism. In recent years, Iran has provided a new model of development and civilisation. People are fed up with the hypocrisy of the West and are looking for an Islamic, Eastern or Middle Eastern civilisation.

Despite strong support for Iran in Palestine, the post-2009 election uprising in Iran raised questions for many Palestinians. Although many people felt suspicious of the Western, Israeli and Arab media's support for the democracy movement in Iran and wondered if it was an attempt to destabilise the country, the majority were sympathetic to the movement. Rifat, a Palestinian activist in London, explained:

We have always been critical of the role of Iran in Iraq. Now the persecution of the democracy activists in Iran is raising a question for us: how can we trust a regime which is not accountable to its own people? If they are not able to deliver for their own population, how can they deliver for us? Certainly after the revolution their rhetoric was important, but the recent rhetoric is not useful for Palestinians.

Hamas in power

Hamas in power is different from Hamas in opposition. It is not a homogenous organisation; it has a military wing, a religious wing and a political wing. Hamas has used violence against Israel and Fatah, but, as was discussed above, in the 2006 election it stood on a platform of law, order and social welfare. Prior to the election, Hamas dropped from its election manifesto the call for the destruction of Israel, bringing them closer to the Fatah position of a two-state solution that it had previously denounced. Since the election, its nationalist position on the liberation of historic Palestine from the River Jordan to the Mediterranean Sea has been toned down. Mahmoud al-Zahhar, Hamas's foreign minister, wrote to Kofi Annan, the UN secretary general, declaring that his government was willing to accept the two-state solution based on the 1967 borders, with Jerusalem as its capital with genuine sovereignty.[26] Thus the organisation is moving towards a pragmatic nationalism and away from militant Islamism (Hroub 2006: 21–30, 40, 108; Masalha 2007: 230–31). However, this is a concern for many Palestinians. Leila, a Palestinian activist whom I talked to in London, argued that

Recent discussions about recognising the State of Israel were like a bomb dropped on the heads of the majority of the Palestinians and the people of the Middle East. If the idea is not to truly represent the aspirations of the Palestinians, but rather to play to the tune of the USA, then Fatah is a better model than Hamas for this job. Hamas was supposed to deliver on the Palestinians' political vision and agenda. But now it is moving away from this model and embracing a Fatah model. If Hamas does not deliver in power, it will lose its image as a resistance movement.

The role of Iran has also been modified. In 2006, Ayatollah Khamenei stated that Iran and the Arab countries share a common view on the issue of Palestine, implying that Iran accepts the Arab League's 2002 Beirut Declaration calling for normalisation of relations with Israel. Nasrallah has also repeatedly stated that, although as a Lebanese organisation Hezbollah does not recognise the legitimacy of the State of Israel, it would not oppose a Palestinian decision in favour of a two-state solution (Chomsky 2007: xvi).

For Iran, Hamas's victory in the 2006 election was important. Iran's relationships with the Iraqi government, the Syrian government, Hezbollah in Lebanon and Hamas in Palestine are a strong bloc against US and Israeli policies in the region. This support, together with grassroots support for Iran's policy against the USA and Israel, put Iran in a strong position to defend itself against possible attacks from these two countries. Hamas also benefits from Iran's support as it allows them to entice Iran's rivals, Egypt, Saudi Arabia and Turkey, to support them. Indeed, these countries are concerned about Hamas falling into Iran's sphere of power and influence (Hroub 2006: 103–4, 154).

For Hamas, its relationship with Turkey is more important than its relationship with Iran. Turkey is a member of NATO and has invited a high-level Hamas delegation to Ankara. Although the USA and Israel have put pressure on Turkey, the country has offered mediation between Israel and Hamas. In 2009, Erdogan argued that an Israeli–Palestinian agreement would have to include Hamas as a party of change and reform.[27] Hamas, with its roots in the Muslim Brotherhood, and within the context of Palestinian nationalism, has demonstrated its readiness to adopt pragmatic and conciliatory programmes and follow the ruling party in Turkey.

When Israel attacked the Gaza aid flotilla in international waters in June 2010 and killed nine Turkish activists, Turkey became even more popular in Palestine and throughout the region. By standing up to Israel, the Turkish government benefited domestically and regionally.[28]

As is argued by Hilal, Islam provides ideological cover for all sorts of political and social formations (Hilal 2007: 6–7), and this is apparent in Iran's and Hezbollah's foreign policies. Socio-economic and political circumstances have constantly shifted the boundaries between conservative Islam and liberal-democratic Islam in the Middle East; these diverse Islamists are in different ways seeking compromise with liberal democracy. Their commonality is their anti-imperialist and anti-Zionist stance; however, they are prepared to collaborate with neoliberalism and imperialism, so long as the barriers to building independent states and societies are removed.

SEVEN

The relationship between
Iran and Egypt

Since 1500, Egypt has been host to many peoples and cultures, including Iranians, Turks, Greeks and Italians (Bayat and Baktiari 2002: 305). The relationship between Iran and Egypt dates back to 550–486 BCE when the construction of the Suez Canal, which began under the reign of Necho II, was completed by Darius I of Persia, linking the Red Sea to the River Nile, thus connecting the Mediterranean to the Indian Ocean (Kadivar 1994: 96–100; Katouzian 2009: 34). The Ismaili Shi'a movement, led by Abdullah, son of Meimun, known as al-Qaddah, who was of Iranian descent, was influential in the establishment of the Fatimid Caliphate (909–1171 CE) in Egypt and North Africa. During the reign of al-Mustansir (1035–1094 CE), an important era of Fatimid rule, the great Iranian poet and thinker Nasser Khosraw visited Cairo and was converted to the Isma'ili Shi'a[1] (Katouzian 2009: 79, 97). As was discussed in Chapter 3, Shi'ism was strong in North Africa and Southern Syria in this period, while Iran was at the centre of Sunni theology. As Shi'ism declined in North Africa and Syria, Iran became the centre of Shi'ism.

Capitalist development in nineteenth-century Egypt was similar to that in Iran. These developments were fundamentally driven by the European capitalist markets' need to import from these countries. As was discussed in Chapter 1, the process of integrating Iran into the world economy was through oil. In Egypt, this process was driven by the cultivation of cotton and its export to Europe. The rapid expansion of cotton cultivation transformed agricultural land into private property and restructured agrarian social relations (Beinin and Lockman 1987).

As in Iran and Iraq, Egypt's ulema played the role of intermediary between religion and the people, and many participated in the anti-colonial movement. Muhammad Ali, the Ottoman governor of Egypt between 1805 and 1848, shaped the modern economy and society of Egypt and challenged European economic domination. Under his rule, the ulema were offered income from farm taxes and endowments and were consulted politically. However, he later subordinated them to paid employees of the state (Bayat 2005: 36–7).

European investors developed a modern infrastructure, including the reconstruction of the Suez Canal, which was completed in 1869. Economic development in this era was, therefore, facilitated by foreign capital. Industries and transport enterprises were mainly owned and controlled by non-Egyptians. Egypt was pushed into significant debt to European creditors. As a result, a massive resistance movement against European political and cultural domination emerged, and in 1881 Britain invaded Egypt to safeguard foreign interests. By the end of the nineteenth century, the vast majority of the Egyptian peasantry were landless, while a new class of large landowners had emerged to become the dominant class until the land reform of 1952 (Hourani 1991: 283, 287; Beinin and Lockman 1987: 8–9).

The impact of market relations was not just economic but also involved the distribution of power and culture. Throughout the late nineteenth and early twentieth centuries, workers and peasants challenged exploitative social relations. The protests and strikes of service workers, in particular, played a significant role in the development of nationalism (Chalcraft 2004, 2008: 69–90). Lord Cromer was the British colonial administrator in Egypt from 1879 to 1907. Although he believed that Egyptian women should be liberated from Islam and Muslim men, he was against women's education and opposed to women being treated by female doctors, as he believed that 'throughout the civilised world attendance by medical men is still the rule'. Women therefore also played an important role in the nationalist movement (Ahmed 1992: 153).

Sayyid Jamal al-Din al-Afghani (1838–1897), who was born in Iran and received a Shi'a education, was a pioneer of Islamic modernism. He changed Islam from merely a religious faith into a religio-political ideology and emphasised resistance to Western domination. He wrote in Arabic and lived in Egypt from 1871 to 1879, where he taught Islamic philosophy and advocated anti-colonial activities. In 1879, he was expelled from Egypt for his anti-British speeches. After his expulsion, his followers continued their involvement in nationalist politics. Muhammad Abduh (1849–1905) and Rashid Rida (1865–1935) were influenced by Afghani and, despite their differences,[2] worked together to pioneer the Islamic modernist school of thought which became prominent from the late nineteenth century (Hourani 1991: 307–8, 1962: 130–244; Keddie 2005: 11–29).

Abduh and Rashid Rida opposed the British rule of Egypt. They were Islamist reformers who believed in the compatibility of Islam with modernism. As is argued by Asef Bayat, the historical evidence demonstrates that this tradition of reform existed in Sunni'ism as much as in Shi'ism (Bayat 2005: 36–7). Abduh advocated the acquisition of modern science, gender equality and women's education, which was curbed by the British. He was critical of the closing of *ijtihad*, and his work amounted to a reinterpretation of Islam for the modern world. His ideas have continued to shape many Muslim reformers throughout Muslim-majority societies and beyond (Ahmed 1992: 137–41; Haddad 2005: 11–29).

As in Iran, Lebanon, Iraq and Palestine, women have played an important role in the socio-history of Egypt. Evidently, the women's movement in Egypt can be traced back to the nineteenth century when educated women, such as Malak Hifni Nassef, regularly wrote articles for newspapers. Women's activism once again was intensified in the early 1900s, when a variety of feminist activist movements emerged, with women establishing women's organisations and participating in the 1919 national revolution and its 1923 constitution.

Sofiya Zaghlul was given the title of Um al-Masriyiin (the mother of the Egyptian nation) for playing a leadership role in the movement. Hoda Sha'rawi established the Egyptian Feminist Union in 1923. Christian women, in particular, played a significant role in this movement. The debate over the emancipation of women also took place among Muslim reformers; and in women's journals, issues such as polygamy, arranged marriages and women's education were debated (Ahmed 1992: 169–88).

The secular nationalists and the left have also played an important role. In 1919 the nationalist al-Wafd Party embodied the struggle for independence. It enjoyed massive support among the rural and urban working classes. However, the organisation lost its hegemony over the labour movement and the majority of the population became disillusioned with liberal nationalism. Its legitimacy was further diminished by its conciliatory attitude towards the monarchy and its inability to resist domination by the large landowners. After World War II, al-Wafd failed to mobilise the people, who were demanding an end to British domination, and could not provide leadership for the mass nationalist resistance movement (Beinin and Lockman 1987: 218–56, 310–94).

In this period, communist organisations grew in strength and influence. In the 1930s and early 1940s, the communists championed workers' demands through strikes, hunger strikes, protest marches and sit-ins. They also provided nationalist legitimacy for the labour movement. However, by the mid-1940s, the communist movement was factionalised and failed to develop grassroots support. Political repression also inflicted major setbacks on both nationalist and communist movements, and they dissolved themselves into the Nasserite state. The communist movement, in particular, lost its influence because it followed the Soviet Union and Stalin's endorsement of a partitioned Palestine and the establishment of the State of Israel (Beinin and Lockman 1987: 310–11, 327–62).

A new political force, Jama' at al-Ikhwan al-Muslimun, the Society of Muslim Brotherhood, which was established by Hassan al-Banna in 1928, emerged as a rival to the nationalist al-Wafdists and the communists. Hassan al-Banna, a follower of Afghani and Abduh, and his discourse of sharia-minded Sufism gave an added dimension to the tradition of Islamic political struggle. He was a charismatic leader, and under his direction the Muslim Brotherhood played an important role against the British occupation. Al-Banna believed in electoral politics, and ran unsuccessfully in the 1942 and 1945 parliamentary elections (Commins 2005: 125–53; El-Ghobashy 2005: 377). Women's issues were also important within the Brotherhood. The Brotherhood's first women's division, Ferqat al-Akhawaat al-muslimaat (the Muslim Sisters Group), was set up in 1932. During this period, the Sisters' activities were concentrated on charity work, health care and education (Abdel-Latif 2008: 2–3). In the 1930s, the Muslim Brotherhood provided financial aid to the unemployed. They were committed to the mobilisation of civil society through mosques, schools, youth associations, sports, women's organisations, clinics and work co-operatives. The failure of secular liberalism and communism in the 1940s left the Muslim Brotherhood as the viable alternative (Bayat 2005: 40–41).

Iran and Egypt

The relationship between Iran and Egypt at state level was cemented in 1939 when Mohammad Reza, Shah of Iran, married Fauziya, the sister of King Faruq of Egypt. Both monarchies were unpopular with their people for their capitulations to foreign domination, and since the defeat of the Egyptian army in Palestine, King Faruq had been increasingly unpopular in Egypt. During this period the Iranian and Egyptian Islamists also cemented their relationship. In 1947, the Iranian cleric Mohammad Taqi Qommi and Shaykh Mahmud Shaltutu, the rector (1958–63) of Al-Azhar,[3] attempted to effect a rapprochement between Sunnism and Shi'ism. Qommi taught the fiqh of Zaydi[4] and Twelver Shi'a Islam alongside the fiqh of the four Sunni Maddhabs (Traditional Jurisprudence). Following on from these attempts at unification, in 1954 the Muslim Brotherhood invited Navab Safavi, the leader of Iranian Fedayan-e Islam[5] (the Devotees of

Islam), to a conference at Cairo University. In 1959, Twelver Shi'ism was recognised as the fifth school of Islam, and Iranian Studies and the Persian language and literature were promoted by Al-Azhar University. Then, in 1948, a member of the Muslim Brotherhood assassinated the Egyptian prime minister, and the Egyptian authorities' assassinated al-Banna in response (Bayat and Baktiari 2002: 306, 312; Kadivar 1994: 82–94).

As was discussed in Chapter 1, the nationalisation of oil in Iran by Mossadeq in 1951, which was followed by the CIA and MI6 coup d'état and Gamal Abdel Nasser's nationalisation of the Suez Canal in 1956, made Nasser and Mossadeq popular in the region. Nasser was as popular as Mossadeq in Iran, and Mossadeq was as popular as Nasser in Egypt. As is argued by Anne Alexander,

> the sight of British technicians leaving the Abadan oil installations following the nationalisation of the Anglo-Iranian Oil Company by the Iranian government in August 1951 was greeted with jubilation by many Egyptians who saw in the Iranian case a potential model for their own fight for national liberation. British officials and military commanders, as they debated whether to send troops to Abadan, noted with consternation, however, the difficulties of doing so, while dealing simultaneously with popular protest across Egypt and guerrilla attacks in the Canal Zone.[6]

After the CIA coup in Iran, the Shah considered Nasser to be an instrument of communism, and Nasser viewed the Shah as an instrument of imperialism (Katouzian 2009: 278). In 1952, Egypt's King Faruq (1936–52) was forced to abdicate; the monarchy was abolished in 1953 and the movement for national liberation allowed the Free Officers[7] to mobilise and take control. In 1954, the strength of the mass movement forced the British to withdraw from the Suez Canal, but Nasser guaranteed international right of passage through the Canal and compensated many foreign shareholders. In the early years, Nasser and his associates shared many views with the communists and the Muslim Brotherhood. But soon the communists were driven underground, and by 1954 the Muslim Brotherhood leaders were sent to jail. Nasser initially saw Sayyid Qutb, an influential Muslim

Brotherhood ideologue, as a useful ally. But in 1954, the Muslim Brotherhood was banned and members of the organisation were imprisoned and executed. Qutb was also arrested and was executed in 1966 (Tripp 2005: 154–83).

Despite his persecution of the communists and his anti-imperialist stance, Nasser accepted economic aid from both the Soviet Union and the USA. Nevertheless, in the minds of most Egyptians, Nasser overthrew the monarchy, ended British occupation, nationalised the Suez Canal, and carried out land reform and economic development (Alexander 2005: 46–67, 116, 123, 142). Women's activism also continued under Nasser, concentrating on women's rights, advocacy, NGOs and challenging the discourses of male domination (Pratt 2005: 123–50).

In 1956, Britain, France and Israel attacked the Canal, leaving Britain and France in control, with Israel occupying the Sinai Peninsula. Although the movement for democracy continued, defeat in the 1967 war with Israel marked the failure of nationalist and communist movements, not just in Egypt but also elsewhere in the region, and gave rise to guerrilla movements. In 1970, Nasser accepted UN Resolution 242 to bring peace between Israel and the Arab countries (Alexander 2005: 135–51).

As was discussed in the previous chapter, Iran during this period also recognised the State of Israel and supplied it with oil. Although Egypt broke off diplomatic relations with Iran over Israel under Nasser. When Nasser died in 1970, Feraidon Hoveyda, the prime minister of Iran, attended his state funeral (Chubin and Zabih 1974: 140–69). Nasser was replaced by Anwar Sadat (1970–81), who reversed Nasser's economic policy of state subsidies in housing, health care and other benefits and opened up the Egyptian economy to foreign investment. In 1979, he signed a peace treaty with Israel at Camp David. From 1971 to 1973, the secular left and the nationalists continued their struggle for democracy, national sovereignty, and social and economic justice; they also had some impact on the labour movement (Abdallah 1985: 152, 189–91, 224–6).

Sadat released the Muslim Brotherhood leaders who had been in jail under Nasser. The organisation remained illegal, but in 1979 Sadat allowed the Brotherhood to publish the monthly journal al-Dawa (The Call) and rendered the Egyptian penal code compatible with sharia (Abdel-Latif 2008: 5). The journal openly supported Sadat's liberalisation polices, and the organisation was both anti-communist and anti-secular. It built its grassroots support from Islamic student associations and those who were influenced by Sayyid Qutb (Naguib 2009: 109). By the late 1970s and early 1980s, the Muslim Brotherhood, Islamic Jihad and al-Jama'a al-Islamiyya (the Islamic Group), who were also challenging the state, emerged as strong Islamic social movements, active in particular in the context of the media, education and health-care institutions (Bayat 2005: 34–5).

Under Sadat, the diplomatic relationship between Iran and Egypt was restored. Sadat, who was fluent in Farsi, had a close relationship with the Shah. Iran provided loans to Egypt for the reconstruction of Port Said and supported Sadat's decision to make peace with Israel. Nevertheless, the 1979 Iranian Revolution was popular with most Egyptians as well as with the left and the secular nationalists and Islamists. For them, this revolution demonstrated the possibility of defeating a powerful dictator, and Iran was the response of a Muslim nation to imperialist and Zionist aggression (Chubin and Zabih 1974: 140–69; Bayat and Baktiari 2002: 305–16; Kadivar 1994: 187–95). The Shah of Iran fled to the USA and later to Cairo. Sadat, who by this time was becoming unpopular in Egypt for his 'open door' policy to the West and his peaceful attitude towards Israel, welcomed the Shah, who eventually was to die and be buried in Cairo. So revolutionary Iran broke diplomatic relations with Egypt. During the Iran–Iraq war, Egypt became an ally of Iraq and together they joined the Arab Cooperation Council alongside Jordan and Yemen. In 1991, however, Egypt participated in the US-led coalition that drove Iraq out of Kuwait, and after the 2003 Iraq invasion and the fall of Saddam Hussein, Egypt was reluctant to have a relationship with the now Shi'a/Kurd-dominated state with its link to Iran.

After the Iran–Iraq war, industrial and trade cooperation began between Iran and Egypt. By the end of Rafsanjani's presidency (1989–97), bilateral trade between the two countries had reached $80 million. During Khatami's presidency, there were attempts to improve the relationship through diplomatic visits and the establishment of the Iran–Egypt Friendship Society in Iran. The victory of the reformists in the parliamentary election of 2000 was significant for many Egyptians as they saw Iran as a model for democracy in the Muslim Middle East. This was especially pertinent for them at that time as President Hosni Mubarak had extended the Emergency Law in Egypt. Even Al-Azhar, which is critical of Iran, emphasised that the election had demonstrated that Islam can embrace democracy (Bayat and Baktiari 2002: 320–21).

The June 2009 election in Iran and the ensuing post-election political repression have also been debated by the secular left, nationalists and Islamists in Egypt. The support of the mainstream Arab and Egyptian media for the democracy movement in Iran has raised many issues for Egyptians. Omaima Abou-Bakr, an academic and women's rights activist, commented:

> The June election in Iran was very disappointing because we felt that there were real elections and democracy in Iran. We saw brutality in the streets against the demonstrators. We also witnessed the support of the Western and regional governments for the democracy movement. We were confused and suspicious and are still wondering whether the hand of America is at work in Iran.

Under Ahmadinejad's government there have also been attempts to restore the relationship between Iran and Egypt. In December 2009, Ali Larijani, the speaker of the Iranian parliament, a conservative centrist, attended a meeting of the Parliamentary Union of the Organisation of the Islamic Conference. Although there have been no diplomatic relations between the two countries since 1980, and despite the objection of Iranian conservative hardliners, Larijani met with Mubarak and discussed Palestinian issues, peace and security in the region, and possible trade between the two countries.[8]

The rise of the Islamists

In the preceding chapters, I have examined the influence of Iran in Lebanon, Iraq and Palestine in terms of the wider historical context, such as socio-economic developments, nationalisms, Islamisms and the political trajectory of these experiences, in order to demonstrate how they have produced distinct changes in these societies. In this light, we shall examine here the fall of the secular left and nationalism; the rise of Islamisms as an alternative force; and the contradictions, limitations and dynamic nature of political Islam in Egypt.

Nasser, Sadat and Mubarak exploited the popularity of Islamists in order to consolidate their own hegemony. They also used the Islamists to suppress the secular left and nationalists. Under the governments of Sadat and later Mubarak, who took power in 1981, the secular left and the nationalists were weakened as a result of the disunity between the two groups. Political oppression and the absence of a coherent political programme also contributed to lack of support for them among the majority of the population. In places where they had some support, such as within the labour movement, they were unable to contribute effectively; and they also remained a minority within the pro-government-majority-led unions[9] (Makram-Ebeid 2009).

For Egyptian women's rights activists, the position of the secular left and the nationalists was, and still is, problematic, as they have never prioritised gender equality. In 1982, Nawal El-Saadawi, one of the founders of the Arab Women's Solidarity Association (AWSA), challenged gender inequalities within the home and wider society (El-Saadawi 1980: 235–41). Under Mubarak, several women's rights activists have continued their struggle for gender rights (Hatem 2000: 33–57; Philipp 1978: 277–94; Al-Ali 2000: 51–86). As is argued by Abu-Lughod (1998: 243–69), by appropriating modernist conceptualisations of women's role in society, marital relations and the family, the Islamists thereby began to compete with the secular left, the liberals and the nationalists. Under Mubarak's presidency, UN organisations and international funding bodies have been shaping state policies and the agenda of contemporary women's activism (Al-Ali 2000: 219–21). In the eyes of most people, this has had a negative impact and has increased the popularity of Islamist women's organisations that do not rely on the state and international funding.

Today the aggression of the secular left and nationalists against Islamists has been seized upon by Mubarak's regime as an opportunity to exclude Islamists; these secular forces therefore have often found themselves on the side of the repressive state (Abdelrahman 2009: 117). For all these reasons, the secular left and nationalists have been unable to provide an alternative to Islamism and so have been marginalised, opening the way for Islamist activism. In the early 1970s, the secular left and the nationalists challenged Sadat's regime through cycles of protests. But four decades later, although they are still an important part of the democratic movement against Mubarak, the influence of the Islamists is much greater (Naquib 2006, 2009).

Islamist women's rights activism

Since the beginning of the twenty-first century, the presence of Islamist women's rights activists has been significant. They have played an important role in the growing Islamist movement that believes in the compatibility of Islam, modernism and democracy. They reinterpret Islamic precepts and have thereby struggled for gender equality within the Islamic paradigm, which is popular with many educated young women. They have taken women's rights as their main activity and use religious language and practice to extend these rights. Depending on context, they negotiate gender in different ways. They sometimes find themselves in positions of dominance, able to exercise power within the family and society; at other times they are subordinate.

Omaima Abou-Bakr is a professor of English and Comparative Literature at Cairo University and a leading member of the Women and Memory Organisation in Cairo. Like the Iranian women activists discussed in Chapter 2, Egyptian women here read the history of Islam from an Islamic feminist viewpoint, with the aim of making women in Islam visible. Women have played important political and cultural roles in the history of Egypt, Iraq, Syria, Lebanon and Saudi Arabia; by making these historical examples visible, women activists challenge both Mubarak's secular pro-Western regime and the conservative clergy. This is a difficult task, as they are under attack by both camps. But the younger generation of both women and men respond positively to their call to challenge the regime and the conservative Islamists in the media and in the mosques.[10]

Many Islamist women activists are also engaged in the provision of social welfare. The failure of the state to provide resources to the poor has opened up opportunities for women to provide health care and education for poorer women throughout the country who live in desperately marginalised positions. For these activists, women's participation in the community is essential to the creation of a better Egypt. In this context, changing the erroneous perceptions of Muslim women as passive mothers and wives is an important part of women's religious duty. They are not associated with any Islamist groups and receive no funding from the state. By relying on their own resources and female volunteers such as doctors, nurses and other professional women, they look after orphans and distribute food and other necessities to many poor women and their families. In many cases the women who receive help and whose conditions are ameliorated become volunteers themselves, in order to help others in their communities.

The provision of resources by Islamists

As is the case with Hezbollah in Lebanon and Hamas in Palestine, Islamists in Egypt are engaged in the provision of resources, community development and a social network. They have thus won the support of the majority of Egyptians by becoming a political, cultural and economic alternative to a regime committed to neo-liberalism, authoritarianism, Zionism and imperialism. Under President Mubarak, the process of economic liberalisation has accelerated. In the 1990s, in particular, the private sector expanded through the sale of state industries. In the late 1980s and early 1990s, after the implementation of neoliberal policies, the state withdrew from its role as welfare provider, causing networks of hundreds of aid societies, Islamic charities, and Islamic and secular NGOs to spring up in Egypt. The majority of these NGOs were, and still are, run by various Islamist organisations providing social welfare to poor communities. Many mosques began to provide social services. The funds for these organisations came from zakat and from businesses and migrant workers in the Persian Gulf. It is said that Islamic NGOs have been better financed and managed than the secular NGOs (Wickham 2002: 75; Bayat 2005: 43–4).

In the 1980s, one-third of voluntary organisations were run by Islamists, providing social welfare to millions; by the 1990s, the proportion had increased to half. In the 1980s, these Islamist organisations provided health care for 4.5 million people; by the 1990s, the total had risen to 15 million. They have also provided mosques, schools, video clubs and computer training centres. Secular NGOs have also been engaged in resource provision. However, the involvement of Al-Azhar, together with the Muslim Brotherhood, Jihad and al-Jama'a al-Islamiyya, has made the Islamists' social welfare provision more effective (Bayat 2009: 79–80).

Welfare provision by Islamists is particularly significant. Since the beginning of the twenty-first century, foreign investment has increased and, from 2005 onwards, economic growth has reached 7 per cent per annum. However, an inflation rate of 15 per cent and the high price of imported food have created extreme hardship for much of the population, and the poor in particular. In 2008 there were demonstrations over the long queues for subsidised bread, in which six people died and thirty-five were injured. Informal settlements in Greater Cairo, home to the urban poor, are lacking education, employment and health care; meanwhile in other parts of Cairo gated residential communities with private security services are expanding (Sabry 2009).

Privatisation schemes and drastic cuts in welfare mean that 26.3 per cent of the population of Egypt is unemployed, and the rate is much higher among the 15 to 29 age group. Those in employment face the continuous erosion of real wages, decline in consumption and deteriorating living standards. By World Bank standards, 95 per cent of Egypt's 5.8 million state employees are categorised as poor. Meanwhile the wealthiest 10 per cent of the population receives 29.5 per cent of the nation's income (El-Naggar 2009: 34–50).

Under these economic circumstances, the Islamists became the dominant oppositional force among the urban poor, professionals, students and workers. A range of organisations, such as the Muslim Brotherhood, al-Jama'a al-Islamiyya, Jihad, Tabligh and al-Dawa, contribute to the growing influence of Islamists. The power of Islamic writers, thinkers and preachers who are not affiliated to any particular group is also growing. Israel's violence against Palestinians, the US 'war on terror' and the US call for democracy from above have fuelled nationalist-religious sentiments and have further delegitimised the government (Bayat 2005: 21, 182).

The Muslim Brotherhood and electoral politics

The Muslim Brotherhood is currently the largest of the organisations mentioned above. They have mobilised tens of thousands in opposition to Mubarak. Their support comes from rich and poor, women and men, young and old, although mainly in urban areas. Many of the educated lower classes who in the 1970s benefited from the expansion of the education system have faced unemployment since the 1980s and have become supporters of the Muslim Brotherhood (Bayat 2005: 34–5, 44; Naquib 2006). Thus, the Brotherhood has expanded its mass base in poor urban neighbourhoods among graduates, workers and sections of the urban poor. They have won support by providing social services, and thereby present themselves as an alternative to a state that has failed to provide for them because of its total commitment to neoliberalism and its alliance with the West (Naquib 2009: 114–16).

Since the beginning of the twenty-first century, the Brotherhood's support for the Palestinian intifada, its close relationship with Hamas, and its opposition to the war on Iraq have been popular with the majority of Egyptians. It has even criticised the Gulf countries for not challenging American aggression in the region. In the absence of a secular left and nationalists as an alternative to US and Israeli policies in the region, the Muslim Brotherhood has led mass opposition against the war on Iraq and in protest at Israeli brutality in Palestine. In 2006, it even suggested that it would support Hezbollah against Israel (Naguib 2009: 116–17).

In response to support from diverse communities, the Brotherhood has declared equal citizenship rights for men and women and for Christians and Muslims. This is despite party policy that prevents women and Copts from becoming head of state. There are factions within the Brotherhood who would prefer a more militant confrontation with the state and more cooperation with the secular opposition (El-Hamalawy 2008). But, as is argued by Naguib, the Muslim Brotherhood's change in position is the result of ideological tensions within the organisation and the leadership's determination to satisfy their diverse support base (2009: 117–18).

However, the January 2010 election of a new ultra-conservative leadership was a defeat for the reformist wing of the Muslim Brotherhood. It is especially disappointing for the young members and supporters who have been calling for the organisation's democratisation and for it to join ranks with the secular left and nationalists against the Mubarak regime.[11]

Israel's attack on the Gaza aid flotilla in June 2010 had enormous political ramifications in Egypt. Although the Muslim Brotherhood directed all criticisms at Israel, its young members joined with the secular socialists and nationalists and put demands on Mubarak's government. It wanted a reversal of what has appeared to be the government's slavish support for Israel's Gaza policy and, more generally, the democratic aspirations of the Egyptian people to be respected.[12]

In this regard, Mohamed ElBaradei, the Nobel Peace Prize winner and the former head of the UN's nuclear weapon agency, who is expected to stand in 2011 presidential elections against Mubarak, argued that 'Western governments needed to open their eyes to the realities of Egypt's "sham" democracy, or risk losing all credibility in the battle against extremism. Western governments risk creating a new generation of Islamist extremists, if they continue to support repressive regimes in the Middle East.'[13] Notwithstanding their defeat, this growing reformist current could eventually cause the self-destruction of the conservatives within the Muslim Brotherhood.

In the same vein as Hezbollah in Lebanon and Hamas in Palestine, the Muslim Brotherhood has been challenging the Egyptian state through electoral politics and has been effective in winning support. In the 1970s, it started out as a modern political organisation through electoral politics in professional organisations and local and national assemblies. Over the decades, changes in the social composition of the organisation, internal debates between the older and younger generations on gender issues, attitudes towards the Coptic community, socio-economic circumstances, and regional and international issues have all changed the organisation politically. Throughout the 1980s and 1990s, other Islamist organisations, such as Jihad, that continued their guerrilla activities were subject to more severe state repression and lost their support among ordinary people. The Brotherhood survived as the only significant Islamist organisation, and was particularly strong within the student movement. In 1984, it began participating in doctors' association elections, gaining seven of twenty-five seats on the governing board (El-Ghobashy 2005: 373–4; Wickham 2002: 184).

In the 1980s, the organisation decided to participate in local and national assemblies. But since it was not a political party, it entered into an electoral alliance with the al-Wafd. In 1984, this alliance gained 15.1 per cent of the national vote, while other opposition parties failed to reach the 8 per cent threshold required to qualify for parliamentary representation. In 1987, the Brotherhood switched partners and forged an alliance with both the Labour Party and the Liberal Party, gaining 17.1 per cent of the vote. Meanwhile, the al-Wafd gained 10.9 per cent and the National Progressive Unionist Party (NPUP) only 2.2 per cent. Hence, in these elections, the party bloc encompassing the Brotherhood received more votes than all other opposition parties combined (Wickham 2002: 90; Bayat 2005: 34; El-Ghobashy 2005: 378–81).

By the late 1980s and early 1990s, the Muslim Brotherhood controlled Egypt's major professional associations and unions, including those of doctors, engineers, pharmacists, lawyers, dentists, businessmen and university students. Under their influence, association leaders fought corruption and created social welfare systems and consumer co-operatives. They were also involved in political activities, organising pilgrimages to Mecca to defend Palestine and other human rights issues (Bayat 2005: 44; Naguib 2009: 112–14).

A number of Muslim Brotherhood supporters in the past owned and controlled private enterprises. By the late 1980s, 40 per cent of all private enterprises in Egypt were connected to the Brotherhood. These investment companies subsidised low-income families. The Brotherhood supported the Sadat regime's liberalisation policies, and throughout the 1980s called for more extensive market reform. In 1991, under pressure from the IMF and the World Bank, the state accelerated its neoliberal reform programme through a structural adjustment programme. This led to contradictions emerging in the Brotherhood's economic discourse. In the trade-union elections of 1991 the Brotherhood criticised the neoliberal economic programme and supported workers' right to strike (Naquib 2009: 114; Beinin 2005: 133).

In 1990, the Brotherhood protested against political repression and boycotted the election. But it participated in the 1995 election, securing one seat in parliament; and in the 2000 election it secured seventeen seats (Abdel-Latif 2008: 5–12). In the February 2001 Lawyers Association elections, the Muslim Brotherhood won eight out of twenty-four seats on the executive board, allied itself with secular candidates and avoided any association with Jihad and the al-Jama'a al-Islamiyya (Wickham, 2002: 224–5). In the parliamentary election of November 2005, the Brotherhood won eighty-eight seats – nearly 20 per cent of the seats in parliament. This is despite political restrictions that allowed the organisation to put forward only 150 candidates. In the same election the leftists and liberals won fourteen seats, representing just over 3 per cent of the total vote (Naguib 2009: 103).

In 1996 a number of young Brotherhood members challenged the authoritarianism of the Brotherhood and established the Hizb al-Wasat (the Centre Party) and welcomed gender equality and political pluralism. They gained the support of some prominent secular intellectuals, who saw the organisation as representing a more moderate and enlightened form of political Islam.

As was discussed above, the Muslim Brotherhood, which has supported neoliberal economic policy, criticised the privatisation and dissolution of the public sector in its 2007 electoral programme for the upper house of parliament, under pressure from supporters in the unions and among the poorer sections of society (Naquib 2009: 114–16).

Since the 2000 election the Brotherhood has put forward a number of female candidates for local Egyptian elections, but so far none of them has been elected. In the 2000 parliamentary elections the nomination of Jihan al-Halafawi was significant. She outperformed her ruling party (National Democratic Party, NDP) rival in the first round of the election. In response, the Ministry of the Interior cancelled the result, postponed the election for two years and then allegedly rigged the result in the 2002 election, announcing the victory of two NDP candidates (El-Ghobashy 2005: 374). Jihan al-Halafawi's nomination generated debate within the Muslim Brotherhood about the future of women's activism. Nevertheless, in her constituency even the conservative Islamists organised rallies in her support and mobilised votes for her. In the parliamentary and municipal elections in 2000, 2005 and 2007, women played an important role within the Muslim Brotherhood. They were actively involved in its political activities and demonstrations. A young generation of educated women activists who are critical of their marginal position in the Brotherhood's power structure are challenging the male leadership over their subordinate status. There are a number of Brothers who support the Sisters and there is debate within the organisation on the ban against women running for the presidency (Abdel-Latif 2008: 15–18).

As is the situation in Iran, Lebanon and Palestine, the change in the discourse of the Islamists in Egypt is significant. However, as Bayat argues (2005: 178), the Muslim Brotherhood and other Islamists in Egypt, including al-Wasat, have not yet gone further than the Islamists of the nineteenth and twentieth centuries, such as Muhammad Abduh and Rashid Rida, and they have not matched the Iranian 'religious new thinkers' discussed in Chapter 3. Nevertheless, as is discussed below, the political opposition movement in Egypt has shown the way forward through joint political work and coordination between leftists, nationalists and Islamists. Despite antagonisms between these diverse groups, a younger generation is open to cooperation and is actively calling for the democratisation of society by engaging in campaigns against Western domination and the political repression of their own regime (Abdelrahman 2009).

The client state of the West strengthens Islamists

In 2006, in response to Mubarak's policies, the most politically significant industrial strike took place at the Misr Spinning and Weaving Company in Mahalla al-Kubra. Some 22 per cent of the workforce is female (as two-thirds of all Egyptian families cannot survive on a single income). Women also played an important role in the Mansura-Espana Garment Factory strike. These workers, along with tax collectors, who had managed to organise their own independent union, have played a key role in the movement for democracy, and despite political repression have challenged Mubarak's regime (Beinin 2009: 68–86).

During the tax collectors' strike, many women workers, including those who are heads of their households, joined the street demonstrations. They were criticised by the authorities, including the minister of the labour force Aisha Adel Hadi, but they continued their protests and demonstrations. For many nights they slept in the streets alongside the male workers. Poverty and economic crisis united workers across gender and occupation, and they were optimistic that any victory for the tax collectors would be beneficial to all workers. In the face of poverty and state repression, gender solidarity strengthened. At the same time, many women workers recognised their ability to stand up against the authorities shoulder to shoulder with male workers.[14]

People are also struggling against the state in rural areas. Millions face the threat of losing their land as a result of the implementation of a law permitting landowning families from the colonial era to reclaim their properties – a shift in favour of larger landowners and a consequent increase in the absolute and relative number of landless peasants. These latter are struggling by refusing to return the land (Bush 2009: 51–67).

The Movement for Change (Kifaya, meaning 'Enough'), an umbrella group comprising intellectuals, rights activists, journalists, judges, artists, workers, students, university professors, NGOs, women's groups, Muslims and Coptic Christians, embraced activists of all persuasions – nationalists, socialists, liberals and Islamists. Kifaya, Muslim Brotherhood supporters and other Islamists took to the streets calling for an end to the Emergency Law. Women activists constituted almost half of the demonstrators; Islamist women activists wearing the hijab were particularly visible. The movement went beyond the demand for change in Egypt; they supported the Palestinians, Iraqis and Lebanese and argued against globalisation and US hegemony (Kamel al-Sayyid 2006). Egyptian judges, one of the three arms of the state, also challenged the state, demanding full supervision of elections and real judicial independence. They received the support of NGOs, political parties, the Muslim Brotherhood, professional associations, intellectuals, university professors and students (Bernard-Maugiron 2006).

The Cairo anti-war and anti-imperialist conferences (2003–08), in collaboration with the Journalist Syndicate, brought together the nationalist al-Karama Party, the Muslim Brotherhood, Hizb al-Wasat, Al-Ishtiraqiyiin Al-Thawriyyin (the Socialist Revolutionaries) and Hizb Al-I'mar (the Development Party). These conferences were significant as cooperation between Islamists, nationalists and the left reveals an important feature of the new political activism in Egypt: on the one hand, many Islamist political activists are open to political argument; on the other hand, many secular leftists and nationalists, although critical of the Islamists' projects, refuse to support the regime's suppression of Islamists. This new form of cooperation between different forces provides a new challenge for Mubarak's regime (Abdelrahman 2009).

Islamists as well as secular and socialist anti-war activists from the Middle East, Europe, North America and beyond attended these conferences. In the face of the deepening chaos and crisis throughout the Middle East, and as a result of the catastrophic failure of US, UK and Israeli policies in the region, the conferences provided an opportunity for networking and exchanging ideas and arguments. Zeinab, a supporter of the al-Karama Party and a Kifaya activist, said to me:

> In 1997 and 1998, during the sanctions on Iraq, we established a committee – the 'People's Committee for the Rescue of Iraqi Children'. This committee arranged seven convoys of medical aid for Iraqis as well as political support. We were against the American invasion of Iraq. We believed that the Iraqis themselves should deal with Saddam Hussein's regime. Later, this committee was transformed into the 'International Campaign Against Zionist and American Occupation', which organized The Annual Cairo Anti-War conference, an international summit attended by global anti-war organisations. We have also discussed anti-Zionism and the role of Arab governments in relation to Israel, the West and human rights issues.

Rabab El-Mahdi argues that the first stage of the Egyptian Movement for Change began by challenging Mubarak's fifth six-year term in office and rejecting the prospect of the president's son replacing him. This movement for change was followed by the pro-Palestinian intifada mobilisation of 2000–2001, where one slogan used was 'the road to Jerusalem passes through Cairo',[15] and the anti-war movement of 2003. The Kifaya movement was the 'third cycle' of activism. In 2005 the Kifaya movement began to fade, but in 2006 Egypt's judges mobilised for the independence of the judiciary. As the judges' campaign subsided a new wave of activism developed, this time among workers and professionals (El-Mahdi 2009: 87–102).

In response to the protest movements, the state has intensified political repression. Workers and political activists face imprisonment and torture. The notorious Emergency Law has been renewed until 2010, giving security agencies the authority to detain without charge or trial, and this has led to further brutality. Besides political prisoners, street children are arrested and are physically and sexually abused. Journalists, activists, judges and even members of parliament are subject to imprisonment and violence (Seif El-Dawla 2009: 120–35). Despite the rhetoric of political reform and calls for democracy by the USA and EU, the Egyptian government is currently holding 10,000 people in prolonged detention without charge (Bush 2006).

In 2006, Egypt received US$1.3 billion in military aid and US$490 million in economic aid. This military and economic assistance, together with the joint action plan between the EU and Egypt to promote a Middle East Peace deal and wage the 'war on terror', are determining US and EU influence on Egypt. It is argued that Mubarak's regime extracts rent from the international community for its role in the 'war against terror' and as a broker in the Palestinian–Israel conflict. For many Egyptians who face economic hardship and political repression, the regime's close collaboration with the USA and Israel legitimises their opposition, especially as the country is approaching presidential elections in 2011 (Alexander 2009: 136–50; El-Mahdi and Marfleet 2009: 151–5).

Iran's popularity in Egypt

As was discussed in previous chapters, Iran's relationships with the Syrian government, Hezbollah and Hamas form a strong bloc against US and Israeli policies in the region. And, as we have seen, although the Iraqi government is now a client state of the USA, Iran's good relationship with the Iraqi government and its support for both anti-occupation and pro-occupation forces have earned it security against possible threats from the USA and its allies. More importantly, grassroots support in the region for Iran's anti-US and anti-Israel policies puts the country in a strong position to defend itself against possible attacks. Despite the Sunni and Shi'a divide, the Egyptian government's hostility towards Iran, and the mainstream Egyptian and Arab media's portrayal of Iran as a Shi'a force in the region that threatens Sunni culture and identity, Iran enjoys significant popularity in Egypt. Many see Iran as a model for the conquest of state power, a model for revolutionary practice. Moreover, despite the importance of Arab-nationalist, Iranian nationalist and Sunni–Shi'a divisions, Hezbollah's victory over Israel has changed the nature of these relationships. Hezbollah's Al Manar Television and Secretary General Hassan Nasrallah have become popular in Egypt. In this context, Shaykh al-Qaradawi's speech about the threat of Iran and Shi'ism in the region certainly found an echo, but it also generated debate in Egypt.[16] In 2008, al-Qaradawi, a Qatar-based Egyptian Sunni scholar and influential preacher, who believes in the compatibility of Islam with modern society, argued that Iran is spreading Twelver Sh'ia Islam and thereby threatening Sunni societies. These comments came not from the Egyptian regime or the mainstream media, but from an influential modernist preacher who had issued a fatwa during the 2006 Israeli war on Lebanon, calling for all Muslims to support Hezbollah in their fight against Israel. He was well known for his argument that the Sunni and Shi'a branches of Islam agree on the important principles. His popularity therefore increased, especially when he also called upon the Sunni and Shi'a communities in Iraq to end their conflict. However, his comments about Iran raised debates in Egypt among secular and Islamist intellectuals. Even some of his supporters are critical of his comments and believe that, despite important historical and theological differences between Sunni Islam and Shi'a Islam, these differences are political rather than religious today. For them, unity against US-backed Zionism is more important than the Sunni–Shi'a divide. Mustafa, a member of the Muslim Brotherhood in Cairo, argued thus:

> I do not believe that the Sunni and Shi'a divide is an important issue. Hassan al-Banna was among the first people to encourage rapprochement between the Sunnis and Shi'as. He said that they are the other wing of the umma (Islamic community) and that

there should be a strong relationship between the two. Ordinary
Egyptians do not know much about Shi'a Islam. Some of them
confuse Shi'ism with communism (shiyoui'a) which sounds similar
to Shi'a or Shi'ism. Educated Egyptians, on the other hand,
consider Shi'as to be an important part of the Islamic umma. Prior
to the invasion of Iraq there was no division between Sunnis and
Shi'as. The American invasion of Iraq created the perception of a
serious divide. We need to unite against Zionism in the region.
The war on Lebanon in 2006 brought the Sunnis and Shi'as close
together. Hezbollah's victory in this war was very important and
eye-opening for the Egyptians.

Ahdaf, an Islamist NGO activist and supporter of Hezbollah whose
son married a Shi'a from Lebanon, explained to me:

> As long as someone believes that there is no God but Allah, and
> that the Prophet is the messenger of God, then one is automatically
> a Muslim. We teach our grandchildren to pray in both ways. It is
> good that Iran has power in the region; Muslim nations have to
> have power in the region to stand up to Israel. We must not allow
> foreign powers to divide us; we must unite. The mainstream media
> are against Iran and the Shi'a people, but the majority of people
> look at Hezbollah's struggle and Iran's stand against Israel and do
> not believe the media.

Palestine is an important issue for the Egyptians. Campaigns in
support of Palestinians are popular, despite internal socio-economic
and political crises, although mainstream media and politicians
attempt to distance themselves from the Palestine–Israel issue by
arguing 'we have our own problems, why should we support the
Palestinians?' Support for the Palestinians has increased since 2005,
when Israel withdrew from Gaza, and every time Israel attacks
Palestine and Lebanon Egyptians' support for the Palestinians and
Lebanese increases. The Egyptian government's response in early
2009 was to deploy 750 armed border guards in the northern Sinai
to patrol the border.[17] With the Egyptian government demonstrating
its inability to promote the country's economic or political interests,
Egyptians' grievances are brought into focus by Iran's support for

Palestine and Lebanon. Jihan, a member of the nationalist al-Karama Party in Cairo who has been engaged in a campaign in support of the Palestinians in Gaza, said:

> We organised 40 tonnes of medical supplies to Rafah for our brothers and sisters in Gaza. We demanded the expulsion of the Israeli ambassador and the opening of the Rafah border in order to transport medical aid and rescue supplies to the people of Gaza. The convoys included construction workers, electricians and architects in order to reconstruct Gaza. The closing of the Rafah crossing and the refusal to allow these emergency supplies to the people of Gaza is a crime committed by the Egyptian regime. Unlike Egypt, Iran is in opposition to America and Israel; although it is not an Arab country, it gives strength to Arab demands in the region. It is a country seeking independence, able to build its armaments capabilities to confront America and the Zionist enemy in Palestine. The Egyptian government tries hard to portray Iran as a danger to the Arab umma and as a bigger threat than Israel. But the majority of Egyptian people do not buy this propaganda. We must strengthen our presence and confront America and Israel as two distinct – Arab and Iranian – forces. The mainstream media try to create a bigger gap between Sunni'ism and Shi'ism. But for most Egyptians Iran is the only country which opposes Israel and they admire it for this.

Amany, from the Al-Ishtiraqiyiin Al-Thawriyyin Socialist Revolutionaries, reflected:

> For most Egyptians, Iran is the country which closed down the Israeli embassy after the 1979 revolution, expelled the Israeli ambassador, opened up the Palestinian embassy and supported the Palestinians. In this context, the relationship between the Sunni and Shi'a is now stronger than ever before.

Hossam from the Muslim Brotherhood expressed similar views:

> Iran is a country which does not surrender to American hegemony in the region. It is able to make independent decisions. Egyptians respect Iran for supporting liberation movements in the region and see Iran as a complete contrast to the Egyptian regime. I wish that our regime in Egypt would do the same. Governments in the

region and the Arab media try to portray Iran as the enemy. But Israel's constant attacks on the Palestinians create a more positive image of Iran. Many Egyptians support Iran's nuclear capabilities and think that Egypt should have some because we are next door to Israel, a country with nuclear bombs that is a real threat to us. Iran, Turkey and the Arab World should unite against Zionism and American imperialism.

Despite their admiration for Iran, many Egyptians are critical of the country's role in Iraq. Like the Palestinians, they see Turkey as the real model, particularly since its change in position and support for the Palestinians. Sameh argued:

I commend Iran for supporting liberation movements in the region, but I am critical of its role in Iraq. I am also critical of the Turkish government's military and economic ties with Israel. But the war on Gaza has changed Turkey's relationship with Israel. Turkey is a good model as it has shown that an Islamic movement can come to power. I also admire the Turkish way of secularizing society. In this context I also prefer Turkey to Iran.

Egyptian nationalism and Arab nationalism remain powerful forces in Egypt. Many people make a distinction between nationalism and the state – they have lost faith in the state as their protector. At the same time, nationalism coexists with Muslim identity and a strong feeling of belonging to the non-Arab Muslim world. The ideal of a good relationship between Iran, Turkey and the Arab world is popular. After the 2003 US-led invasion of Iraq and the fall of Saddam Hussein, Egypt was reluctant to have a relationship with the Iraqi regime given its links to Iran. However, in late 2009 and early 2010, the Egyptian government opened up trade links with Iraq to reduce Iranian influence in Iraq.[18] But for many Egyptians, ties between Iran, Turkey and the Arab world would strengthen the region against Zionism and its Western backers. As so many Egyptians, as well as Palestinians, Iraqis and Lebanese, have repeatedly stressed: 'Me and my brother against my cousin, but me and my cousin against the stranger.'

EIGHT

The global context
of Iranian state and society

This book is about the internal socio-economic and political dynamics of Iran and its regional influence, created by its character as a religio-political state. The informed voices of Iranians, Lebanese, Iraqis, Palestinians and Egyptians it records serve to demonstrate how the pressure from diverse communities within Iran and throughout the region has been shaping Iran's domestic, regional and international roles.

The first three chapters concentrate on the complexity of Iran's institutional structures. They demonstrate socio-economic and political developments as well as the undeniable shortcomings of the Iranian state and society since the 1979 revolution. These developments have created contradictions within the Islamic state and society and have led to the formation of a strong democracy movement since the mid-1990s. This is not new, but is the continuation of historical movements from the 1906–07 Constitutional Revolution to the Iranian oil nationalisation of 1951 and the 1979 revolution, all of which have in common the struggle for democracy and independence from imperial domination.

For decades, this struggle threatened the West's economic and political interests in Iran. The global players, particularly the USA, have responded by suppressing the secular left and nationalist movements in Iran, and indeed in the wider region, and in more recent years have moved against the Islamist movements. They have supported dictatorial regimes and have created extremists such as the Taliban and al-Qaeda to secure their economic and political interests. The Islamist movements that have replaced the secular left and nationalist social movements have won the support of the majority of the people in the region precisely by expressing opposition to US and Israeli policies. The West has, therefore, continued its hostility towards these movements, despite the fact that, under pressure from the majority, the dominant Islamist movements believe in the compatibility of Islam, modernism and democracy.

Such perceived Islamophobia has reinforced a profound feeling of outrage among a majority of the people across the Middle East. As they feel their culture under intense attack, they have embraced further religiosity and nationalism. The US call for democracy from above has fuelled nationalist-religious sentiment and has delegitimised the pro-Western governments in the region. The examples of Iraq and Afghanistan, the 'war on terror', Guantánamo, Abu Ghraib in Iraq and Bagram in Afghanistan have all exposed the West's flawed rhetoric regarding the installation of liberal democracy in the Middle East. As discussed in this book, where people have been given the chance to vote, they have voted overwhelmingly for Hezbollah, Hamas and the Muslim Brotherhood. As is argued by Arrighi (2005), the West, in particular the USA, is facing a crisis of regional and international legitimacy. The rhetoric of human rights, women's rights and democracy no longer has an echo in the Middle East and beyond.

In this context, Chapters 4 to 7 have focused on how Iran is perceived in various communities in Lebanon, Iraq, Palestine and Egypt. To conceptualise the influence of Iran in the region, we have looked at the response of different communities to both Iran's and US foreign policy. The conclusion is that the failure of Israeli and Western policies in the region has served to strengthen Iran's position in relation to its neighbours – its regional influence and role are now greatly enhanced by its defiant stance. A majority of the population in the region view their own national governments as client states of the USA, which are sacrificing the economic, political and cultural interests of their people to that of neoliberalism and Zionism. Many see Iran as a model for the conquest of state power, a model of revolutionary practice. In this context, despite diverse forms of nationalism, the Sunni–Shi'a divide, and powerful global media portraying Iran as a Shi'a force threatening Sunni culture and Arab nationalist identity, Iran's popularity continues to grow. This concluding chapter concentrates on the global context of the Iranian religio-political state, and how, since the 1979 revolution, the popularity of Iran's foreign policy with the people in the Middle East has alienated the West and has led to hostility towards Iran.

'You are either with us or with the terrorists'

The 1979 revolution threatened the economic and strategic interests of the USA and its allies as Iran withdrew from military and commercial cooperation with the West and the region. The revolution also challenged the socio-political interests of the West, as the majority of the people across the Middle East were inspired to question their own pro-Western regimes. This continuing lack of care regarding issues such as poverty, unemployment and the lack of basic human rights today is leading the people of the region's pro-Western regimes to challenge their leaderships. In this context the popularity of Iran is threatening the political influence of the West in the region.

In January 1980, US president Jimmy Carter announced that any attempt to gain control of the Persian Gulf was an assault on the interests of the USA and would be confronted by any means necessary, including military force (Callinicos 2009: 182). Henry Kissinger, US secretary of state 1972–77, has repeatedly argued that the USA is willing to cooperate with Iran as long as the country's policies matched Washington's views, otherwise Washington would take action to damage Iran's influence in the region (Bennis 2009: 99). In the early

1990s, Paul Wolfowitz, undersecretary of defence 2001–05, outlined the neoconservative strategy in the Middle East and Southwest Asia as 'to remain the predominant power in the region and preserve US and Western access to the region's oil'.[1] In January 2010, at the London Chilcot Iraq Inquiry, which was meant to draw lessons from the war on Iraq, Tony Blair, UK prime minister 1997–2007, mentioned Iran fifty-eight times. Without showing remorse for the bloodshed his policies had helped to produce in Iraq, he called for a war against Iran by arguing that, with its link to terrorist groups, it posed a particularly dangerous threat and was responsible for much of the destabilisation of the Middle East today.[2]

The common denominator in all such comments is that expressed in George W. Bush's infamous statement of September 2001, in an address to the US Congress, when he told countries around the world: 'You are either with us or with the terrorists.' In other words, a country in the Middle East faces the threat of retaliation if it challenges the West's interests economically and politically.

War on Iran

During the Iran–Iraq war of 1980–88 the USA backed the regime of Saddam Hussein as a means of containing the Iranian Revolution. During 1986–88, in response to the prospect of an Iranian victory over Iraq, American naval and air power was deployed to ensure that Iraq did not lose the war. However, as was discussed in Chapter 5, Saddam Hussein (whom the USA promoted as a counterweight to Iran) stepped out of line of the global hierarchy of economic and military power by seizing Kuwait in 1990. Consequently Iraq was invaded and occupied, which led to the fall of Saddam. The war on Iraq did not produce a reconciliation with Iran, but was a policy of 'dual containment' aimed at both countries, pursued by Bush Senior, and followed by Bill Clinton after the 1991 Gulf War (Callinicos 2003: 42–4, 2006).

As was discussed in Chapter 1, the consequence of the Iran–Iraq war for Iran was the creation of a state of emergency, leading to a far

more centralised and authoritarian state, which imposed further Islamisation and repression of women, the secular left and nationalists.
The war years led to the decline of Iranian nationalism, intensifying
instead religiosity. Thus, as is often the case, war produced a strong
state and served to shape national and foreign policies. It allowed the
more conservative factions of Islamists to consolidate power, and in
time the constant threat of war and sanctions from the West translated
into an intensified level of political repression. Throughout the 1990s
and up to today, under both the reformist government of Khatami
(1997–2005) and the conservative government of Ahmadinejad since
2005, the West's hostility towards Iran has continued, despite the fact
that both regimes embraced neoliberalism and on many occasions
called for improvements in the relationship.

Since 11 September 2001, there have been reports that the USA
is planning a military strike against Iran. Seymour Hersh, author,
investigative journalist and a regular contributor to the New Yorker has
argued that preparations for war with Iran began in 2003.[3] George
Bush (2001–09), shortly after his re-election, explicitly argued for
'regime change' in Iran. In 2005, US vice president Dick Cheney
was reported to have prepared a war plan for Iran, including the use
of nuclear weapons. The plan was to deploy 200 strategic bombers
against 10,000 targets, in which it is estimated that more than 2
million people would be killed in a short period of time (Plesch and
Butcher 2007: 6, 44).

Despite the constant threats of war, in 2001 and 2003 under Khatami's administration and in 2008 under Ahmadinejad, Iran has offered
the USA a set of proposals for stability in Afghanistan and a solution
to the Israel–Palestine conflict. What Iran demanded in return was a
guarantee that the USA would not attack the country or attempt to
enforce 'regime change', and lifting of the ban on Iran's membership of the World Trade Organization. Paradoxically, the reaction on
the part of Bush's administration was further hostility. Israel was
equipped with special weaponry to threaten Iran. Israel's air force
(which is more sophisticated than that of any NATO country apart
from the USA) operates from American bases in Eastern Turkey and

constantly flies around the Iranian border to threaten Iran (Chomsky and Achcar 2009: 138).

Furthermore, with the US occupation of Iraq and the NATO invasion of Afghanistan, as well as the massive US troop deployment to the Persian Gulf, Turkey and Pakistan, and the permanent US military presence in Azerbaijan,[4] Iran is surrounded by US and allied military troops. In 2007 the USA began the construction of a military base in Iraq, less than 5 miles from the Iranian border (Bennis 2009: 68).

The aggressive hostility of the West towards Iran has brought diverse communities from the Middle East region together in its support. For many in Lebanon, Palestine and Egypt no country except Iran has challenged Israel since Gamal Abdel Nasser. All other governments in the region have so far supported peace with Israel without addressing the interests of the Palestinians. A majority of people in the Middle East perceive Iran's position as legitimised by its being on the side of the oppressed people, while the West they perceive as illegitimately interfering in their affairs. It is for this reason that the USA, Israel and the UK claim that Iran is influencing movements in the region and that it represents a threat to the stability of the (pro-West) states.

Of course the pro-West regimes in the region are concerned about the influence of Iran economically and politically. But they have a much greater fear of the consequences of a US attack on Iran. Even Saudi Arabia, a close ally of the West, takes a different perspective on Middle Eastern relations to that of the West and Israel. This is mainly because, as was discussed in Chapter 3, Shi'a communities constitute a large majority in Bahrain and the oil-producing region of Saudi Arabia. They are, therefore, open to engagement with Iran and Hezbollah and see Hamas as a legitimate player in Palestinian politics. It is on this basis that Baker and Hamilton's 'Iraq Study Group Report' addresses Iran's influence (Chomsky and Achcar 2009: 244).

Iran has also strengthened its relationship with its Arab neighbours in the Persian Gulf, in particular the United Arab Emirates, Kuwait, Oman and Qatar, as a way of countering any possible military attack (Ehteshami 2008: 135; Fathollah-Nejad-Asl forthcoming). In fact, no country other than Israel has stated that it would be prepared to back a US attack on Iran unequivocally. Even France and the UK, which do not absolutely rule out a US military attack, have not in the past backed the USA in its overt calls for a military attack on Iran. Policy failure in Iraq, Afghanistan and Palestine was one of the main causes of the rapid decline in the fortunes of George W. Bush in the USA and Tony Blair in the UK, and public opinion in Europe remains strongly anti-war.[5] Nevertheless, as this book goes to press, the possibility of war on Iran is once again on the table.

Under the terms of Article 51 of the UN Charter, an attack on Iran would be illegal; Iran could challenge its attackers in the International Court of Justice or request a special session of the United Nations Security Council. However, the USA could manipulate the Security Council, as it did before the war on Iraq and Afghanistan. In any case, the Iranian state would defend itself not only inside Iran but also outside its borders. Iran would retaliate by attacking US forces in Iraq, Oman, Kuwait, Qatar, Bahrain, Afghanistan and elsewhere in the region. It could attack Israel and oil tankers in the Strait of Hormuz, through which 45 per cent of the world's oil passes. Hence, the impact of such an attack would be catastrophic not only in humanitarian and environmental terms but also for the global economy (Bennis 2009: 34–35; Plesch and Butcher 2007: 65–71).

SANCTIONS

As was discussed in Chapter 2, Hashemi Rafsanjani's administration (1989–97) embraced neoliberalism and invited large-scale investment by the USA in Iran's oil and gas sector. However, Bill Clinton's administration (1993–2001) rejected this offer. Instead, Clinton not only imposed harsh unilateral trade sanctions against Iran, but also pressurised US trade partners not to engage with Iran. This policy continued under the Bush presidency (2001–09) and is continuing under Obama. As a result Iran has deepened its trade ties with Russia, China and some European countries which prefer to pursue their own economic interests. Therefore sanctions have not unduly affected trade with Iran; indeed the country's overall trade has increased.[6] In 2007, the Anglo-Dutch Shell Oil Company signed an agreement with

Iran to develop a major natural gas field.[7] In the same year that Iran began to sell its oil in euros, Japan and China accepted its request to purchase its crude oil in the currency, and by the end of 2007 Iran had succeeded in eliminating its reliance on the dollar for its oil. Even with sanctions prohibiting the exports to Iran of any nuclear material for its power reactors, Mohamed ElBaradei, in 2007, called again for engagement between Iran and the USA. However, instead the USA put pressure on the Security Council for further sanctions (Bennis 2009: 60, 80–87).

Rather than producing political change, these sanctions have simply caused suffering for the Iranian people. Iran's infrastructure, particularly its oil industry and civilian airlines, was constructed under the Shah's regime and still relies on US-made parts, which are unavailable under the sanctions regime. As a consequence, civilian lives have been put in grave danger from airline accidents. Moreover, sanctions have had a devastating impact on Iran's ability to rebuild and improve its oil refinery capacity, thus reducing not its export of crude oil to the global market but its domestic use. Even the so-called 'smart sanctions', designed to target state institutions, including the Revolutionary Guards, have in the end negatively affected large numbers of ordinary people, as these institutions are ultimately part of Iran's state and economy (Bennis 2009: 82–3).

REGIME CHANGE

The West has continued to be engaged in the discourse of 'regime change' in Iran in a variety of ways. In 2005, the neoconservative Michael Ledeen of the American Enterprise Institute advocated the idea that Iran should be federalised (Adib-Moghadam 2008: 123–54; Plesch and Butcher 2007: 32–9, 60). US Special Forces and Israeli intelligence and military operatives have been running covert operations inside Iran fuelling ethnic unrest in several provinces.[8] Seymour Hersh argues that in 2007 the US Congress agreed to a major escalation of covert operations against Iran, allocating US$400 million to destabilise the country, by spying on its nuclear programme and infiltrating ethnic minorities.

In the name of funding democracy in Iran, in 2007 Condoleezza Rice allocated a further $75 million to the existing propaganda effort, which included satellite television broadcasts such as *Voice of America* in Farsi, aimed at 'regime change' in Iran. In response the Iranian government arrested activists and closed down many NGOs. In 2008, USAID also allocated $20 million aid to 'promote democracy, human rights and the rule of law in Iran'.[9] Many Iranian civil society activists have consistently condemned such funding as counterproductive, arguing that the money does not reach the people of Iran, and mainly goes to the Western-based groups such as the Iranian Mujahideen (MKO) and monarchist groups. The funding, which was expanded under George W. Bush, is continuing under Barack Obama, despite statements from him that the USA will not interfere in Iran's affairs.

Since the June 2009 presidential election in Iran, the Western-supported groups of the MKO and monarchists have attempted to infiltrate the Green Movement. The leadership of the Green Movement has repeatedly disassociated itself from such actions and the influence of Western governments, in the belief that their aim is not to promote democracy but to turn Iran once more into a client regime of the West, and to oppose the country's nuclear programme and its stance against Israel. As was discussed in Chapter 2, the leaders of the reform and democracy movement have repeatedly announced that they do not advocate a dismantling of the Islamic state, recognition of the State of Israel, or a reduction in Iran's influence in the region. In the meantime, overt and covert operations against Iran are continuing, and this can only weaken the democracy movement.

THE NUCLEAR BOMB

Iran's nuclear programme is another issue that has been used by the West to support its threats. In this context, it is important to recognise that the programme started in the 1950s and 1960s with the technological assistance and political encouragement of the USA. After the fall of the Shah and the 1979 revolution, Iran's nuclear programme was halted for five years. During the Iran–Iraq war,

Saddam Hussein repeatedly bombarded the nuclear sites. After the war, Iran and the USSR signed a nuclear cooperation treaty to build the Bushehr nuclear site in the south of the country. In 1995 Iran signed another agreement with Russia to rebuild the nuclear reactor and provide technological support for developing nuclear energy (Lotfian 2008: 158–60).

Since then Iran has been accused by the USA and Israel of developing 'weapons of mass destruction'. Iran, however, is a signatory to the non-proliferation treaty (NPT), where, like other signatories, it asserts its right under Article 11 to develop nuclear energy for peaceful purposes. Iran has repeatedly stated that it is committed to replacing confrontation with negotiations in good faith, as an equal partner, to find a peaceful solution to the nuclear issue. It has stated its commitment to non-proliferation and to the elimination of nuclear weapons, and indicated that it considers nuclear weapons detrimental to its security. It has declared its readiness to abide by its obligations under the NPT and to work for the establishment of a zone free from WMD in the Middle East. In return, under pressure from neoconservatives in the USA and their supporters globally, Iran has faced intimidation based on unfounded speculation about its intention to produce WMDs.

Ahmadinejad's Holocaust-denial statement has also been used by Western media and politicians to demonise Iran and pave the way for the extension of war and conflict to Iran. The president's posture represents a crude attempt to assert his leadership within the region. Whilst such statements must be condemned unconditionally, it must be recognised that Holocaust denial and anti-Semitic rhetoric are now very popular throughout the region (Achcar 2009). This is deeply troubling. This type of anti-Semitism, with its roots in Europe, was once unknown in the Islamic world. There is plenty of evidence illustrating close cooperation between Muslims and Jews at the height of Islamic civilisation. As was discussed in Chapter 6, the rise of anti-Semitism in the region must be laid firmly at the door of Israel and its aggressive Zionist policies. By making such statements, Ahmadinejad seeks to enhance Iran's position in the Muslim-majority world, especially at a time when Western politicians and mainstream global media have been trying to whip up anti-Shi'a feeling in the region.

Despite the media hype about Iran's nuclear weapon programme, in 2007 the National Intelligence Estimate (NIE) on Iran made clear that Iran did not have a nuclear weapon and, contrary to US intelligence agency claims, indicated that Iran was not determined to build such weapons. In 2008, Bush's administration and Israel announced that the NIE report would not change their policies towards Iran.

Saideh Lotfian, an Iranian anti-nuclear specialist, argues that the threat of Israeli and US military aggression has led Iranian policymakers, scholars and politicians to debate the nuclear issue within Iran. Analysing the debate, she finds that Iranians, across the political spectrum, are divided into two camps: a pro-nuclear faction and an anti-nuclear faction. From an anti-nuclear position she emphasises that 'It is the responsibility of the international community to avoid any action that could make Iran react either by withdrawing from the NPT or by speeding up the pace of its military modernisation' (2008: 158–75).

The majority of people in Iran, of all political persuasions, and regardless of their criticisms of the government, support the country's right to defend itself against the threat from Israel and the USA. At the regional level, the occupation of Iraq and the invasion of Afghanistan have increased public support for the acquisition of nuclear weapons. The people of Iran perceive Israel as a major nuclear power, which has a regional monopoly on nuclear deterrence and blackmail. As a nuclear power,[10] Israel has constantly violated international law, has attacked Palestinians, Lebanese and Syrians, and constantly threatens Iran. In this context, many people in the Middle East support their countries' acquisition of nuclear power and ask why calls by Egypt, an ally of the West and a signatory to the NPT, for a nuclear-weapons-free zone throughout the Middle East, have been ignored by the USA and Israel (Bennis 2009: 29). In the preface, I described the comment made to me by a middle-aged shoe keeper in a mosque in Cairo, saying 'Iran good, Bomb Inshaallah', indicating that he wished Iran to obtain the bomb. Similar sentiments indicating the popularity of Iran in the region demonstrate how many people view Iran's technological advance and possible development of nuclear weapons as a positive response by Islam to the aggression of the West and Israel in the region.

The USA and Israel want to prevent Iran possessing nuclear weapons not because they believe that Iran will attack them or the countries in the region – clearly this would be suicidal – but because possessing such weapons would make Iran an effective counter-deterrent against them (Chomsky and Achcar 2009: 139). Precedent relationships between the West and Pakistan, India and Israel clearly demonstrate that if Iran was to become a client regime of the West it would gain more support for its nuclear programme and possibly even for nuclear weapons. It is clear that hostility towards Iran over the nuclear issue is really about the desire to return the country to the status of a client state of the West (which would in particular benefit the US oil corporations) and discourage Iran from developing independent electricity-generation capacity and energy security.

STATE-SPONSORED TERRORISM

Since the 1979 revolution and the overthrow of the Shah, Iran has been accused by the USA, the UK and Israel as being responsible for 'state-sponsored terrorism', another factor deployed to legitimise their attacks on the country. The notion that Iran has been involved in terrorism or supporting terrorism, and therefore that the USA and Israel have the right to attack Iran, has no legitimacy or legal status, as there is no evidence for such claims (Bennis 2009: 20–24; Adib-Moghadam 2009).

As is discussed in this book, Iran's support for Hamas and Hezbollah has been of a political nature, and since the 1980s these organisations have turned into mainstream political parties. They both have military wings and some of their activities have involved attacks on civilians in violation of international law, which might qualify as 'terrorism'. However, as discussed in Chapters 4 and 6, Iran's financial support for these organisations has been minimal, and they do not need the country's military support. Their support comes from the majority of the people in the region, who are opposed to the aggressive policies of the USA and Israel.

Western politicians and mainstream media portray the Middle East as being dominated by extremists, all supported by Iran. On the contrary, the dominant Islamist political groups in the region have sought to use political and electoral processes to achieve their objectives. Those who wish to pursue their objectives through violence and extremism have been in the minority.

In fact, for decades, the rise of extremism in the region can be seen as resulting from international policies and relations. Besides Israel, the most important ally of the USA in the region is Saudi Arabia. During the Cold War era, the USA quite deliberately worked with the conservative Islamists attached to Saudi Arabia to combat the secular left and nationalists in the Middle East, a policy that continued throughout the Soviet war in Afghanistan where the USA mobilised the Afghan Mujahideen against the USSR. Thus the USA created al-Qaeda and the Taliban. Later these forces turned against them, resulting in the 11 September 2001 attacks on New York and the Pentagon (Chomsky and Achcar 2009: 6–30; Callinicos 2009: 217).

Furthermore, the occupation of Iraq and the invasion of Afghanistan have led to the creation of new training grounds for terrorism, which is spreading around the world. And it is argued that control of the energy resources of the Middle East and political and cultural control over the region are actually more important than combating terrorism that threatens the USA and the UK. The recent evidence for this is the London conference on Afghanistan in January 2010 where the heads of Western states, the UN and NATO announced that, with the help of Saudi Arabia, they could do business with the Taliban and even share power with this ultra-conservative guerrilla force. So, after eight years of occupying Afghanistan, the deaths of thousands of civilians and military personnel, escalating corruption, and with very little change for the people in terms of access to health, education, employment and improvement in women's position (Rostami-Povey 2001, 2004), the West is once again planning to collaborate with the Taliban, who cooperate and share funding with al-Qaeda, and who together control much of the country and have the capability to overthrow Karzai's government.[11] As Seumas Milne has argued,[12] this is not a policy to end the war, as Barack Obama is sending tens of thousands more troops to Afghanistan. The policy is designed to split the Taliban and al-Qaeda in order to secure US economic and political interests in the region.

The decline of American hegemony

As is argued by Callinicos (2003) and Harvey (2003), the USA possesses military superiority, but economically faces competitive challenges in the Middle East from Europe, Russia, China and Japan, who are also dependent on the export of oil from the region. The USA's influence over China (as an emerging global economic power and the USA's hegemonic rival) is hugely overshadowed by its dependence on a massive inflow of capital from China and other countries in the East. The 'global war on terror', the occupation of Iraq and the invasion of Afghanistan were intended to use American military superiority to reinforce Washington's domination of the region, and also be a reminder of the costs of challenging American hegemony. However, although this military power was strong enough to invade and occupy Afghanistan and Iraq, the USA has not been able to control these countries and their resources. In both Iraq and Afghanistan the USA, its allies and NATO are bogged down in unwinnable wars.

The decline of US hegemony also has implications for the alliance between Israel and Washington. Such an alliance represents a formidable military power in terms of containing the threat posed by Islamism (similar to the threat of Arab nationalism in the past) and guaranteeing the West's interests in the region. However, the growth of Islamism throughout the region, Hezbollah's victory against Israel in 2006, and Hamas's success in Palestinian parliamentary elections pose identical difficulties for both the USA and Israel. When Israel attacked Lebanon in 2006, the Bush administration saw the war on

Lebanon and Hezbollah, a powerful ally of Iran, as an opportunity to weaken Iran. However, the defeat of Israel by Hezbollah highlighted America's crisis of international legitimacy, since only Israel and Britain supported US efforts. The victory of Hezbollah in Lebanon strengthened its position, as well as that of Iran, and consequently weakened the hand of Israel and the USA. Furthermore, Israel's withdrawal from Gaza strengthened the position of Hamas. As is argued by Achcar (2006), 'The defeat of Israel by Hezbollah, instead of helping in raising the sinking ship of the US Empire, the Israeli rescue boat has actually aggravated the shipwreck, and is currently being dragged down with it.'[13]

The replacement of the discredited administration of George W. Bush with that of Barack Obama was an event welcomed across the globe, as many desired to heal the wounds created by slavery and racism in US society. However, the power of the US president is interwoven with the country's foreign policy, especially in the Middle East. This is especially important today when the USA is grappling with the crisis of its declining hegemony over the world system, which is being challenged by China. Therefore the US policy of asserting global control over strategic resources – especially oil – and expanding its power militarily, economically and politically is continuing under Barack Obama. This was demonstrated in Obama's pre-election speech to the American Israel Public Affairs Committee (AIPAC), a key pro-Israel lobbying organisation, in which he reiterated that Israeli security is sacrosanct and non-negotiable, and that Jerusalem will remain undivided. He has also promised Israel US$30 billion of support over the next ten years. Following his election victory, his Persian New Year speech on 21 March 2009 and speech at the University of Cairo on 4 June 2009 indicated a move away from Bush's policies and showed an understanding of the causes of resentment and mistrust of the West in the Middle East. However, many were sceptical and felt his speech lacked substance.[14] They have so far been proved right. The Obama administration has seemingly not learned the lessons of the failure of these policies and of the death and destruction they have brought to the people of the Middle East as well as to the US military. Therefore, sanctions, 'regime change' and democratisation Iraq- and Afghanistan-style are on the agenda, and the threat of war with Iran persists. Although unilateralism is unlikely under Obama's administration, multilateralism is just a tactical adjustment, reflecting an accommodation to the limits of American power rather than a strategic reorientation (Callinicos 2006).

In February 2010, Obama reverted to a policy that his predecessor, George W. Bush, had followed on Iran. While the neoconservative Daniel Pipes argued that the only way for Obama to save his presidency was to 'bomb Iran', Israel renewed its threats of war against Iran's allies, Lebanon's Hezbollah and the Palestinian Hamas. When Iran agreed to ship most of its enriched uranium abroad to be reprocessed and returned to Iran in the form of fuel rods for research purposes, a deal which was agreed in Geneva in October 2009, US and European officials dismissed the offer and escalated their military build-up in the Persian Gulf. Obama has supplied tens of billions of dollars worth of new weapons to Kuwait, the United Arab Emirates, Qatar, Saudi Arabia and Bahrain.[15]

In May 2010, the Tehran Joint Declaration, between Brazil, Turkey and Iran, promoted a solution that would ensure the full exercise of Iran's right to its peaceful use of nuclear energy, while providing assurances that Iran's nuclear programme is exclusively for peaceful purposes. This declaration removed political obstacles to the October 2009 IAEA proposal. President Obama, who in April 2010 welcomed such a negotiation (to persuade Iran to send 1,200 kg of its low enriched uranium to Turkey in exchange for fuel rods for the Tehran Research Reactor), completely changed his position. His secretary of state, Hillary Clinton, dismissed the Brazil–Iran–Turkey offer and announced instead a draft UN Security Council Resolution to impose a new round of sanctions on Iran.[16]

The constant threat of military strikes, sanctions, covert operations and funding for 'regime change' could destroy the grassroots democratic movement in Iran and will increase the Iranian regime's influence in the region. The impact of sending more ships and missiles to the Persian Gulf by Obama has been negative for the democracy movement in Iran, as the conservatives within the regime have used the pressure from outside as an additional pretext to clamp down even more fiercely. In this context, history is repeating itself: the West in the past destroyed the secular and nationalist movements that were fighting for democracy and independence in Iran and in the wider region; now they are destroying the Islamist modernists through the constant threat of military intervention.

As this book argues, the people of the region are struggling for democracy and freedom from Zionism and imperialism. Their historical experience has shown that without democracy and independence their governments lack the will and legitimacy to carry out sustainable socio-economic and political development. The West's hostility towards Iran and the modern Islamist movements in the region will increase political hostility against the West and their client states, and will ultimately strengthen Islamic conservatism in the region and globally. The history of past struggles and the trajectory of contemporary movements in the region demonstrate that the local and global systems of domination and exploitation, which only work to the advantage of a few, will be resisted. In this context, should Iran, Hezbollah, Hamas and the Muslim Brotherhood see fit to fashion their policies to conform with those of the USA, thereby ensuring that the economic and political interests of the USA take precedence over those of their peoples, then the resistance to national governments, imperialism and Zionism will continue.

Notes

INTRODUCTION

1. There are different forms of both Arab nationalism (Egyptian, Iraqi, Palestinians, Lebanese) and Iranian nationalism (Kurds, Azeris, Baluchis, Arab and Turkmen). These identities have also shifted during the history of nationalist struggles according to the degree of religiosity (Muslims, Christians, Jews) and secularity.
2. See also Uma Narayan's concept of 'Travelling Modernity', which suggests a constant state of transformation and flux. For local modernities, see Miller 1994, 1995; Abu-Lughod 1998; Ali-Ali 2000; Deeb 2006a.
3. As is argued by Gramsci (1976), these authoritarian regimes rule hegemonically.
4. For the discussions, I am indebted to Tara Povey.

ONE

1. This was the celebration of the 2,500th anniversary of the Iranian monarchy.
2. This Shi'a culture is discussed fully in Chapter 3.
3. For this discussion, see Chapter 3.
4. For this discussion I am indebted to John Rose.
5. For the history of secular (nationalist and communist) movements in Iran, see Abrahamian 1982; Bayat 1987; Cronin 2004.
6. For a full discussion of temporary marriage in Iran, see Haeri 1989.
7. I am indebted to Arshin Adib-Moghadam for translating these concepts into English.
8. *Jihad* is a broad concept which can be interpreted as war and as peaceful

opposition to repressive values and actions; as resistance to oneself and as resistance to repressive systems and regimes. According to such interpretations, jihadist movements have existed throughout history in different contexts, from anti-colonial movements to anti-dictatorial movements, opposition to state repression and anti-imperialism. The term *qital* (to kill) is also used as a form of jihad, but in the sense of last resort. For discussion, see Ramadan 2007.

9. For this discussion I am indebted to John Rose.

TWO

1. www.payvand.com/news/09/oct/1090.html.
2. www.etemaad.com/Released/86–05–18/252.htm.
3. www.advarnews.U.S.A/ and www.autnews.com.
4. For this discussion I am indebted to a number of members of Tahkime Vahdat and Advare Tahkime Vahdat.
5. For this discussion I am indebted to Attaollah Mohajerani and Jamileh Kadivar.
6. A great deal has been written about Babi and Bahai religious beliefs. See Sanasarian 2000: 50–53.
7. Simon Tisdall and Robert Tait, *Guardian*, 27 June 2006.
8. Afary 2009; Afshar 1991; Bahramitash 2003; Haeri 2009; Honarbin-Holliday 2009; Hoodfar 2000; Kian 2005; Mir-Hosseini 2002; Moallem 2005; Moghadam 2000; Moghissi 2001; Mojab 1998; Naghibi 2007; Najmabadi 1991; Osanloo 2009; Paidar 1997; Poya 1999; Tohidi 2002; Torab 2002.
9. Ian Black, *Guardian*, 3 August 2009, and Mark Tran, *Guardian*, 15 August 2009.
10. Arshin Adib-Moghadam, *Guardian*, 28 July 2009.
11. Robert Tait, *Guardian*, 11 August 2009.
12. The Revolutionary Guard is a branch of Iran's military, founded to safeguard the 1979 revolution. It has 125,000 personnel, including ground, air and naval forces. There is also the paramilitary Baseej militia, which was founded after the Iran–Iraq war to mobilise and recruit for the war; it has 90,000 personnel. As discussed in Chapter 1, in recent years these security forces have developed into business empires.
13. Julian Borger, *Guardian*, 9 July 2009.
14. Robert Tait, *Guardian*, 7 November 2009; 22 and 28 November 2009; Ian Black, *Guardian*, 12 February 2010; Ali Ansari, *Guardian*, 13 February 2010.
15. Mark Tran, *Guardian*, 17 August 2009; Bagher Moin, *Guardian*, 2 July 2009.
16. www.insideiran.org.

THREE

1. For this discussion I am indebted to Ibrahim Salahi.
2. Asef Bayat argues that the Islamic movement in this period in Iran was a

late bloomer. Before evolving into a mass movement it was interrupted by the revolution (2005: 27–32).

3. Ayatollah Montazeri has a large following, his arguments have been published by reformist media, and he has an official website, www.amontazeri. com.

4. For this discussion I am indebted to Eisa Saharkhiz.

5. This quotation is from Mir Hosseini and Tapper 2006: 109. See also Kadivar 1999, 2002, and www.kadivar.com/index.asp.

6. Ayatollah Saanei also supported the post-June 2009 demonstrations and in this regard issued a number of declarations: www.saanei.org.

7. www.amontazeri.com.

8. Baqer Moin, *Guardian*, 21 December 2009.

9. *Der Spiegel*, 1 July 2009.

FOUR

1. As is discussed in Chapter 6, the creation of Israel destroyed Palestine in 1948 and Palestinians were driven out of their country in a terrifying mass exodus to Lebanon, Syria, Jordan and Egypt.

2. As is discussed by Rahimi (2007: 6), religious taxes donated by believers (*zakat*) are intended to assist the poor, needy, orphans and those in debt. Part of *zakat* is paid to cover the expenses of collecting taxes by religious administrators. *Khums*, on the other hand, is a special annual tax that Shi'as pay at one-fifth of the value of their wealth, which is spent mostly on the needy, orphans, and on the Prophet and his family. However, one-tenth of *khums* must be paid to a high-ranking cleric, *marja' al-taqlid* (the source of imitation), who is the most knowledgeable and pious among the clerics and whom the believers (*moqalids*) are expected to imitate in everyday life and follow on religious matters. The role of *marja' al-taqlid* is crucial in the institution of religious taxation since it is under his authority (as the definitive representative of the Hidden Imam, the twelfth male descendant of Muhammad, who has been hiding since 874 CE and whose return is expected at the end of time) that the collected money is distributed to pious causes.

3. In 1978 al-Sadr mysteriously disappeared on a visit to Libya. This contributed to the popularity of AMAL.

4. Despite the illegality of the invasion, Israel continued to ignore the UN Security Council and pumped precious water out of Lebanon. For discussion, see Harik 2005: 48–50.

5. Hezbollah's first secretary-general was Shaykh Subhi al-Tufayli.

6. Michel Aoun and his supporters were part of the March 14 Alliance but, although anti-Syrian, they joined with the March 8 Alliance in opposition to Prime Minister Fouad Siniori.

7. *Financial Times*, 8 September 2009. I am indebted to Mona Harb, Judith Harik and Laleh Khalili for drawing my attention to this issue.

8. For Hezbollah's finances, see also Hamzeh 2004.
9. Ayatollah al-Khoi was of Iranian origin and lived in Najaf. See Chapter 5.
10. Nasrallah's speech was broadcast by Al Jazeera.
11. Ian Black, *Guardian*, 16 May 2008.
12. Ian Black, *Guardian*, 22 May 2008.
13. Ian Black, *Guardian*, 5 March 2009; Hugh Macleod, *Guardian*, 8 June 2009.
14. Ian Black, *Guardian*, 27 June 2009, 7 November 2009; Simon Tisdall, *Guardian*, 9 June 2009.
15. *Daily Star*, Lebanon, 3 October 2009.
16. Omayma Abdel-Latif, Al *Ahram*, 19–25 November 2009.
17. For this discussion I am indebted to Laleh Khalili.

FIVE

1. The father-in-law of Muqtada al-Sadr and cousin of Imam Musa al-Sadr. His grandfather was born in Isfahan in Iran in 1842.
2. One of the sisters of Imam Reza, the eighth Shi'a Imam, whose shrine is in Mashhad in Iran.
3. For this discussion I am indebted to Hassan Yousefi Eshkevari, an Iranian cleric.
4. Sadr City was built by Abd al-Karim Qasim in 1959 and was called Madinat al Thawra (Revolution City). Under Saddam it was called Saddam City, and in April 2003 was renamed Sadr City to commemorate Muhammad Sadiq al-Sadr, Muqtada's father, who was assassinated by Saddam in 1999. In the 1990s Ayatollahs Muhammad Sadiq al-Sadr, Abol-Qasim al-Khoi and Ali al-Sistani provided social services to the Shi'a poor in the area.
5. These two main Iraqi Kurdish Parties allied themselves periodically either with Saddam or with the Iranian government in order to control Iraqi Kurdistan.
6. He followed his predecessor, Ayatollah Abol-Qasim al-Khoi, who was the spiritual leader of much of the Shi'a world until his death in 1992, and challenged Ayatollah Khomeini's *Velayat-e faqih*.
7. I am indebted to Anne Alexander for this discussion
8. See also Sami Ramadani: www.guardian.co.uk/profile/samiramadani.
9. For this discussion I am indebted to Sami Ramadani.
10. In 2007, the SCIRI changed its name to Islamic Supreme Council of Iraq (ISCI), dropping the term 'Revolution', which implied that the revolution was the overthrow of the Saddam regime.
11. Martin Chulov, *Guardian*, 27 and 29 March 2010.
12. Jonathan Steele, *Guardian*, 4 April 2008.
13. In 2008, the Mahdi Army was infiltrated by its enemies, including the occupation authorities. Muqtada al-Sadr abandoned politics and retired from political activities for the time being. See Sami Ramadani: www.guardian.co.uk/profile/samiramadani.
14. Steele, *Guardian*, 4 April 2008.

15. For this discussion, see Seymour Hersh, 'Plan B', *New Yorker*, 28 June 2004.
16. Jonathan Steele, *Guardian*, 30 May 2008.
17. Haifa Zangana's speech at the Stop the War Coalition meeting, London, March 2009.
18. Amnesty International, 'Iraq: Nine Women Face Imminent Execution', 23 July 2009.
19. Charles Tripp, 'Prospects of State Building in Iraq', speech at SOAS, 11 May 2009.
20. See also *Iraq Occupation Newsletter* 125, 2009; Sami Ramadani, www.guardian. co.uk/profile/samiramadani.
21. Cath Clarke, *Guardian*, 1 May 2009.
22. Jonathan Steele, *Guardian*, 30 June 2009; Seumas Milne, *Guardian*, 26 June 2009; Martin Chulov, *Guardian*, 1 July 2009; Ramadani, 28 March 2008, www.guardian.co.uk/profile/samiramadani.
23. See also Jonathan Steele, *Guardian*, 2 January 2009.
24. *Iraq Occupation Newsletter* 125, 2009: www.iraqoccupationfocus.org.uk. See also https://lists.riseup.net/www/arc/iraqfocus and http://solidarityiraq. blogspot.com.

SIX

1. For this discussion, see Chapter 7.
2. Nur Masalha, the Palestinian academic and writer, argues that there is no evidence of Israel's support for this movement, except that in 1973 Israel allowed Sheikh Ahmed Yassin, the leader of the Muslim Brotherhood, who later founded Hamas and became the spiritual leader of the organisation, to set up the Islamic Centre, Al-Mujamma' al-Islami, and gave the organisation some financial support (Masalha 2007: 219).
3. Rabin was assassinated by a right-wing Zionist who believed that he was selling out the 'land of Israel'.
4. UN Resolution 194 was a direct application of Article 13 of the Universal Declaration of Human Rights, which states that 'everyone has the right to leave any country, including his/her own country and return to his/her own country'.
5. Amnesty International reported that more than 1,000 Palestinian prisoners were ill-treated in the PA's prisons. See www.amnestyusa.org/countries/ israeland_occupied_territories/document.do?id=19024C93E884246A80256A 0F005BCC96; Rory McCarthy, *Guardian*, 6 October 2009.
6. For this discussion, see also Rory McCarthy, *Guardian*, 11 December 2009.
7. The Israel Lobby in America had the political endorsement of the powerful 50–60 million evangelical block votes, most of whom are Christian Zionists.
8. Marwan Barghouti is the single most important leader of a young generation of Fatah that grew out of the first intifada.

9. *Daily Star*, Lebanon, 3 October 2009.
10. See also Right to Education Campaign e-Bulletin: http://right2edu.birzeit.edu, and BRICUP: www.bricup.org.uk.
11. See www.stopthewall.org, and Electronic Intifada. http://electronicintifada.net.
12. Roula Khalaf, Albeer Alliam, Najmeh Bozorgmehr and Tobias Buck, *Financial Times*, 5 June 2009; Rory McCarthy, *Guardian*, 13 October 2009.
13. Simon Tisdall, *Guardian*, 19 October 2009; Ewen MacAskill, *Guardian*, 19 March 2010.
14. Rory McCarthy, *Guardian*, 12 May 2008.
15. Nicolas Pelham, *London Review of Books*, 22 October 2009.
16. On Friday 9 April 2004, Hamas appealed to the population of the Gaza Strip to raise funds to combat the US, European, Israeli and PA blockades. On that day they collected US$1.2 million.
17. Paulo Freire's concept of conscientisation is popular with many NGO activists. For full discussion, see Mayo 1999.
18. http://electronicintifada.net.
19. Peter Beaumont, *Guardian*, 14 August 2009; Clancy Chassey, *Guardian*, 24 March 2009.
20. International Action Centre, www.iacenter.org/Palestine. See also Rory McCarthy on the UN inquiry accusing Israel of war crimes, *Guardian*, 17 September 2009.
21. Nick Clegg, *Guardian*, 22 December 2009.
22. For discussion of Hamas, see Gunning 2007.
23. www.pacbi.org.
24. See also Rory McCarthy, *Guardian*, 19 October 2009.
25. *Daily Star*, Lebanon, 3 October 2009.
26. Rory McCarthy, *Guardian*, 12 May 2008
27. Robert Tait, *Guardian*, 25 February 2009.
28. Harriet Sherwood and Ian Black, *Guardian*, 8 June 2010.

SEVEN

1. The Isma'ilis are a Shi'a community that believe in Seven Imams. In their belief, the Seventh Imam is Ismai'l, the elder son of the sixth Imam, Ja'far al-Sadiq. Conversely, the Twelver Shi'a (mainly in Iran) believe that the Seventh Imam was Musa al-Kazim, the younger son of the sixth Imam. They ruled in North Africa and Egypt from 909 until they were overthrown by Saladin in 1171. They are known as Fatimid, as they claimed to have descended from the Prophet's daughter Fatima. See Katouzian 2009: 97–9.
2. Abduh believed in Islamic social order and justice rather than Islamic state and government, while Rida believed in Shari'a as the law. Thanks to Tara Povey for this discussion.

3. Al-Azhar is the pillar of established Islam in Egypt; it was created by the Fatimids for the teaching of Islam in its Isma'ili form and continued as an important centre of Sunni religious learning. See Hourani 1991: 122–5.

4. Zaydis are another branch of Shi'ism who historically played an important role in Iran. They are followers of Zayd ibn Ali, son of Imam Hussein. See Katouzian 2009: 71–2.

5. This was a conservative religious nationalist group, opposing foreign domination. They assassinated a number of people in Iran who were critical of Islam. Their leaders, including Navab Safavi, were executed in 1955.

6. I am indebted to Anne Alexander for allowing me to use this quotation from her forthcoming book, *Leadership, Democracy and Collective Action in Egypt and Iraq: 1945–63*. See also Thornhill 2006: 35; Wilson et al. 1986: 87.

7. The Free Officers Movement, founded by Gamal Abdel Nasser, was a group of young and educated urban men who were committed to end the monarchy and British colonialism; they succeeded in bringing about the 1952 Revolution.

8. *Monthly Review*, 22 December 2009; *Tehran Times*, 24 December 2009.

9. The Egyptian Trade Union Federation (ETUF), is a state-controlled organisation.

10. For full discussion of this topic, see Tara Povey forthcoming.

11. See Fawaz Gerges, *Guardian*, 21 January 2010.

12. See Hossam el-Hamalawy, www.arabawy.org.

13. Jack Shenker, *Guardian*, 1 April 2010.

14. For full discussion of this movement, see Tara Povey forthcoming.

15. See el-Hamalawy 2008.

16. For this discussion I am indebted to Heba Raouf and Dina Samak.

17. See Rory McCarthy, *Guardian*, 11 December 2009.

18. See Saleh Hemeid, 'Face to Face with Iran', *Al-Ahram*, 19–25 November 2009.

EIGHT

1. Jim Vallette, 'Cheney's Oil Change at the World Bank', *Energy Bulletin*, 30 March 2005, www.energybulletin.net/5009.html.

2. See Robert Tait, *Guardian*, 1 February 2010; Seumas Milne, *Guardian*, 4 February 2010.

3. Seymour Hersh, 'The Iran Plans', *New Yorker*, 17 April 2006. See also 'The Next Act', *New Yorker*, 27 November 2006; 'The Coming Wars', *New Yorker*, 24 January 2005, 'Shifting Targets: The Administration's Plan for Iran', *New Yorker*, 8 October 2007.

4. Azerbaijan's parliament has ruled out foreign bases in the country. However, since Azerbaijan needs US assistance in its dispute with Armenia, as well as with development of oil and gas resources, it has allowed the USA to use Azerbaijan territory to attack Iran.

5. See Campaign Against Sanctions and Military Intervention in Iran (CASMI), www.campaigniran.org/casmii; Campaign Iran. http://campaigniran.blogspot.com.
6. General Accounting Office, 'Iran Sanctions: Impact in Furthering US Objectives Is Unclear and should be Reviewed', December 2007, www.gao.gov/new.items/do858.pdf.
7. Terry Macalister, 'Shell Defies US Pressure and Signs £5bn Iranian Gas Deal', *Guardian*, 29 January 2007.
8. See Seymour Hersh, 'Plan B', *New Yorker*, 28 June 2004; 'Preparing the Battlefield', *New Yorker*, 7 July 2008; 'Israeli Agents Operating in Iraq, Iran and Syria', www.democracynow.org/2004/6/22/seymour_hersh_israeli_agents_operating_in.
9. www.usatoday.com/news/pdf/usaid.pdf.
10. Israel's nuclear weapon was first tested jointly with apartheid South Africa in 1979. This was disclosed by Mordechai Vanunu in 1986. In December 2006 Israeli prime minister Ehud Olmert stated that Israel did belong to the club of nuclear weapons states.
11. Rory Stewart, *New York Review*, 14 January 2010.
12. *Guardian*, 28 January 2010.
13. G. Achcar, 'The Sinking Ship of US Imperial Designs', 7 August 2006, www.zmag.org.
14. Ian Black, *Guardian*, 5 June 2009.
15. See Robert Tait, *Guardian*, 1 February 2010, 3 February 2010; Seumas Milne, *Guardian*, 4 February 2010.
16. See CASMII press releases, 28 May 2010 and 10 June 2010, www.casmii.campaigniran.org.

References

Ababneh, S. (forthcoming) 'Islamic Political Parties As a Means of Women's Empowerment? The Case of Hamas and the Islamic Action Front', Ph.D. thesis, St Antony's College, Oxford University.

Abdallah, A. (1985) *The Student Movement and National Politics in Egypt*, Saqi Books, London.

Abdel-Latif, O. (2008) 'In the Shadow of the Brothers, The Women of the Egyptian Muslim Brother', *Carnegie Papers* 13, October, Carnegie Middle East Centre.

Abdelrahman, M.M. (2004) *Civil Society Exposed: The Politics of NGOs in Egypt*, Tauris Academic Studies, London and New York.

Abdelrahman, M.M. (2009) 'With the Islamists? – Sometimes. With the State? – Never! Cooperation between the Left and Islamists in Egypt', *British Journal of Middle Eastern Studies* 36(1): 37–54.

Abdollahi, S. (2008) 'Eterazate moaleman bar bastary az nakaramady doloat' (Teachers protests in the context of government's neglect), conference paper presented at the international conference, 'Thirty Years of Islamic Republic: Workers Organisations, Social Study and the Formation of Civil Society in Iran', CERI/CNRS, Centre d'études et de recherches internationals, Paris.

Abrahamian, E. (1982) *Iran between Two Revolutions*, Princeton University Press, Princeton NJ.

Abrahamian, E. (2004) 'The Islamic Left, From Radicalism to Liberalism', in S. Cronin (ed.), *Reformers and Revolutionaries in Modern Iran: New Perspectives on the Iranian Left*, Routledge Curzon, London and New York.

Abrahamian, E. (2008) *A History of Modern Iran*, Cambridge University Press, Cambridge.

Abu-Lughod, L. (1998) 'The Marriage of Islamism and Feminism in Egypt: Selective Repudiation as a Dynamic of Post-colonial Cultural Politics', in

Abu-Lughod (ed.), *Remaking Women: Feminism and Modernity in the Middle East*, Princeton University Press, Princeton NJ.

Abu-Rabi I.M. (2004) *Contemporary Arab Thought: Studies in Post-1967 Arab Intellectual History*, Pluto Press, London.

Achcar, G. (2006) 'Eleven Theses on the Resurgence of Islamic Fundamentalism', *International Viewpoint*, www.internationalviewpoint.org.

Achcar, G. (2009), *Arabs and the Holocaust: The Arab–Israeli War of Narratives*, Saqi Books, London.

Achcar, G., and M. Warschawski (2007) *The 33-Day War: Israel's War on Hezbollah in Lebanon and its Aftermath*, Saqi Books, London.

Adelkhah, F. (1998) *Being Modern in Iran*, Hurst, London.

Adib-Moghadam, A. (2008) *Iran in World Politics: The Question of the Islamic Republic*, Columbia University Press, New York.

Adib-Moghadam, A. (2009) 'Discourse and Violence: The Friend–Enemy Conjunction in Contemporary Iranian–American Relations', *Critical Studies on Terrorism* 2(3), December.

Adib-Moghadam, A. (2010) 'The Future of Islam and Democracy in Iran', *Bitterlemons-international Org* 3(8), 28 January.

Afary, J. (2009) *Sexual Politics in Modern Iran*, Cambridge University Press, Cambridge.

Afshar, H. (1991) 'The Emancipation Struggles in Iran: Past Experiences and Future Hopes', in H. Afshar (ed.), *Women Development And Survival in the Third World*, Longman, London and New York.

Ahmad, H. (1994) *From Religious Salvation to Political Transformation: The Rise of Hamas in Palestinian Society*, Passia, Jerusalem.

Ahmed, L. (1992) *Women and Gender in Islam*, Yale University Press, New Haven.

Al-Ali, N. (2000) *Secularism, Gender and the State in the Middle East: The Egyptian Women's Movement*, Cambridge University Press, Cambridge.

Al-Ali, N. (2007) *Iraqi Women: Untold Stories from 1948 to the Present*, Zed Books, London.

Al-Ali, N., and N. Pratt (2009) *What Kind of Liberation? Women and the Occupation of Iraq*, University of California Press, Berkeley.

Alexander, A. (2005) *Nasser*, Haus, London.

Alexander, A. (2009) 'Mubarak in the International Arena', in R. El-Mahdi and P. Marfleet (eds), *Egypt: The Moment of Change*, Zed Books, London.

Alexander, A. (forthcoming) *Leadership, Democracy and Collective Action in Egypt and Iraq: 1945–63*.

Alexander, A., and S. Assaf (2005) 'Iraq: The Rise of the Resistance', *International Socialism* 105.

Alexander, A., and J. Rose (2008) *The Nakba: Why Israel's Birth Was Palestine's Catastrophe and What's the Solution?*, Bookmarks, London.

Algar, H. (1969) *Religion and State in Iran 1785–1906*, University of California Press, Berkeley.

Amin, S. (2001) 'Political Islam', *Covert Action Quarterly* 71.

Ansari, A.M. (2003) *Modern Iran since 1921: The Pahlavis and After*, Longman, London and New York.

Ansari, A.M. (2006) *Confronting Iran*, Hurst, London.

Ansari, A.M. (2009a) 'Preliminary Analysis of the Voting Figures in Iran's 2009 Presidential Election', Chatham House and the Institute of Iranian Studies, University of St Andrews.

Ansari, A.M. (2009b) 'The Revolution Will Be Mercantalised', *The National Interest*, Nixon Centre, Washington DC.

Appadurai, A. (1996) *Modernity at Large: Cultural Dimensions of Globalization, Public Worlds*, vol. 1, University of Minnesota Press, Minneapolis.

Arrighi, G. (2005) 'Hegemony Unravelling', *New Left Review*, II/32–33.

Bahramitash, R. (2003) 'Islamic Fundamentalism and Women's Employment in Iran', *International Journal of Politics and Society* 16(4): 551–68.

Baker, R. (2003) *Islam without Fear: Egypt and the New Islamists*, Harvard University Press, Cambridge MA.

Batatu, H. (2004) *The Old Social Classes and the Revolutionary Movements of Iraq: A Study of Iraq's Old Landed and Commercial Classes and of Its Communists, Ba'athists and Free Officers*, Saqi Books, London.

Bayat, A. (1987) *Workers and Revolution in Iran*, Zed Books, London.

Bayat, A. (1997) *Street Politics: Poor People's Movements in Iran*, Columbia University Press, New York.

Bayat, A. (2005) *Making Islam Democratic: Social Movements and the Post Islamist Turn*, Stanford University Press, Stanford CA.

Bayat, A. (2008) 'Workless Revolutionaries: The Unemployed Movement in Revolutionary Iran', in S. Cronin (ed.), *Subalterns and Social Protest: History from Below in the Middle East and North Africa*, Routledge, London and New York.

Bayat, A. (2009a) *Life as Politics: How Ordinary People Change the Middle East*, American University in Cairo Press, Cairo.

Bayat, A. (2009b) 'Iran: A Green Wave for Life and Liberty', www.opendemocracy.net.

Bayat A., and B. Baktiari (2002) 'Revolutionary Iran and Egypt: Exporting Inspirations and Anxieties', in N.R. Keddie and R. Matthee, *Iran, and the Surrounding World*, University of Washington Press, Seattle.

Beck, L. (1990) 'Tribes and State in Nineteenth- and Twentieth-Century Iran', in P. Khoury and J. Kostiner (eds), *Tribes and State Formation in the Middle East*, University of California Press, Berkeley.

Behrouz, M. (2004) 'The Iranian Revolution and the Legacy of the Guerrilla Movement', in S. Cronin (ed.), *Reformers and Revolutionaries in Modern Iran: New Perspectives on the Iranian Left*, Routledge Curzon, London and New York.

Beinin, J. (2005) 'Political Islam and the New Global Economy: The Political Economy of an Egyptian Social Movement', *New Centennial Review* 5(1): 111–39.

Beinin, J. (2009) 'Workers' Struggles under "Socialism" and Neoliberalism', in R. El-Mahdi and P. Marfleet (eds), *Egypt: The Moment of Change*, Zed Books, London.

Beinin J., and Z. Lockman (1987) *Workers on the Nile: Nationalism, Communism, Islam, and the Egyptian Working Class, 1882–1954*, Princeton University Press, Princeton NJ.

Bennis, P. (2009) *Understanding the US-Iran Crisis: A Primer*, Olive Branch Press, New York.

Bernard-Maugiron, N. (2006) 'Judges as Reform Advocates: A Lost Battle?', in N.S. Hopkins (ed.), *Political and Social Protest in Egypt*, Cairo Papers in Social Science 29(2/3), Summer/Fall.

Bosworth, C.E. (2009) 'The Persistent Older Heritage in the Medieval Iranian Lands', in V. Sarkhosh Curtis and Sarah Stewart (eds), *The Rise of Islam*, I.B. Tauris, London.

Britannica World Data Analyst 2004, 2005, 2006, 2007, 2008, www.britannica.com.

Browne, E.G. (1910) *The Persian Revolution of 1905–1909*, Cambridge University Press, Cambridge.

Bulliett, R.W. (2009) 'Economy and Society in Early Islamic Iran: A Moment in World History', in V. Sarkhosh Curtis and S. Stewart (eds), *The Rise of Islam*, I.B. Tauris, London.

Burgat, F. (2003) *Face to Face with Political Islam*, I.B. Tauris, London.

Bush, R. (2006) 'When "Enough" is not Enough: Resistance during Accumulation by Dispossession', in N.S. Hopkins (ed.), *Political and Social Protest in Egypt*, Cairo Papers in Social Science 29(2/3), Summer/Fall.

Bush, R. (2009) 'The Land and the People', in R. El-Mahdi and P. Marfleet (eds), *Egypt: The Moment of Change*, Zed Books, London.

Callinicos, A. (2003) *The New Mandarins of American Power*, Polity Press, Cambridge.

Callinicos A. (2006) 'Imperial Assault on and Tasks for the Left', Ardeshir Mehrdad interviewing Alex Callinicos, *Iran Bulletin – Middle East Forum*, www.iran-bulletin.org/.

Callinicos, A. (2009) *Imperialism and Global Political Economy*, Polity Press, Cambridge.

Canby, S.R. (2009) *Shah, Abbas, The Remaking of Iran*, British Museum Press, London.

Chalcraft, J. (2004) *The Striking Cabbies of Cairo and Other Stories: Crafts and Guilds in Egypt, 1863–1914*, State University of New York Press, Albany NY.

Chalcraft, J. (2008) 'Popular Protest, the Market and the State in Nineteenth- and Early Twentieth Century Egypt', in S. Cronin (ed.), *Subalterns and Social Protest: History from Below in the Middle East and North Africa*, Routledge, London and New York.

Chehabi, H.E., and H.I. Mneimneh (2006) 'Five Centuries of Lebanese–Iranian Encounters', in H.E. Chehabi (ed.), *Distant Relations: Iran and Lebanon in the last 500 years*, Centre for Lebanese Studies and I.B. Tauris, London.

Chit, B. (2008) 'Lebanon', *Socialist Review* 9.

Chomsky, N. (1999) *Fateful Triangle: The United States, Israel and the Palestinians*, Pluto Press, London.

Chomsky, N. (2007) 'Foreword', in R. Sayigh, *The Palestinians: From Peasants to Revolutionaries*, Zed Books, London.

Chomsky, N., and G. Achcar (2009) *Perilous Power: The Middle East and U.S. Foreign*

Policy, Dialogues on Terror, Democracy, War and Justice, Paradigm, Boulder CO and London.

Chubin, S., and C. Tripp (1988) Iran and Iraq at War, I.B. Tauris, London.

Chubin, S., and S. Zabih (1974) The Foreign Relations of Iran, A Developing State in a Zone of Great-Power Conflict, University of California Press, Berkeley.

Cockburn, P. (2006) The Occupation, Verso, London and New York.

Cockburn, P. (2008) Muqtada al-Sadr and the Fall of Iraq, Faber & Faber, London.

Commins, D. (2005) 'Hassan al-Banna (1906–1949)', in A. Rahnema (ed.), Pioneers of Islamic Revival, Zed Books, London.

Cronin, S. (2004) 'Introduction', in S. Cronin (ed.), Reformers and Revolutionaries in Modern Iran: New Perspectives on the Iranian Left, Routledge Curzon, London and New York.

Cronin, S. (2008) 'Resisting the New State: The Rural Poor, Land and Modernity in Iran, 1921–1941', in S. Cronin (ed.), Subalterns and Social Protest: History from Below in the Middle East and North Africa, Routledge, London and New York.

Cronin, S. (ed.) (2003) The Making of Modern Iran: State and Society under Reza Shah (1921–1941), Routledge Curzon, New York and London.

Dabashi, H. (2007) Iran: A People Interrupted, New Press, New York.

Davis, E. (2005) Memories of State: Politics, History, And Collective Identity in Modern Iraq, University of California Press, Berkeley.

Deeb, L. (2006a) An Enchanted Modern: Gender and Public Piety in Shi'a Lebanon, Princeton University Press, Princeton NJ.

Deeb, L. (2006b) 'Deconstructing a "Hezbollah Stronghold"', in R. Leenders, A. Ghazal and J. Hanseen (eds), 'The Sixth War, Israel's Invasion of Lebanon', MIT Electronic Journal of Middle East Studies.

Ebadi, S. (2006) Iran Awakening. From Prison to Peace Prize: One Woman's Struggle at the Crossroads of History, Rider, London.

Ehteshami, A. (2008) 'Iran and its Immediate Neighbourhood', in A. Ehteshami and M. Zweiri (eds), Iran's Foreign Policy: From Khatami to Ahmadinejad, Ithaca Press, Ithaca NY.

El-Ghobashy, M. (2005) 'The Metamorphosis of the Egyptian Muslim Brothers', International Journal of Middle East Studies 37: 373–95.

El-Hamalawy, H. (2008) 'More than Bread and Butter', Socialist Review 18, May.

El-Mahdi, R. (2009) 'The Democracy Movement: Cycles of Protest', in R. El-Mahdi and P. Marfleet (eds), Egypt: The Moment of Change, Zed Books, London.

El-Mahdi, R., and P. Marfleet (2009) 'Conclusion, What's Next?', in R. El-Mahdi and P. Marfleet (eds), Egypt: The Moment of Change, Zed Books, London.

El-Naggar, A. (2009) 'Economic policy: From State Control to Decay and Corruption, in R. El-Mahdi and P. Marfleet (eds), Egypt: The Moment of Change, Zed Books, London.

El Saadawi, N. (1980) The Hidden Face of Eve: Women in the Muslim World, Zed Books, London.

Evans, P. (1995) Embedded Autonomy: States and Industrial Transformation, Princeton University Press, Princeton NJ.

Farhadpour, L. (2000) *Zanane Berlin* (Berlin's Women), Jamee Iranian, Tehran.

Farhadpour, L. (2006) 'Women, Gender Roles and Journalism in Iran', paper presented at the Development Studies Women and Development Study Group, York University.

Fathollah-Nejad, A. (forthcoming) 'A Critical Geopolitics of Iran's International Relations in a Changing World', Ph.D. thesis, School of Oriental and African Studies, University of London.

Fattouh, B., and J. Kolb (2006) 'The Outlook For Economic Reconstruction in Lebanon After the 2006 War', in R. Leenders, A. Ghazal and J. Hanseen, 'The Sixth War, Israel's Invasion of Lebanon', *MIT Electronic Journal of Middle East Studies*.

Fisk, R. (2005) *The Great War for Civilisation: The Conquest of The Middle East*, Fourth Estate, London.

Gheissari, A., and V. Nasr (2006) *Democracy in Iran: History and the Quest for Liberty*, Oxford University Press, Oxford.

Gheissari, A., and K.C. Sanandaji (2009) 'New Conservative Politics and Electoral Behaviour in Iran', in A. Gheissari (ed.), *Contemporary Iran: Economy, Society, Politics*, Oxford University Press, Oxford.

Ghouchani, M. (2004) *Shi'a As Jonbesh to Dolat* (Shi'a From Movement to Government), Shargh Salaneh, Iran.

Gramsci, A. (1976) *Selections from the Prison Notebooks*, ed. Quintin Hoare and Geoffrey Nowell-Smith, Lawrence & Wishart, London.

Gunning, J. (2007) *Hamas in Politics: Democracy, Religion, Violence*, Hurst, London.

Haddad, Y. (2005) 'Muhammad Abduh: Pioneer of Islamic Reform', in A. Rahnema (ed.), *Pioneers of Islamic Revival*, Zed Books, London.

Haeri, S. (1989) *Law of Desire: Temporary Marriage in Iran*, I.B. Tauris, London and New York.

Haeri, S. (2009) 'Women, Religion, and Political Agency in Iran', in A. Gheissari (ed.), *Contemporary Iran: Economy, Society, Politics*, Oxford University Press, Oxford.

Hamzeh, A.N. (2004) *In the Path of Hezbollah*, Syracuse University Press, New York.

Harb, M. (2007) 'Faith-Based Organisations as Effective Development Partners? Hezbollah and Post-War Reconstruction in Lebanon', in G. Clarke and M. Jennings (eds), *Development Civil Society and Faith-Based Organisations: Bridging the Sacred and the Secular*, Palgrave, London.

Harb, M., and R. Leenders (2005) 'Know Thy Enemy: Hezbollah, "Terrorism" and the Politics of Perception', *Third World Quarterly* 26(1): 173–97.

Harik, J. (2005) *Hezbollah: The Changing Face of Terrorism*, I.B. Tauris, London.

Harik, J. (2006) 'Hezbollah's Public and Social Services and Iran', in H.E. Chehabi (ed.), *Distant Relations, Iran and Lebanon in the Last 500 Years*, Centre for Lebanese Studies and I.B. Tauris, London.

Harman, C. (1994) 'The Prophet and the Proletariat', *International Socialism* 64.

Harman, C (2006) 'Hezbollah and the War Israel Lost', *International Socialism* 112.

Harvey D. (2003) *The New Imperialism*, Oxford University Press, Oxford.

Hasso, F. (2005) 'Discursive and Political Deployments by/of the 2002 Palestinian Women Suicide Bombers/Martyrs', *Feminist Review* 81.

Hatem, M. (2000) 'The Pitfalls of the Nationalist Discourses on Citizenship in Egypt', in S. Joseph (ed.), *Gender and Citizenship in the Middle East*, Syracuse University Press, Syracuse NY.

Hilal, J. (2007) *Where Now for Palestine? The Demise of the Two-State Solution*, Zed Books, London.

Hillenbrand, R. (2009) 'What Happened to the Sassanian Hunt in Islamic Art?', in V. Sarkhosh Curtis and S. Stewart (eds), *The Rise of Islam*, I.B. Tauris, London.

Hiro, D. (1990) *The Longest War: The Iran-Iraq Military Conflict*, Paladin Grafton Books, London.

Hoffmann, C. (2002) 'The Unrest is Growing: Habermas in Iran', Interview with Jürgen Habermas, *Frankfurter Allgemeine Zeitung*, 18 June, www.pubtheo. com/page.asp?pid=1073.

Honarbin-Holliday, M. (2009) *Becoming Visible in Iran: Women in Contemporary Iranian Society*, I.B. Tauris, London.

Hoodfar, H. (2000) 'Iranian Women at the Intersection of Citizenship and the Family Code', in S. Joseph, *Gender and Citizenship in the Middle East*, Syracuse University Press, Syracuse NY.

Hourani, A. (1962) *Arabic Thought in the Liberal Age, 1798–1939*, Cambridge University Press, Cambridge.

Hourani, A. (1991) *A History of the Arab Peoples*, Faber & Faber, London.

Hourani, A. (2006) 'From Jabal Amil to Persia', in, H.E. Chehabi (ed.), *Distant Relations, Iran and Lebanon in the Last 500 Years*, Centre for Lebanese Studies and I.B. Tauris, London.

Hroub, K. (2000) *Hamas: Political Thought and Practice*, Institute for Palestine Studies, Washington DC.

Hroub, K. (2006) *Hamas: A Beginner's Guide*, Pluto Press, London.

Huntington, S. (1998) *The Clash of Civilisations and the Remaking of World Order*, Touchstone Books, New York.

ICRC (International Committee of the Red Cross) (2008) 'Iraq: No Let-Up In The Humanitarian Crisis', www.icrc.org.

Iran Statistical Year Book, 2006–2007 and 2007–2008, Iran Statistical Centre, Iran.

Iraq Occupational Newsletter, www.iraqoccupationfocus.org.uk.

Ismael, T.Y. (2005) *The Communist Movement in the Arab World*, Routledge Curzon, London and New York.

Ismail, S. (2006) *Political Life in Cairo's New Quarters: Encountering the Everyday State*, University of Minnesota Press, Minneapolis.

Issawi, C. (1971) *The Economic History of Iran*, University of Chicago Press, Chicago.

Jad, I., P. Johnson and R, Giacaman (2000) 'Gender and Citizenship under the Palestinian Authority', in S. Joseph (ed.), *Gender and Citizenship in the Middle East*, Syracuse University Press, Syracuse NY.

Joseph, S. (1978) 'Women and the Neighbourhood Street in Borj Hammoud, Lebanon', in L. Beck and N. Keddie (eds), *Women in the Muslim World*, Harvard University Press, Cambridge MA.

Joseph, S. (2000) 'Civic Myths, Citizenship, and Gender in Lebanon', in S. Joseph (ed.), *Gender and Citizenship in the Middle East*, Syracuse University Press, Syracuse NY.

Kadivar, J. (1994) *Mesr az Zaviehee Digar* (Egypt from a Different Angle) Ettellaat Publishers, Tehran.

Kadivar, J. (1997) *Entefazeh Hemase Moghavemat Felestin* (Intifada, The Epic Resistance in Palestine), Etellaat Publishers, Tehran.

Kadivar, J. (2000) *Tahavole Goftemane Siasie Shi'a dar Iran* (Transformation in Shi'a Political Discourse in Iran) Tarhe Naw, Tehran.

Kadivar, J. (2007) *Poshte Parde Solh* (Behind the Curtain of the Peace) Etellaat Publishers, Tehran.

Kadivar, M. (1999) *Bahaye Azadi: Defaiyate Mohsen Kadivar dar Dadgahe Vizhehe Rouhaniyat* (The Price of Freedom: Mohsen Kadivar's Defence in the Special Clergy Court), Nashre Ney, Tehran.

Kadivar, M. (2002) *Andishe Siasi dar Eslam Vol. 3, Hokumat e Entesabi* (Political Thinking in Islam – Government by Appointment), Nashre Ney, Tehran.

Kamel al-Sayyid, M. (2006) 'Kefaya at a Turning Point', in N.S. Hopkins (ed.), *Political and Social Protest in Egypt*, Cairo Papers in Social Science 29(2/3), Summer/Fall.

Karshenas, M., and H. Hakimian (2008) 'Managing Oil Resources and Economic Diversification in Iran', in H. Katouzian and H. Shahidi (eds), *Iran in the 21st Century, Politics, Economics & Conflict*, Routledge, London and New York.

Katouzian, H. (2009) *The Persians: Ancient, Mediaeval and Modern Iran*, Yale University Press, New Haven.

Keddie, N. (1966) *Religion and Rebellion in Iran: The Tobacco Protest of 1891–1892*, Frank Cass, London.

Keddie, N. (1981) *Roots of Revolution: An Interpretive History of Modern Iran*, Yale University Press, New Haven CT.

Keddie, N. (2005) 'Sayyid Jamal al-Din 'al-Afghani'', in A. Rahnema (ed.), *Pioneers of Islamic Revival*, Zed Books, London.

Kennedy, H. (2009) 'Survival of Iranianness', in V. Sarkhosh Curtis and S. Stewart (eds), *The Rise of Islam*, I.B. Tauris, London.

Khalili, L. (2006) 'The Refugees Who Give Refuge', in R. Leenders, A. Ghazal and J. Hanseen (eds), 'The Sixth War, Israel's Invasion of Lebanon', MIT *Electronic Journal of Middle East Studies*.

Khalili, L. (2007a) *Heroes and Martyrs of Palestine: The Politics of National Commemoration*, Cambridge University Press, Cambridge.

Khalili, L. (2007b) 'Standing with My Brother: Hezbollah, Palestinians, and the Limits of Solidarity', *Comparative Studies in Society and History, An International Quarterly* 49(2), April.

Khalili, L. (2010) 'Palestinians: The Politics of Control, Invisibility, and the

Spectacle', in M. Ali Khalidi (ed.), *Manifestations of Idenity: The Lived Reality of Palestinian Refugees in Lebanon*, Institute for Palestine Studies, Beirut.

Khosrokhavar, F. (2009) 'Iran's New Scientific Community', in A. Gheissari (ed.), *Contemporary Iran: Economy, Society, Politics*, Oxford University Press, Oxford.

Kian, A. (2005) 'From Motherhood to Equal Rights Advocates: The Weakening of Patriarchal Order', *Iranian Studies* 38(1).

Koolaee, E. (forthcoming) ' Women and the Parliament', in E. Rostami-Povey and T. Povey (eds), *Women, Power and Politics in 21st Century Iran*, Ashgate, Aldershot.

Lajevardi, H. (1985) *Labour Unions and Autocracy in Iran*, Syracuse University Press, Syracuse NY.

Lewis, B. (2003) *What Went Wrong? The Clash between Islam and Modernity in the Middle East*, Oxford University Press, New York.

Lotfian, S. (2008) 'Nuclear Policy and International Relations', in Iran', in H. Katouzian and H. Shahidi (eds), *Iran in the 21st Century: Politics, Economics & Conflict*, Routledge, London and New York.

Machini, F. (2008a) 'Mogheeyate Zanan Iran 30 sal pas az enghelab: yek negahe be din' (Women's situation in Iran, 30 years after the revolution: A view of religion), conference paper presented at the international conference, 'Thirty Years of Islamic Republic: Workers Organisations, Social Study and the Formation of Civil Society in Iran', CERI/CNRS, Centre d'études et de recherches internationales, Paris.

Machini, F. (2008b) 'Zarorate tarhe zan va noandishi dini' (The necessity of projecting women and religious intellectualism), *Aeen Monthly Journal* 15, Farsi, Iran.

Mafinezam, A., and A. Mehrabi (2008) *Iran and its Place amongst Nations*, Praeger, Westport CT.

Makdisi, K. (2006) 'Israel's 2006 War on Lebanon', in R. Leenders, A. Ghazal and J. Hanseen (eds), 'The Sixth War, Israel's Invasion of Lebanon', *MIT Electronic Journal of Middle East Studies*.

Makdisi, U. (2000) *The Culture of Sectarianism: Community, History, and Violence in Nineteenth-Century Ottoman Lebanon*, University of California Press, Berkeley.

Makdisi, U., and P. Silverstein (eds) (2006) *Memory and Violence in the Middle East and North Africa*, Indiana University Press, Bloomington.

Makram-Ebeid, D. (2009) '"Changing History?" Everyday Labour Relations at the Egyptian Iron and Steel Plant and Implications on Workers' Collective Action', paper presented at the conference, 'Egyptian Labour Movement: Possibilities and Constraints', School of Oriental and African Studies, University of London, July.

Maljo, M. (2008) 'Kaheshe Taharokate Kargary dar doreh dolat nohom: sarkhordegi ya emkanate siasi' (Decline of workers' actions during the Nine's Government, demoralisation or political possibilities), conference paper presented at the international conference, 'Thirty Years of Islamic Republic: Workers Organisations, Social Study and the Formation of Civil Society in Iran', CERI/CNRS, Centre d'études et de recherches internationales, Paris.

Mallat, C. (2005) 'Muhammad Baqer as-Sadr', in A. Rahnema (ed.), *Pioneers of Islamic Revival*, Zed Books, London.

Maloney, S. (2000) 'The Bonyads and Privatization in Iran', *Goft-O-Gu Political Economy Journal* 28, Farsi, Tehran.

Martin, V. (1989) *Islam and Modernism: The Iranian Revolution of 1906*, Syracuse University Press, Syracuse NY.

Martin, V. (2000) *Creating an Islamic State: Khomeini and the Making of a New Iran*, I.B. Tauris, London.

Masalha, N. (2007) *The Bible and Zionism: Invented Traditions, Archaeology and Post-Colonialism in Israel-Palestine*, Zed Books, London.

Mayo, P. (1999) *Gramsci, Freire, and Adult Education: Possibilities for Transformative Action*, Zed Books, London.

Milani, M.M. (2009) 'Iran's Persian Gulf Policy in the Post-Saddam Era', in A Gheissari (ed.), *Contemporary Iran: Economy, Society, Politics*, Oxford University Press, Oxford.

Miller, D. (1994) *Modernity — An Ethnographic Approach: Dualism and Mass Consumption in Trinidad*, Berg, Oxford .

Miller, D. (ed.) (1995) *Worlds Apart: Modernity through the Prism of the Local*, Routledge, London and New York.

Mir-Hosseini, Z. (2002) 'Islam, Women and Civil Rights: The Religious Debate in the Iran of the 1990s', in S. Ansari and V. Martin, *Women, Religion and Culture in Iran*, Curzon and Royal Asiatic Society of Great Britain and Ireland, Richmond, Surrey.

Mir-Hosseini, Z., and R. Tapper (2006) *Islam and Democracy in Iran: Eshkevari and the Quest for Reform*, I.B. Tauris, London.

Mishal, S., and A. Sela (2000) *The Palestinian Hamas: Vision, Violence, and Coexistence*, Columbia University Press, New York.

Moallem, M. (2005) *Between Warrior Brother and Veiled Sister: Islamic Fundamentalism and the Cultural Politics of Patriarchy in Iran*, University of California Press, Berkeley.

Moghadam, V. (2000) 'Hidden from History? Women Workers in Modern Iran', *Iranian Studies* 33(3–4), Summer/Fall.

Moghissi, H. (1999) *Feminism and Islamic Fundamentalism: The Limits of Post-modern Analysis*, Zed Books, London.

Moin, B. (2005) 'Khomeini's Search for Perfection: Theory and Reality', in A. Rahnema (ed.), *Pioneers of Islamic Revival*, Zed Books, London.

Mojab, S. (2001) 'International Feminist Movements', in H. Kapoor (ed.), *Women Living under Muslim Laws, Dossier* 23, 24.

Moloudi, A. (n.d.) 'Barresie Mizane Entebagh Pazirie Shahrhaye Kordneshine Jonobe Ostan Azarbaijane Gharbi, Az Tahavolate Kordestane Aragh' (An analysis of the extent of the adaptability of the Kurdish southern cities in the Western Azarbaijan Province to the changes in the Iraqi Kurdistan), unpublished paper.

Naghibi, N. (2007) *Rethinking Global Sisterhood, Western Feminism and Iran*, University of Minnesota Press, Minneapolis.

Naguib, S. (2006) 'The Muslim Brotherhood: Contradictions and Transformations', in N.S. Hopkins (ed.), *Political and Social Protest in Egypt, Cairo Papers in Social Science* 29(2/3), Summer/Fall .

Naguib, S. (2009) 'Islamism(s) Old and New', in R. El-Mahdi and P. Marfleet (eds), *Egypt: The Moment of Change*, Zed Books, London.

Najmabadi, A. (1991) 'Hazards of Modernity and Morality: Women, State and Ideology in Contemporary Iran', in D. Kandiyoti (ed.), *Women, Islam & State*, Macmillan, London.

Narayan, U. (1997) *Dislocating Cultures: Identities, Traditions and Third World Feminism*, Routledge, New York and London.

Nasr, V. (2007) *The Shia Revival: How Conflicts within Islam Will Shape the Future*, W.W. Norton, New York and London.

Nomani, F., and A. Rahnema (1994) *Islamic Economic Systems*, Zed Books, London.

Norton, A.R. (1987) 'The Origins and Resurgence of Amal', in Martin Kramer (ed.), *Shi'ism, Resistance and Revolution*, Westview Press, Boulder CO.

Norton, A.R. (2007) *Hezbollah*, Princeton University Press, Princeton NJ.

Osanloo, A. (2009) *The Politics of Women's Rights in Iran*, Princeton University Press, Princeton NJ.

Paidar, P. (1997) *Women and the Political Process in Twentieth-Century Iran*, Cambridge University Press, New York.

Pappe, I. (2004) *A History of Modern Palestine: One Land, Two Peoples*, Cambridge University Press, Cambridge.

Pappe, I. (2006) *The Ethnic Cleansing of Palestine*, One World, Oxford.

PENGON, Jerusalem (2003) *Stop the Wall in Palestine: Facts, Testimonies, Analysis and Call to Action*, Palestinian Environmental NGOs Network.

Philipp T. (1978) 'Feminism and Nationalist Politics in Egypt', in L. Beck and N. Keddie (eds), *Women in the Muslim World*, Harvard University Press, Cambridge MA.

Plesch, D., and M. Butcher (2007) 'Considering a War with Iran: A Discussion Paper on WMD in the Middle East', www.cisd.soas.ac.uk.

Povey, T. (forthcoming) 'Forces of Change: Social Movements in Egypt and Iran' Ph.D. thesis, University of Sydney.

Poya, M. (1987) 'IRAN 1979: Long Live Revolution!... Long live Islam?', in C. Barker (ed.), *Revolutionary Rehearsals*, Bookmarks, London.

Poya, M. (1999) *Women, Work and Islamism: Ideology and Resistance in Iran*, Zed Books, London.

Pratt, N. (2005) 'Hegemony and Counter-hegemony in Egypt: Advocacy NGOs, Civil Society, and the State', in S. Ben Nefissa, N. Abd al-Fattah, S. Hanafi and C. Milani (eds), *NGOs and Governance in the Arab World*, American University in Cairo Press, Cairo.

Quilty, J. (2006) 'Politics and Business, State and Citizenry: Preliminary Thoughts on the Response to Lebanon's Humanitarian Crisis', in R. Leenders, A. Ghazal and J. Hanseen (eds), *The Sixth War, Israel's Invasion of Lebanon*, MIT Electronic Journal of Midde East Studies.

Rahimi, B. (2003) 'Cyberdissent: The Internet in Revolutionary Iran', *Middle East Review of International Affairs* 7(3).

Rahimi, B. (2007) 'Ayatollah Sistani and the Democratisation of Post-Ba'athist Iraq' *United States Institute of Peace*, Special Report 187, www.usip.org.

Rahnema, A. (1998) *An Islamic Utopian: A Political Biography of Ali Shariati*, I.B. Tauris, London.

Rahnema, A. (2005a) 'Introduction to First Edition', in A. Rahnema (ed.), *Pioneers of Islamic Revival*, Zed Books, London.

Rahnema, A. (2005b) 'Ali Shariati: Teacher, Preacher, Rebel', in A. Rahnema (ed.), *Pioneers of Islamic Revival*, Zed Books, London.

Rahnema, A., and F. Nomani (1990) *The Secular Miracle: Religion, Politics and Economic Policy in Iran*, Zed Books, London.

Rahnema, S. (2004) 'The Left and the Struggle for Democracy in Iran', in S. Cronin (ed.), *Reformers and Revolutionaries in Modern Iran: New Perspectives on the Iranian Left*, Routledge Curzon, London and New York.

Ramadan, T. (2007) *The Messenger: The Meanings of the Life of Muhammad*, Allen Lane, London.

Ramadani, S. (2007) 'Iraq: This is Not a Communal War', *International Socialism* 114.

Ramadani, S., and H. Zangana (2006) 'Resistance and Sectarianism in Iraq', *International Socialism* 109.

Richter-Bernburg, L. (2009) 'Oranges, Quiddities and Algorisms', in V. Sarkhosh Curtis and S. Stewart (eds), *The Rise of Islam*, I.B. Tauris, London.

Robinson, G. (1997) *Building a Palestinian State: The Incomplete Revolution*, Indiana University Press, Bloomington.

Rose, J. (2002) 'Israel: The Hijack State, America's Watchdog in the Middle East', *Socialist Worker*.

Rose, J. (2004) *The Myths of Zionism*, Pluto Press, London.

Rostami-Povey, E. (2001) 'Feminist Contestations of Institutional Domains in Iran', *Feminist Review* 69.

Rostami-Povey, E. (2004) 'Political Social Movements: Unions and Workers' Movements in Iran', in S. Joseph (ed.), *Encyclopedia of Women and Islamic Cultures*, vol. 2: *Family Law and Politics*, Brill Academic, Leiden.

Rostami-Povey, E. (2005) 'Trade Unions and Women's NGOs, Diverse Civil Society Organisations in Iran', in D. Eade and A. Leather (eds), *Development NGOs and Labour Unions: Terms of Engagement*, Kumarian Press, London.

Rostami-Povey, E. (2007a) four entries in *Biographical Encyclopaedia of the Modern Middle East and North Africa*, Vol. 1, ed. Michael R. Fischbach, Gale, Detroit.

Rostami-Povey, E. (2007b) *Afghan Women: Identity and Invasion*, Zed Books, London.

Saad-Ghorayeb, A. (2002) *Hezbollah: Politics and Religion*, Pluto Press, London.

Saad-Ghorayeb, A. (2003) 'Factors Conducive to the Politicization of the Lebanese Shi'a and the Emergence of Hezbollah', *Journal of Islamic Studies* 14(3), September.

Sabry, S. (2009) 'Poverty Lines in Greater Cairo, Underestimating and Misrepresenting Poverty', *Poverty Reduction in Urban Areas*, Working Paper 21, International Institute for Environment and Development, London; www.iied.org.

Sadria, M. (2009) 'Modernities: Reposing the Issues', in M. Sadria (ed.), *Multiple Modernities in Muslim Societies*, I.B. Tauris, London.

Said, E. (1978) *Orientalism*, Routledge & Kegan Paul, London.

Said, E. (1980) *The Question of Palestine*, Routledge & Kegan Paul, London.

Said E. (1994) *The Politics of Dispossession: The Struggle for Palestinian Self-Determination 1969–1994*, Chatto & Windus, London.

Said, E. (1995) *Peace and Its Discontents, Gaza–Jericho 1993–1995*, Vintage, London.

Said, E. (2000) *The End of the Peace Process, Oslo and After*, Granta, London.

Said Makdisi, J. (1999) *Beirut Fragments: A War Memoir*, Persea Books, New York.

Salibi K.S. (1976) *Cross Roads to Civil War, Lebanon 1958–1976*, Ithaca, London.

Salibi, K.S. (2005) *A House of Many Mansions: The History of Lebanon Reconstructed*, I.B. Tauris, London.

Salvatore, A. (2009) 'From Civilisations to Multiple Modernities: The Issue of the Public Sphere', in M. Sadria (ed.), *Multiple Modernities in Muslim Societies*, I.B. Tauris, London.

Sanasarian, E. (2000) *Religious Minorities in Iran*, Cambridge University Press, Cambridge.

Sayigh, R. (2007) *The Palestinians: From Peasants to Revolutionaries*, Zed Books, London.

Sayigh, Y. (1997) *Armed Struggle and the Search for State: The Palestinian National Movement 1949–1993*, Clarendon Press, Oxford.

Seif El-Dawla, A. (2009) 'Torture: A State Policy', in R. El-Mahdi and P. Marfleet (eds), *Egypt: The Moment of Change*, Zed Books, London.

Shabestari, M. (2000) *Naghdi Bar Ghera'at e Rasmi az Din* (A critique of the official reading of religion), Tarh e Naw, Tehran.

Shaery-Eisenlohr, R. (2008) *Sh'ite Lebanon: Transnational Religion and The Making of National Identity*, Columbia University Press, New York.

Shahidi, H. (2002) 'Women and Journalism in Iran', in S. Ansari and V. Martin, *Women, Religion and Culture in Iran*, Curzon Press and Royal Asiatic Society of Great Britain and Ireland, Richmond, Surrey.

Shariati, A. (2000) *Shi'a, Majmoee Asar 7* (Shi'a, Collective Work 7), Elham, Tehran.

Sharoni, S. (1995) *Gender and the Israeli–Palestinian Conflict: The Politics of Women's Resistance*, Syracuse University Press, Syracuse NY.

Shlaim, A. (2000) *The Iron Wall: Israel and the Arab World*, Penguin Books, London.

Tabari, A. (1983) 'The Role of Clergy in Modern Iranian Politics', in N. Keddie (ed.), *Religion and Politics in Iran*, Yale University Press, New Haven CT.

Tabari, A., and Yeganeh, N. (1982) *In the Shadow of Islam: The Women's Movement in Iran*, Zed Books, London.

Tamimi, A. (2007) *Hamas: Unwritten Chapters*, Hurst, London.

Tohidi, N. (2002) 'Culture in the Islamic Republic in Relation to the World, International Connections of the Iranian Women's Movement', in N.R. Keddie and R. Matthee (ed.), *Iran and the Surrounding World*, University of Washington Press, Seattle and London.

Tohidi, N. (2009) 'Ethnicity and Religious Minority Politics in Iran', in A. Gheissari (ed.), *Contemporary Iran: Economy, Society, Politics*, Oxford University Press, Oxford.

Thornhill, M. (2006) *Road to Suez: The Battle of the Canal Zone*, Sutton, Stroud.

Torab, A. (2002) 'The Politicisation of Women's Religious Circles in Post-Revolutionary Iran', in S. Ansari and V. Martin (eds), *Women, Religion and Culture in Iran*, Curzon and the Royal Asiatic Society of Great Britain and Ireland.

Tripp, C. (2005) 'Sayyid Qutb: The Political Vision', in A. Rahnema (ed.), *Pioneers of Islamic Revival*, Zed Books London.

Tripp, C. (2008) *A History of Iraq*, Cambridge University Press, Cambridge.

Tripp, C. (2009) 'Prospects of State Building in Iraq', lecture, 5 May, SOAS, University of London.

UNCTAD (2006) *The Palestinian War Torn Economy: Aid, Development and State Formation*, UNCTAD Assistance to the Palestinian People Unit, Geneva.

UNDP (2000) *NGOs in the Islamic Republic of Iran: A Situation Analysis*, United Nations Development Programme, Iran.

Vali, A. (2002) 'The Kurds and Their Fragmented "Others": Fragmented Identity and Fragmented Politics', *Comparative Studies of South Asia, Africa, and the Middle East* 21(1/2).

Von Sponeck, H.C. (2006) *A Different Kind of War: The UN Sanctions Regimes in Iraq*, Berghahn Books, New York.

Wickham, C.R. (2002) *Mobilising Islam: Religion, Activism, and Political Change in Egypt*, Columbia University Press, New York.

Wilson, I.T.C., et al. (eds) (1986) *History of the Corps of Royal Engineers*, vol. X: 1945–60, Institution of Royal Engineers, Chatham.

WLUML (Women Living Under Muslim Laws) (2006) 'Iraq, Women's Rights under Attack, Occupation, Constitution and Fundamentalism', Occasional Paper 15.

Yarshatar, E. (2009) 'Re-emergence of Iranian Identity after Conversion to Islam', in V. Sarkhosh Curtis and S. Stewart (eds), *The Rise of Islam*, I.B. Tauris, London.

Zabih, S. (1966) *The Communist Movement in Iran*, University of California Press, Berkeley.

Zangana, H. (2007) *An Iraqi Women's Account of War and Resistance*, Seven Sisters Press, London.

Zubaida, S. (1993) *Islam, the People and the State: Essays on Political Ideas and Movements in the Middle East*, I.B. Tauris, London.

Index